MISTER JIU'S IN CHINATOWN

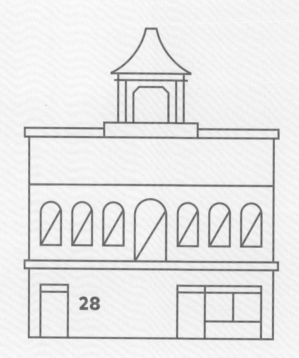

MISTER JIU'S IN CHINATOWN

Recipes and Stories
from the Birthplace of
Chinese American Food

BRANDON JEW
TIENLON HO

Photographs by Pete Lee
Recipe Development by Christine Gallary

TEN SPEED PRESS
California | New York

RESEARCH YOUR OWN EXPERIENCE;

ABSORB WHAT IS USEFUL,

REJECT WHAT IS USELESS,

AND ADD WHAT IS ESSENTIALLY YOUR OWN.

—BRUCE LEE (李小龍),
CHINATOWN SON

TO OUR FAMILIES' FIRST AMERICANS,

FOOK SOON JEW (周福順), SIT YING CHUNG (張雪燕),
FOOK JANG (鄭福), AND LING HING JANG (鄭莲馨)

WENHUEI KAO (高文慧) AND KEN HO (何坤)

RECIPES

Introduction

Chinatown is just waking up. On Waverly Place, aunties stroll past the colorful facades lining the two-block alley to burn incense at the temple that has served this neighborhood for more than one hundred seventy years. Here, in San Francisco, in the oldest Chinatown in North America, things move on a longer timeline.

I'm meeting Betty Louie, a landlord with a restaurant space—28 Waverly. Only two businesses have stood on this spot. The first was Hang Far Low, which, for decades, beginning in the 1850s, was the city's grandest restaurant. Nearly a century later, this space reopened as the opulent Four Seas. Now, in 2013, the Lim family is beat. They're ready to pass on all 10,000 square feet.

For a kid who trailed his grandma through the markets and did gung fu in the Chinese New Year parade, this building should be legend. But the neglected entrance doesn't look familiar. The dark-red staircase, covered in worn carpeting, is lined with faded photos of past guests—politicians, Chinese dignitaries, and celebrities; near the top, a grinning Vince Vaughn.

Inside, we're greeted by silence. The long, mirrored bar is empty. The dining room too. The signs of life are outside. Out the balcony doors, across the street, pork belly hangs to cure on a fire escape, set against flapping laundry and the tip of the Transamerica Pyramid. The shops on the main streets threaded with red lanterns and gilt are welcoming their first tourists.

The kitchen is missing all the proper sounds, just the drip of faucets over a long wok station. But a cook is hanging his life's work in the kitchen's picture window: a row of beautifully lacquered roast ducks. They are a culinary feat; air pumped between the skin and fat, a boiling water bath, followed by days of continuous basting until they are roasted to a gleaming mahogany. How many lifetimes, centuries ago, did it take for cooks to perfect the process?

There's more, Betty says, pointing up. I follow her upstairs to a massive banquet hall. Everything in it is a throwback. There are murals on the walls, a stage, a parquet dance floor, and golden lotus chandeliers. There's the lingering aroma of celebration—cognac and firecrackers. That's when I remember; I've been here.

My uncle celebrated his wedding with a massive banquet in this room. A legion of staff in black-and-white tended to three hundred guests. Here stands the site of countless red-egg parties for new babies, New Year's feasts, and families catching up over Sunday afternoon dim sum. Everyone connected to the Chinese American community celebrated something here.

But, then, the parties dwindled. A new generation grew up with a taste for quick meals and take-out from other parts of the city, like the Richmond and the Sunset Districts, and from the suburbs. The walls were held up by so much joy, so many memories. The space was too big. It would take so much work to get it back into shape. But I knew I couldn't turn my back on this place.

• • •

I didn't understand that I had to open Mister Jiu's until Ying Ying (人人)—our name for our paternal grandmother in Toisanese—was diagnosed with cancer. She was, at seventy-nine years old, the athletic, hilarious, strong-willed matriarch of our family. I was twenty-six and cooking on the line at Quince, a legendary restaurant in San Francisco, executing perfect Ricotta Sformato with artichokes, radicchio, and Umbrian lentil vinaigrette. I loved my job. I loved to work. I had not taken a vacation in what seemed like years. But my Ying Ying was dying, and with her a history in recipes and love. Ying Ying was our family's head cook. She and I spoke the same language: heat, time, taste. But Ying Ying's noh mái gāi was a long way from Ricotta Sformato. Which meant every day at work in the kitchen, I was a long way from home.

I had spent a solid chunk of my childhood in Ying Ying's kitchen in the Richmond. She would cook the northern Chinese food of her childhood and the southern Chinese food of my grandfather's, and I would clean my plate; then she would refill my plate and praise me for being a good, big-boned boy. I did not tire of it. I had grown up speaking English but my culinary language was Chinese.

On her table would be pickled radish, dried shrimp, and slivers of tofu skin on glass noodles. Platters of dumplings, whole steamed bass, or stir-fried crabs served as mains. Her jīn dēui were extraordinarily light puffs of sticky rice dough stuffed with red bean paste. Her noh mái gāi was a treasure of savory chicken and sweet sticky rice to be unearthed from within a parcel of fragrant lotus leaves. The depth of her cooking knowledge was immense.

My parents moved us—my big sister, little brother, and me—thirty minutes south of the city when I was in middle school, so going to Ying Ying's

on the weekends also meant going back to San Francisco. That was a major perk. I loved the city, especially Ying Ying's version of it. When she needed ingredients, she took me shopping. I imagined Chinatown was just like China—red and gold everywhere, with dragons on streetlights.

On special occasions, when the whole family gathered at Ying Ying's—the Toisan relatives (my dad's side) and the Zhongshan relatives (mom's side)—we had two Chinese dialects plus English flying across the table. On those nights, in addition to all the Cantonese fare, we might also see a well-seared steak for Yeh Yeh (爺爺), my paternal grandfather, a paper son, World War II and Korean War veteran, and man of few words. Yeh Yeh loved radios and all-you-can-eat buffets. My dad also had a taste for American standards. We were a household that swung easily between meatloaf and hàahm yú, fermented salted fish. And, always, there was Ying Ying in the kitchen in the middle of everything. Even when we could not come to her, she came to us, braving the trek to the suburbs. While Yeh Yeh hunted for thrift-store treasure in downtown San Carlos, Ying Ying would wait outside our school to walk us home—where she would feed us the necessary after-school snacks. No detail was lost on her, if it was food related. When I was cooking at Quince, Ying Ying would often show up at the one window to the kitchen, just to wave hello.

Ying Ying cooked by memory, taste, and feel. Nothing was written down. She lived for only a few days after I learned she was sick. Her death marked a crossroads in my life and career. I'd climbed the rungs in the fine-dining world and was proud of my accomplishments; but suddenly, mastery of the Art Culinaire mattered less to me than the mysteries of Ying Ying and her kitchen. I quit thinking of ways to reimagine risotto and instead concentrated on combinations of jook. I put down books by Michel Bras and Alain Ducasse and picked up those of Grace Young, Ken Hom, Barbara Tropp, Irene Kuo, Rhoda Yee, Susur Lee, Florence Lin, and Eileen Yin-Fei Lo.

I went deep, fast—reading my way back to the Chinese food my grandmother had mastered, and even regional styles I'd never tried. I read for pleasure late at night, through weekends, and even at the beach. I started practicing recipes as if I was running controlled experiments. So many cookbook recipes were rough approximations. I'd spend days at a stretch trying to read between the lines. I'd re-create the dishes from our family dinners; like noh mái gāi, the chicken and sticky rice in lotus leaf. Instead of the lean chicken that my grandmother had used, I tried different birds, like fatty duck confited with orange zest. Instead of dried scallops to flavor the rice, I smoked fresh scallops and dried them in my oven. I was cooking from flavor memories and bringing the skills that I'd learned in professional kitchens to make something new but still rooted in my past. Then the day came when I knew I needed to go to China. I gave notice at Quince and bought a one-way ticket to Shanghai.

Picking up a wok instead of a sauté pan wasn't a small adjustment. I'd apprenticed in Piedmont and Bologna in Italy, where monuments to food described the exact width and length of a region's beloved pasta. After Italy, I'd worked for a pair of geniuses back in the Bay Area; Judy Rodgers at Zuni, first, and then Michael Tusk at Quince. Judy was in the kitchen every day, tasting all the mise en place and examining the orders that were being dropped off from farmers. Judy set the menu, put me in front of a wood-fired oven, and taught me to turn up all my senses (even as I was sweating like crazy). Michael showed me how to create dishes around ingredients as we collaborated on the day's menu. I'd pester him with why's, and he'd humor my empirical brain. I'd dedicated my entire career up to this point to variations of classical and California-style Italian and Mediterranean cuisine. Chinese cuisine shared many of the same techniques and philosophies, but it had its own as well—beginning with the way you stood and the way you held your knife. There was a lot to learn.

But then Ying Ying. Some things just matter most.

I looked to China for culinary answers and to connect ancestral dots. But I arrived and discovered quickly it would not be the trip I'd planned. I was neither obviously American nor clearly Chinese. Taxi drivers loved guessing where I was from, and they thought I was Korean, Japanese, Mexican, and everything but what I was. The first big stage I sought out fell through, but I stayed in Shanghai anyway, accepting kitchen gigs that afforded me time for Mandarin lessons and eating everything everywhere.

I sought out flavors that reminded me of home and those that were like nothing I'd ever experienced. In Shanghai, dumplings were on every corner, and I ate as many varieties as I could. Each meal was a meditation on the juiciness of the filling and the thickness of the wrapper, how each component related to the other, how the wrapper had to consider the filling and meld in one bite. I ate lamb in the Muslim quarter and braised pork belly on day trips to the Hangzhou countryside.

I got my first huge Chinese cleaver and learned to wield it. After so many years thinking about precious garnishes and cutlery in fine-dining kitchens, I remembered again that the most delicious food can be eaten off the bone, with your hands. I'd fall asleep to the aroma of neighbors' frying lap cheong wafting in through my open windows.

I also got a better understanding of the degree of Chinese specialization. In China, although there are cooking schools now, in the specialty restaurants, cooking is still considered an inherited discipline, where sifu, the masters, pass their knowledge down to their apprentices. Sifu give their lives to one thing, like goose, hairy crab, or xiao long bao. They know how to source ingredients depending on extremely specific definitions of regionality. The best hairy crab comes from one lake in Jiangsu. The most flavorful black vinegar comes from Zhenjiang, a city dedicated to making it for more than 1,400 years, using two specific strains of mold to ferment a blend of rice, wheat, barley, and peas, each of specified origin. Sifu worship seasonality. They think in twenty-four seasons instead of just four. I was overwhelmed by the crowd of chefs representing

China's eight great cuisines and so much more in between. Even with everything I had studied, eaten, and cooked, it was impossible to appreciate how different the styles of Chinese cooking are until I tasted them firsthand.

I returned to San Francisco sure that I was ready to open my own place, but unsure what kind of Chinese restaurant it would be. Also, I was broke. There are dreams and there are realities. I would be tied up with the latter for three more years, completing tours of duty at several fantastic Cal-Med restaurants (Camino, Dopo, Bar Jules, Bar Agricole). At Agricole, if I served Mt. Lassen trout with salsa verde, Chinese-style fermented mustard greens, and lap cheong, it wouldn't satisfy me. I knew I had to open my own place if I was going to use Chinese techniques in a way that would do them justice.

I started introducing potential backers one by one, meal by meal, to my dream. I'd walk them through 28 Waverly and try to paint my picture through the dust and hammering. This would be a restoration, not a renovation, I explained, as we circled the two-story brick building above a flea market. They could see it too.

Where I arrived with Mister Jiu's is exactly where I've always been: in between. A little of this and a little of that. American and Chinese. Modern and traditional. Mister Jiu's connects everything that I've ever learned—from Ying Ying, from my mentors, from all the parts of the world where I've lived and eaten. It is a place that celebrates all those influences, standing in the heart of Chinatown, the place where Chinese American food began.

—Brandon Jew

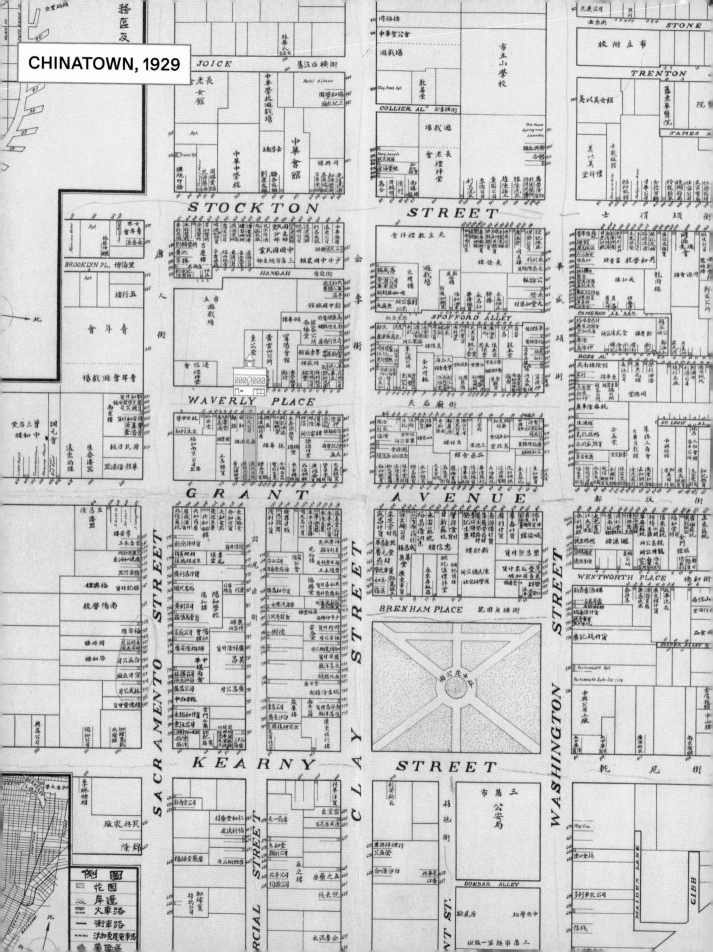

A New Restaurant in Old Chinatown

The building that Mister Jiu's occupies tells the story of Chinatown, the twenty-four blocks roughly bordered by Broadway and California, Stockton and Kearny Streets.

Hang Far Low (1850s–1958)

When 杏花樓 (meaning "apricot blossom restaurant") opened in the 1850s, it stood a few feet from our current location until it burned in 1906 and was rebuilt on this spot. For a century, Hang Far (sometimes Fer) Low, as it came to be known, was Chinatown's grandest establishment and a center of civic life.

In those early years, Hang Far Low's master chefs served classical Cantonese cuisine, using pantry ingredients from China and fresh ingredients raised and caught locally by Chinese farmers and fishermen. Chinatown restaurants specialized in simple stir-fries and rice plates to elaborate banquet fare. The neighborhood chow chows were more affordable restaurants that catered to both Chinese and American tastes. They served all-you-could-eat curries, hashes, ragouts, and fricassees (as Americans then called Chinese-style dishes). Some served steaks, chops, and macaroni. Restaurants were still new in America, and Chinatown's were known for consistently good food and service. Many Chinatown cooks had come through Guangzhou and Hong Kong, where restaurant culture was centuries old, and British and Dutch traders had arrived with a taste for red meat and good coffee.

By 1872, Hang Far Low sold provisions and served quick meals at a counter on the ground floor. On the second floor, it served meals for its boarders and the staff who lived on premises. Lavish banquets were conducted on the third story. In 1902, Harriet Quimby wrote in the *San Francisco Call* of eating a seven-course banquet while perched on a carved ebony stool. The meal began with "rice whisky" and small plates that included century eggs and pickled ginger, and "a sort of transparent plum," followed by soup; brilliantly colored meat dishes; a lacquered, roast fowl; pastries; preserved fruits; and "tea in dear little bowls." From the balcony decorated with giant lanterns, lilies, and dwarf trees, a Chinese orchestra played. "What a feast for an artist in this Chinese kitchen," she extolled.

When Hang Far Low burned with the rest of Chinatown in the Great Quake in 1906, community leaders struck a bargain with city government to be allowed to rebuild, offering to become a tourist destination. Chinatown rose from the ashes in red, gold, and green with curling rooftops and pagodas atop souvenir shops, an idea of Chineseness that didn't actually exist in China. Hang Far Low returned with new dishes and European wines on the menu, a draw for tourists.

Chinatown continued to reach out while anti-Chinese sentiment closed in and exclusionary laws tightened. Chinese people effectively could not work outside of restaurants, groceries, laundries, and housekeeping. A detention center for Chinese immigrants opened on Angel Island in 1910. That year, gas-powered wok ranges also arrived. Gas burners replaced charcoal, hay, and hickory and made the cháau (炒) technique—what we call stir-fry—an easier, more efficient way to cook, especially for those who had never cooked professionally before. More affordable chow chows sprang up, slinging cháau dishes such as chop suey, chow mein, chow fan (fried rice), egg foo young, and moo goo gai pan, among the first Chinese American standards. Stir-fry democratized kitchens for Chinatown cooks, and Chinatown democratized eating out for Americans.

From the first federal Chinese exclusionary law in 1875 until 1943, when Chinese were allowed to naturalize as citizens, Hang Far Low reigned as the king of chop suey palaces. Immigration laws deemed banquet halls and chop suey palaces "high grade" enough to open a door into the United States. If you ran one, you could get a special merchant visa that allowed you to leave the country and bring family back. One uncle could run the business for a while, then help another take over. This is why so many Chinese families from that time got their start in food. Restaurants were the way in and the way up.

Prosperity meant that more families moved from Chinatown to other parts of the city and into the suburbs. Chinese emigrants were limited to just

← Hang Far Low grand
dining room, c. 1882

CHINATOWN, SAN FRANCISCO, CALIF.   68

CHOP SUEY

SA-H1073

Chinese Restaurant,
San Francisco, Cal.

RESTAURANT & TEA-GARDEN

CHOP SUEY

KIN ETOSC ODE

739   739

105 per year from 1943 until 1965. Some trickled in by way of Taiwan, the Philippines, and other parts of the diaspora. But there weren't enough new arrivals to replace the Chinatown exodus, and the neighborhood struggled during this era. Throughout Hang Far Low's history, the families behind it built Chinatown's banks, hospitals, YMCA, and playgrounds, but its final owner was also a gambling kingpin who, after being convicted of tax evasion, disappeared to Hong Kong. In 1958, six-hundred crates of Hang Far Low's history went on the auction block.

Four Seas (1960–2014)

The extravagant Four Seas opened to great anticipation in the summer of 1960. Six partners closely tied to Chinatown poured the equivalent of $2 million into it. Its name came from ancient legends of the universe bounded by four seas, a metaphor for the belief that all people are family and no one is a stranger. There was gold paint, once reserved for emperors, on the outside, and inside, custom everything from carpet to chandeliers. Hand-painted murals spanned the two-story walls in the banquet room that seated five hundred. There had been trips to Hong Kong to recruit certified master chefs and then to India to find the eight largest matching pieces of ivory in the world to be carved into the Eight Immortals for the cocktail lounge. They added a back door on Waverly for slipping in VIPs. But most unique at the time was its menu, which featured "authentic foods from all provinces of China."

It was the start of regional Chinese cuisine in America. Four Seas' eight-page menu was still filled mostly with southern Chinese fare; but even so, its range demanded a team of twelve to prepare. In 1966, its banquet offerings featured a few northern hits such as minced squab in lettuce cups and Peking duck served with thousand-layer buns and the house prawn sauce. Downstairs, you could order everything from winter-melon soup and clay pot to iron platters and dumplings. But the United States had closed trade with China from 1950 to 1972, and key ingredients were hard to come by. This was also an era of imaginative substitutions—sherry for Shaoxing wine, Virginia ham for Jinhua, fresh oranges, and ketchup.

It was also the height Chinatown's cultural heyday. The neighborhood reached out through food,

and people of all walks came to enjoy it. Four Seas' lounge was one of the glamorous places to be seen for dinners and drinks before heading out to one of the theaters, cinemas, or nightclubs. There was R&B at Drag'On A'Go-Go, jazz standards at the Ricksha, and burlesque dancers behind fans at Forbidden City. Hollywood elite flew up on weekends to eat here and at other hotspots, like Kan's just across the street. In its first years, Four Seas hosted banquets for *Flower Drum Song* (the first Hollywood film with Asian Americans in major roles), Miss Chinatown USA, and two-thousand members of the Chin/Chinn family.

In 1965, the Immigration and Naturalization Act lifted quotas based on national origin, and a second wave of Chinese immigrants representing Hunan, Sichuan, Jiangsu, Shandong, and Zhejiang revived Chinatown with new cravings. They created strong Chinese communities in other parts of the city, too, including the Richmond and the Sunset, Hunter's Point, Bayview, and Mission Terrace along San Francisco's southeast edge. After servicemen came home from the Pacific, and Nixon went to China in 1972, nearly every Chinatown restaurant added regional specialties such as hot and sour soup, moo shu pork, and gong bao chicken, alongside the first classics. Diners now had a better understanding of the diversity of Chinese food—the regionally distinct dishes that tasted like what new immigrants remembered—and a new cuisine that began in Chinatown, the Chinese American dishes created from resourcefulness, improvisation, and connecting with America.

As China opened up in the 1990s, a third wave of Chinese representing every region arrived in America to work, explore, and eat. Four Seas welcomed buses of Chinese tour groups curious to taste Chinese American food for the first time.

Mister Jiu's (2016–)

After my handshake with Betty Louie, it was a couple more years before Mister Jiu's opened in this space. First there was a community gathering to meet everyone over tea, explain what I was hoping to build, and get input and their blessing. Then there was two years of major construction to get the structure up to code while saving what we could of the past. It was like inheriting a Porsche that needed a full restoration down to the bolts.

I share a heritage with the people who built this building and this neighborhood. Most, like my family, were Sze Yup, from a region of four counties in Guangdong, just a dot on the southeastern edge of China. The Sze Yup, with other distinct groups from around the Pearl River Delta, came to be known collectively as the Cantonese. Cantonese food came to represent all of China and its food for a good century in America.

Now, in this Chinatown, in between the Chinese American classics on the menus, there are more regional Chinese cuisines represented than ever. And there are fusions of culture you still only find in Chinatown, like the diner that serves pork chops over rice (your choice of gravy, curry or brown), with soup (borscht or minestrone), and a pot sticker. The bakeries offer pork buns and cow's ear cookies (牛耳餅,

a.k.a. smackles), alongside apple pie. Each generation's resourcefulness flavors the food. Chinatown grew out of fear but rose up by reaching across boundaries. And that is how it will continue to thrive.

One change we made to the building was moving our front door to Waverly Place. The earliest restaurants in Chinatown opened up from the alleyways, but eventually they turned to face the main streets to welcome tourists. Every morning when we arrive, the Family Associations greet us. So do our neighbors on their way to the Y or tai chi in the park. In the afternoons, the lion dancers practice while neighborhood kids watch and tourists snap photos. The evenings are filled with someone listening to Canto-pop and the click of mahjong tiles. All day long, people pass by and stop to peek in the window while we work. Waverly is a burst of community life and color.

How We Cook, Here and Now

Mister Jiu's came out of my desire to pay homage to my family traditions and my food memories of growing up Chinese American. I'm not trying to replicate mainland Chinese food with its many genres and distinct regional and subregional cuisines, or the food already in Chinatown, which draws from many facets. I cook food that's a reflection of me and my cooks in this place and time, San Francisco and this neighborhood right now. If you've eaten Chinese food in America, our dishes will feel familiar but different. I want our food to evoke some nostalgia, which is why I dig in to the roots of what we cook. Roots reveal why things are still done a certain way, from techniques to principles of flavor to the subtle details that define the soul of a dish. Context lets food do what it does best—connect us. And not just in the way everyone gathers to appreciate a delicious meal but in how what you cook and eat expresses where you came from and who you are now.

We rely mostly on Chinese equipment and methods, like cleavers, chopsticks, woks, steam, smoking over wood fire, and blanching in oil. We teach our cooks to work with traditional techniques and then experiment. As they find their way in this kitchen, they learn to express their own roots too. Some of them were born in Guangdong or have parents from Shandong. Some experienced Chinese American food for the first time eating General Tso's in a shopping-mall food court. We bring in ingredients and find inspiration in our Chinese, French, Italian, Mexican, Hawaiian, Korean, Japanese, Filipino, Portuguese, and Spanish training and ancestry, and all the other influences that make California cuisine so delicious. It is food rooted in Chinese tradition but not tied down by it. We're riffing on our shared nostalgia as multicultural Americans.

To me, authentic food isn't about a moment in time. People change and move and so does what they eat. China didn't even have chiles until about three hundred years ago, but they are essential to mapo doufu, a now classic Sichuan dish. I also don't believe authenticity has to be dependent on location. The same ingredients will taste different depending on where they're grown. Cooking is about adapting to what's around you. That's how beef-broccoli (instead of beef-gailan) came to be in Chinatown, salt and pepper alligator in New Orleans, and the St. Paul sandwich (egg foo young with pickles, lettuce, and tomato on white bread) in St. Louis. You don't have to be a specific person in a particular place to make food that captures something we all instinctively know has Chinese roots.

There's also a very personal sense of authenticity you feel when you eat something that tastes just how you remember it. My childhood was not identical to yours, so our nostalgia takes us to different places. To me, a more communal way to look at authenticity is in the way a dish embodies cultural traditions; not necessarily in one specific way, but in details that show intention and knowledge. When you cook food that means something to a lot of people, you don't have to look a certain way or have the culture in your blood. (I was, after all, a Chinese American cooking Italian food.) You just have to care. Here is how we cook.

1. Great ingredients first.

Cantonese cuisine and California cuisine are the same in their demand for using only pristine ingredients at the peak of flavor, aroma, and/or texture. Both cuisines are all about showcasing bright, clean flavors and appreciating food that looks like food and tastes of itself. Both honor the seasons. When I'm thinking about a new restaurant dish or deciding what to make with what's in the fridge at home, I start with a great ingredient and, in a way, let it determine its course.

You may not be able to find the exact raw ingredients specified in this book, and that's okay. Many of these recipes are descended from making the best with what was on hand. Northern California is a place of agricultural and wild abundance, but it doesn't matter if you live on another coast, in the mountains, or on the plains, there are ingredients near you that are the best anywhere around. Those are what you need to get to know and cook with. Talk to your farmers and old-school grocers who know what's best when. I'm not saying all substitutions

are a great idea. Substitutions are how cuisines evolve, but they are also how tradition can fade away. If you go through the exercise of breaking down an ingredient's qualities, flavor, shape and color, it will become clearer how to use what's around you to express the essential qualities of a dish, and when to save a specific recipe for another day.

2. More vegetables, less meat.

Chinese food has, out of custom and necessity, traditionally focused on vegetables and grains rather than meat. Early Chinese arrivals led the way for California agriculture to be as diverse and vegetable-focused as it is. It's the way I eat, and it's the way of the future. Pay attention to how things are grown and raised, whether plant or animal, because that affects how they taste. Organic, biodynamic lettuces pack so much flavor, and taste more like lettuce. The cells of a wilted green won't pop open the way they should in a wok over high heat. And, of course, some methods

of agriculture and husbandry are clearly better for all of us.

Cooking vegetables can require more preparation than meat and fish in terms of cleaning and cutting things to the right shape and size, but it also means you're almost done once you bring on the heat.

3. Make what you can.

We fill most of our pantry from scratch using Chinese techniques. Sauces, stocks, spice blends, vinegars, ferments, and pickles are the layers of flavor underlying every recipe. In this way, I can be sure we're starting with the best possible raw ingredients and finishing with clear and bright flavors that are distinctively our own. We want to continue the traditions of making something, and, as the Chinese say, seasoning it with the flavor of skilled hands.

But let's be practical here. Even in our kitchen, with the whole team, we can't make *everything*

ourselves. We'd have to brew five varieties of soy sauce. It also doesn't make sense to prepare certain components that someone else has dedicated a lifetime to making well. At home, maybe start by making some stocks and ferments to quickly kick things up a notch, and go from there. Don't sweat it.

4. Use "grandma wisdom"; cook by principles, not rules.

When it comes to cooking good Chinese food—or good food of any kind, really—there is some grandma wisdom you can't explain. It's knowledge deep in the bones. You only learn it by observing and doing it again and again until you are cooking by feel instead of by numbers. Grandma wisdom comes into play every time you cook, because every vegetable, fish, and cut of meat is unique. Each is shaped by its lineage, where it grew, what nourished it, and how much sun it got. Something you think you know today will be quite different tomorrow. Eggplants at the start of summer are firmer and need more time blanching in oil. The end of tomato season can be as abrupt as the first autumn rain. Every day of every season brings new variables, so cooking requires some judgment calls.

While you are finding your way with any recipe in this book, start by honoring time-tested techniques. (Especially with pastry, fermentation, and charcuterie, which are precisely measured and don't need adjusting.) You're basically riding on several thousand years of development when it comes to Chinese cuisine, plus the work we've done at Mister Jiu's. Many Chinese recipes are really about technique. Take fried rice, which is basically just rice and whatever you want, so long as you know how to use a wok. When you know the way things were done before, it's easier to see what happens as you change the variables. That's when you can start making a dish your own. That's when cooking really gets good.

5. No MSG. But probably not why you think.

Monosodium glutamate (MSG) is everywhere, and research has shown that reasonable amounts have no negative health effects on the overwhelming majority of people. MSG is the salt form of the naturally occurring free glutamates that give savory, craveable taste to Parmesan cheese, seaweed, mushrooms, fish sauce, soy sauce, and breast milk. MSG is added to ranch dressing, canned soup, frozen entrees, chips of almost every brand, fried-chicken sandwiches trending on Twitter, and so on. And it's ridiculous that Chinese restaurants have to post signs saying NO MSG to appeal to customers who consume it in so many other forms. The automatic association of Chinese food with "the mysterious 'white powder' of the Orient," as *The Joy of Cooking* introduced MSG in 1953, has everything to do with race and stereotypes.

The phrase "Chinese restaurant syndrome" first appeared in a headline in the *New England Journal of Medicine* for a letter from pediatrician and researcher Dr. Robert Ho Man Kwok. In the letter, Kwok described experiencing "numbness at the back of the neck" after eating northern Chinese food. (There is a theory that the letter was someone else's prank, but that's another story.) Kwok wrote that he thought it might be the cooking wine, the MSG, or the overall sodium level in the dishes. A flurry of suspect anecdotal evidence soon followed. And it wasn't until 2020, after Ajinomoto (the first major commercial producer of MSG) launched a PR campaign, that *Merriam-Webster's* removed "Chinese restaurant syndrome" from the dictionary.

All that said, MSG is, in my opinion, an intense and flat flavor, all dynamite and no sparkle. If you use too much, there's a sweetness that tastes artificial. I find I have to balance it with more salt (NaCl), which can lead to over-seasoning. MSG comes from a time when fast, convenience cooking took over the world; and for a long time, many Chinese chefs were opposed to using it. Now it is too often utilized as a replacement for flavor that otherwise should have been in the raw ingredients or brought out through technique.

But many chefs, including crazy-famous ones, use MSG! you say. Personally, I just don't believe that MSG goes with the resourceful, cooking-by-hand tradition of Chinese food. I want nuance and layered flavors, not a taste so intense that everyone's palates are strung out and numb. I want ingredients to bring a synergy of flavor, aroma, and texture, not a single, overwhelming taste.

Because sīn meih (鮮味, xián wèi in Mandarin), or umami, is so fundamental to Chinese cuisine,

I bring it about in other ways. I can create flavor synergizers, the magic glutamate + guanylate + inosinate triumvirate that amplify sīn on the tongue by combining ingredients such as cabbage, beef, and mushrooms. Fermentation, drying, and curing also bring them out. As does roasting, slow cooking, and braising. You get richer mouthfeel and more depth of flavor. Through technique you create the space for deliciousness to develop and intensify.

6. Deliciousness through balance.

Everyone says, "good cooking is about balance." Which is like saying, good cooking tastes good. Classical Chinese cooking offers a framework that can help as you're figuring it all out. "Balance" is harmony and contrasts of form (as in the shapes and colors of ingredients), aroma, texture (including the sound of biting into something), and flavor. There's the balance within a single dish and then the balance of everything across the entire meal.

Chinese cooking starts with thinking about the interplay of tastes—salty, sweet, bitter, spicy/pungent, and sour—balanced with sīn. Sīn is described in old Chinese cookbooks as the essence of an ingredient at its absolute peak of flavor, its essential nature. It's the elusive, underlying character that makes us crave something. It's what MSG, first marketed

as "the essence of taste," is meant to capture. In Chinese cooking, you want the sīn to counterbalance and bring out other tastes. Sīn punches up sweetness, sourness, and saltiness while taking the edge off bitterness. It even intensifies some aromas. So think in combinations of flavors.

In Cantonese cooking, there are other combination flavors such as gām (甘), often translated as "golden," which is the unified bittersweet of a kumquat or the aftertaste of good coffee. The sour and astringent taste of a persimmon that makes your mouth pucker is gip (澀). The fragrance of wok hei (see page 25) and fried aromatics on the tongue is hēung (香). There's daahm (淡), or blandness, the idea being that mildness, or the absence of flavor, leaves space to savor and allow other flavors to bloom. Sichuan regional cooking gave us numbing, màh (麻, má in Mandarin), which adds depth to laaht (辣, là in Mandarin), pungent and spicy. There's chūng (冲), that up-the-nose feeling of Chinese mustard that describes a tactile component of flavor. There are many others, and how such flavors interplay with textures is also important. Sourness can neutralize fatty mouthfeel. Slippery and sour can be refreshing. You get the idea. Of course, your preferences will lean certain ways but thinking about cooking as an interplay of flavors, including sīn, and textures that balance, boost, and mellow each other will make your cooking so much more complex and delicious.

麻

MÀH

(NUMBING)

HÀAHM

(SALTY)

甜

TÌHM

(SWEET)

鮮

SĪN

(UMAMI)

淡

DAAHM

(BLAND)

酸

SYÙN

(SOUR)

辣

LAAHT

(PUNGENT/SPICY)

苦

FÚ

(BITTER)

MISTER JIU AND MR. JEW

Yeh Yeh, my father's father, never used my first name. He called all the men in our family, Mr. Jew. Which is why it came as a surprise when he told me that Jew wasn't actually our family name at all.

Before he was an American, Yeh Yeh was toiling on his family's farm in Toisan. Like other young men from that struggling corner of southern China, he heard of opportunity in America. And, so, he bought a boat ticket to San Francisco and with it, a new name.

In America, beginning in 1875 until 1943, the government enacted exclusionary laws barring women, miners, unskilled laborers, and skilled laborers from emigrating from China. These laws made it nearly impossible for Chinese people to enter the United States, or to ever see their families again once they arrived. Even those born in the United States were not American citizens until 1898, when Wong Kim Ark, a Chinatown cook born in San Francisco, took his case to the Supreme Court.

In 1906, the Great Earthquake ignited a fire that burned down Chinatown and San Francisco's hall of records. In this and other parts of the country, people had lit fires to burn Chinese out of their homes. But this time, the San Francisco fire cleared an unintended path to their citizenship. With their paperwork lost, many Chinese claimed they were San Francisco sons. Their new citizenship opened doors for thousands of other Chinese to immigrate to the United States. These new Americans brought over wives and children that they hadn't seen in years. Others returned to their ancestral villages and married,

bringing over new brides. With the help of family, young men looking for opportunity also arrived.

Usually, family shared your blood, but sometimes "family" extended to people willing to trade work for a new name. Those who came to this country under new names were known as "paper sons," and my grandfather became one to an American with the last name 周. You've probably met a Zhou, Zhu, Chiu, Chiau, Chau, Chao, Chew, Chow, Chou, Cho, Chu, Jhou, Jou, Jow, Joo, Jiu, Jue, or Ju? It's all the same name—周—spelled a dozen different ways. Southern China is a region with six major dialects and many subdialects; US immigration didn't have a standard approach for Romanizing those languages. As it happened, my grandfather got the variation, Jew.

In Chinese tradition, your name is your lifeline. Kin will always help you. Shrines, where you pray to ancestors for guidance and protection in life and in death, are in your family name. Community support often comes based on your ancestry through Family Associations and Tongs. In Chinatown, they got you jobs, provided loans, arranged medical care, built schools, funded lawsuits, and became your family when you didn't have any.

You needed kin in San Francisco, the city that the Chinese called Gold Mountain. Life was so hard here that those boarding ships bound for it were known as, jyū jái (豬仔), pigs destined for slaughter. After three weeks at sea, Chinese arrived to be processed at Angel Island in the San Francisco Bay. From 1910 through 1940, the Chinese were separated from the rest of the immigrants there and held in deplorable conditions for weeks, and in some cases, years. (By comparison, it took a few hours to clear immigration at Ellis Island in New York.) During interrogations, detainees were asked about the date of the last typhoon and the number of steps from the family's house to the peach orchard. Everyone hoped their answers matched what others had said before. Those who weren't deported had to then haul themselves from the wharf up the hill to Chinatown, the part of Gold Mountain where Chinese were permitted to live.

Yeh Yeh started his life in America in Chinatown. He learned English, then returned to Toisan to marry my grandmother, Ying Ying. He came back to serve in the army in World War II and Korea and work as a boilermaker, building engines at the Hunter's Point and Mare Island Naval shipyards. He and Ying Ying lived through the Chinese Confession Program in the 1950s, a hunt by the FBI for "paper sons" and communist sympathizers. Eventually, they moved out of Chinatown to the Richmond District to live the American dream of a freestanding house and a big family. My father, Winfred, grew up on 10th Avenue, and nearby he would meet my mom, Mona. And then I showed up.

I started hearing pieces of the story of our family name when I was a teenager. I was shocked, pretty upset actually, and I believed the record needed correcting. Why don't we change it back, I wanted to know? That question didn't fly with anyone in the family. Yeh Yeh and Ying Ying were afraid it might cause our family trouble.

Even after all these years in America, I think that they didn't feel totally secure in their place in this country. Don't rock the boat, they said. Drop it.

Names say a lot though. Those feelings about my family name carried into other parts of my life and how I saw my place in this world. As I learned the history of my family's name, I began making sense of what had been lost and how I wanted to reconnect with the past.

When my wife, Anna Lee, and I were ready to name our restaurant, we wanted one that paid respect to my family's memories and traditions. It also had to be a name that evoked Chinatown in all its glory—as a haven; a booming center of unrivaled hospitality, innovation, and glamour; and a community holding on to tradition while bridging cultures and embracing new ideas.

I spelled Jew as J-I-U for the restaurant, because I wanted to share our family's name but write it the way I choose, not the way it was dictated to us. When you spell out Chinese characters in letters, without tone marks, you lose a lot of context, and jiu takes on a lot of possibilities. It can mean the number 9 (九), a leek (韭), or a dove (鳩). It can mean a stiff drink (酒). It signifies to gather (糾), to hold tight (揪), and to rescue something (救). It can also mean to study something intensely (究). Jiu can describe something very old (久), very ancient (灸). Mister Jiu's is my connection to my past, present, and future.

Losing our name sent me on a journey to recover its meaning. What I found in the end could only have happened because of my grandfather's own journey.

Getting the Most Out of This Book

Often at the restaurant, we do things in a way that aren't so practical for everyday. To season our fried rice, we first cure and dehydrate beef heart over several days, then grate a whisper of it onto the rice. You can make cured beef heart at home (see page 45), but you don't have to. When you can make something delicious by doing less, I'll offer ideas. You can always make things easier by buying some components, or skipping others entirely. You will see what time involvement a recipe requires if you check the **Active Time** and **Plan Ahead** call-outs, which are included at the top of recipes that need them the most.

I want to give you the details, even if maybe you decide to never make some of these recipes. Our cooking is influenced by many food cultures that make California cuisine so delicious. But my personal mission is to make sure traditional Chinese techniques continue by finding new ways to use them, so our palates still crave them and cooks learn to create with them. Simplifying methods to be done in an hour defeats the whole point of teaching you these techniques, some of which I've highlighted in Chef's Notes throughout the book. The chapters in this book follow how we serve meals at the restaurant and roughly the order of courses in a Chinatown banquet. Most ingredient lists are written in units of volume and weight that are open to adjustments—except for pastry, curing meat, and brines for fermenting or pickling. We scaled recipes to what we think is optimum in terms of serving size (4 to 6 people for most individual dishes, more if it's party food) and the physics of cooking. Scaling down any further would create problems with temperatures or equipment, but you can scale up recipes to feed a larger crowd.

This book and the recipes in it are the accumulation of my first three years of cooking at Mister Jiu's. They're not intended to cover every facet of Chinese American cuisine. If we're lucky to have you in, please don't be disappointed if things are different. Our menu depends on what we loved that day at the markets and the good fortune of our farmers and suppliers. Every day surprises us too.

Equipment, in Particular Why You Probably Should Get a Wok

A wok is an incredibly versatile piece of equipment. It is practically required for stir-frying, and it can be used for any recipes that call for blanching, braising, deep-frying, smoking, or steaming. Using a wok gets you in the spirit of cooking Chinese cuisine. The only reason I'm not saying a wok is essential is because I know someone out there has cooked a decent stir-fry in a pan lid over a campfire, and resourcefulness is at the heart of a lot of Chinese American cooking. Also, I know you can achieve really delicious high-temperature cooking without perfect equipment; because at home, I use my trusty 12-inch skillet on a dinky, four-burner range. I developed early versions of many recipes in this book and then convinced people I could run my own restaurant cooking that way. I can't promise that a heavy-bottomed skillet over a burner cranked to 11 will always work perfectly, but if you keep the principles of using a wok in mind, you can make it work.

BUYING A WOK

I suggest getting a 14-inch flat-bottomed, carbon-steel wok with a tight-fitting lid. It will work with both gas-flame and electric burners. It's really tough stir-frying anything on an induction burner. If you're committed, you can invest in an induction burner made just for wok cooking, but otherwise you're going to be really bummed with the results.

A good wok will cost less than every other pot you own. In Chinatown, Tane Chan at the venerable Wok Shop on Grant Avenue can hook you up. You'll also want a wok shovel with a flat edge, or, at least, a very stiff, flat-ended fish spatula. For fried rice, a flat-edged wooden spatula works great. A pair of long bamboo chopsticks is always handy for delicate things, but usually it's enough to have a spider for scooping, especially when oil blanching. You'll need to season a new wok with a scrub and then a high-temperature fry with plenty of oil and aromatics, like scallions, for about 20 minutes until the pan starts to turn golden or darken. The layers of oil that coat a seasoned wok minimize sticking, so water and food skitter across the surface. For the details, I refer you to Grace Young's *The Breath of a Wok*, and Tane at the Wok Shop.

A PAN IS NOT A WOK

Woks are meant to be used with tremendous, steady heat, but most home stoves barely put out 7,000 BTUs. This brings us to the most inconvenient reality of home versus restaurant cooking with a wok. At the restaurant, we use 22-inch, carbon-steel, one-long-handled northern-style woks over dedicated wok holes and huge gas burners that roar like jet engines. Flames shoot up and around the wok. If you're doing everything right and your stir-fry is oily and soggy, or the vegetables dry out before they cook through, you just might not have the right burners for the job. Grace Young says 15,000 BTUs is the minimum power it takes to generate the steady heat required for deep wok hei, which is the point of cooking in a wok.

Wok hei is the flavor, aroma, and resulting texture of heat, smoke, and flame that only a screaming-hot wok can imbue. It's "the breath of the wok," as Young translates it. The word hei is the Cantonese pronunciation of 氣 (qì, in Mandarin), as in the life force that flows in each of us. The hei of a wok is just as ephemeral, disappearing as food cools. Technically speaking, wok hei is created by the caramelization of sugars and the Maillard reaction happening between the proteins and sugars in whatever you're cooking plus the controlled combustion of oil. When you toss your food in a wok, you're not just moving it to cook things evenly, you're also sending tiny beads of oil airborne to kiss your food with bursts of flame.

A wok is a humbling instrument. At Mister Jiu's, no one gets to the wok until they've graduated from every other station in the kitchen, and even then it trips up everyone at first. Think of a wok like a French top or plancha but three-dimensional and moveable. You can play with heat and moisture by moving food in and out of its center and up the sides. It takes practice to understand when to add liquid. Too many flames, and everything tastes burnt. Too much oil, and you're either drenching everything at too low a temperature or, if the pan is hot enough, you're risking a pan fire. Too much heat and not enough oil, and everything tastes metallic and dry. It all happens in a matter of seconds. When you watch someone who's mastered it, their movements look choreographed. They are constantly observing while in motion. They know how long the food should touch down and where to heat, and how long and how often it should be moving through the air to cool. Fair warning, when done right, wok cooking at home is guaranteed to set off a smoke alarm. I do it every time. Turn on your exhaust hood. Open your windows. And maybe take the battery out of your smoke detector for now.

This is what I tell everyone their first day at the wok station.

❶ Your mise en place is everything. Prep all of your ingredients to the proper size and shape for cooking, and line them up in the order they go into the wok. Generally, this means in order of closest to farthest from you will be meat, large veg, small veg, sauce components, and aromatics, combining ingredients that take the same amount of cooking time. Keep proteins cool, but everything else should be about room temperature so as not to cool down the wok. Every vegetable should be dry, and every protein as close to dry as possible, otherwise they will steam and not have any bite. If they aren't dry, pat them with paper towels or set them aside until they are ready. I keep my spatula in one hand at all times and set a spider and a warmed serving platter off to the side.

❷ Choose the right fat and don't use too much of it. You want cooking oils with a high smoke point and a low polyunsaturated-fat content. Cold-pressed rice bran oil is for frying, oil blanching, and any time we're dealing with very high heat. Unrefined peanut oil is also good, but it adds its own strong flavor. Avoid butter (unless clarified) and extra-virgin olive oil because they'll burn in the high heat of the wok. Most of the time, you need only enough just to coat the wok. Pour or wipe out any excess.

❸ Hot wok, warm oil—the Cantonese wok-cook's mantra. Only add the oil right before you are ready to go, because it can't sit alone in a wok too long. Martin Yan told me, deadly serious, "You have not even 10 seconds before it's scorched and ruined." Burnt oil is bitter. Also, avoid waiting until the dry pan is so ripping hot that you might start a fire. You want the oil in the wok the moment a drop of water rolls around and dances away, or you get that first waft of wok hei from a well-seasoned wok. The instant before the oil starts smoking, add the first ingredient.

❹ Stick to the game plan. Adjust the heat as you add ingredients as planned to the wok. In general, you want the flames licking up the sides of the wok but start slightly lower than max, if you can. Adding ingredients to the wok, especially on a typical home stove, can cool things down quickly. Also consider

carryover, the residual heat in the wok that will keep cooking things even after you turn down the heat. This is especially true for electric stoves. You may need to lift the wok completely off the heat occasionally.

⑤ Don't cook too much at once. If your wok is too small to accommodate a recipe, then work in batches. Your food should fill about a third of the wok. You need room for everything to move around, otherwise it will burn or, almost as bad, steam.

⑥ Keep things moving. Get aromatics and most vegetables moving right away. Proteins need a moment undisturbed to sear, otherwise they will stick to the wok. For the sake of wok hei, toss, don't just stir. The gist is to move the wok away from you while tilting it forward (as if scooping toward the flame) and then pulling it back toward you, so that the pan is moving in a circular seesaw motion, and everything you're cooking is sliding in the wok toward you, away from you, and then flipping in the air over the back rim of the wok. The flip is the moment when the flames can kiss the ingredients for max wok hei. It's hard to do this in a sauté pan without risking a stove fire, so use caution.

⑦ Add liquid to a stir-fry only as needed. Add it in an evenly dispersed stream to the ingredients so it doesn't burn or cool everything else down too much. Most vegetables have enough liquid within them already and just need time to release it, but sometimes you need to add more water or stock to create steam to buy more time before ingredients scorch, or to make a sauce.

⑧ Serve a wok'd dish on a hot platter or in a hot bowl immediately.

Everything Else You Need

You can make many of the recipes in this book with the equipment you probably have in your kitchen, but sometimes you will need specialized tools. If there is a way around it, we noted it in the recipe. Otherwise, the best results require what's specified in each recipe as **Special Equipment**.

You don't need a cleaver, but I recommend one. Next to woks and chopsticks, it's the most multifunctional tool in our kitchen. Building up your wrist strength to keep a cleaver steady in motion is a workout at first. The most basic technique is

to cut with the blade moving either straight down, or forward and down. Once you get that motion, the cleaver's weight does the work for you. Get a vegetable cleaver, choi dōu (菜刀), which is relatively lightweight with a thin blade for slicing and dicing vegetables and still enough heft for slicing through meat and cartilage. Look for one with a flat cutting edge that curves just a bit at the heel. A larger cleaver with a strongly curved edge is for serious butchering, which you probably won't need to do often. I still reach for a thin-bladed boning knife for the kind of light butchering required in some recipes in this book. Once the meat is off the bone, I go back to my cleaver for the chopping, slicing, dicing, mincing, smashing, and everything else.

Knife Cuts

Knife skills can make everything look delectable on the plate. Chinese cooks learn to slice a pork kidney so that it cooks up to look like an ear of wheat, a comb, a pine cone, a plump lychee, a fisherman's straw cape, or even the Chinese character for longevity (壽). I love that Chinese fine-dining chefs can cut carrots into the shape of two carps leaping up a waterfall. This isn't our aesthetic at Mister Jiu's, though. When I cut carrots, I'm thinking about how to bring out the essence of the carrot, depending on what I'm cooking it with, and how. I want that carrot to still look and taste like a carrot when it's all over.

How you cut each ingredient depends on how you plan to use it. Cut to enable ingredients to cook evenly, hold sauces and seasonings better, and best express their character. With beef, cut across the grain for tenderness, but keep chicken fibers longer so the pieces don't crumble. You can control how short you want those protein fibers with the angle of your knife. In general, cut everything to about the same size as the thing that takes the longest to cook. Avoid bulky, awkward shapes. Think flat and long (especially for the wok) to maximize the surface area touching heat.

① Here are Maria and Sean to show you the knife cuts in this book.

② BIAS SLICE
Cut slices of vegetables at about 30 degrees on the diagonal. Cut slices of meat at 60 to 90 degrees, depending on the grain and the use.

③ ROLL CUTS
Cut large, regular chunks, generally about 1 inch thick. Slice at about 45 degrees on the diagonal, then roll a third of the way over before the next cut.

④ DICE
Cut cubes or little pieces of regular size. Small dice is ¼ inch, medium dice is ½ inch, and large dice is ¾ to 1 inch.

⑤ THREAD CUT AND ⑥ MATCHSTICKS
Slice thinly into threads or thin strips, 1 to 2 inches long. Threads and strips are thinner than matchsticks, which are ⅛ to ½ inch thick in this book. If preparing a large amount, slice first with a mandoline, then stack and cut into strips.

⑦ FINE MINCE OR ⑧ SMASH
If you're making a garnish, finely dice into tiny cubes. Otherwise, it is usually fine to chop into rough but even little pieces, or smash with the side of the cleaver.

Turning proteins into a paste is a combination of mincing and smashing and goes fastest with a cleaver in each hand. Work with one ingredient at a time. Thinly slice the protein across the grain and then stack the slices. Make close parallel chops while moving the blade from one end of the stack to the other. Flip or fold the mixture over with the flat of the blade and then chop in a 45- to 90-degree angle from before, moving again from one end to the other. Occasionally, with the flat of the blade, smear the mixture into the cutting board, then flip or fold the mixture over again. Continue until the paste is the required texture.

⑨ HAND TEARING
Trim the tough ends of stems from leafy greens and flowering vegetables, then break off bunches by hand into roughly even sizes. Shred rehydrated seafood and braised meats into even pieces.

A Note on Words and Spellings

Everything in Chinatown has many names. For instance, you could say, Mister Jiu's is on Waverly Place. But in Cantonese, you would say it is on Tīn Hauh Gú Míu Gāai, meaning "the street of Tin How Temple," which since 1852 has kept the incense burning in one form or another for the goddess who protects those who cross distant seas. You can write "Tin How Temple" in traditional Chinese characters as 天后古廟. Or in simplified Chinese characters as 天后古庙, depending on when and where you learned to write.

Food can have many names too. Take the strips of fried dough that Chinese people enjoy with soy milk or jook. They are called yóu tiáo (油條, oil sticks) in Mandarin, and yàuh ja gwái ((油炸鬼, oil-fried devils) in Cantonese. In San Francisco, we also call them Chinese donuts, fritters, crullers, or churros. Names and recipes are the stories of people coming together.

In this book, for Chinese words not in common American usage, we mostly use Cantonese terms and traditional characters. But Chinese Americans have roots in every region of China, where more than two hundred, distinct dialects are spoken, so sometimes it made sense to use the term most common to a dish's origins, so you will see Mandarin and other dialects too.

We also included Romanized pronunciations with diacritics—marks that describe a word's tone, pitch, and contour—throughout this book. Keep in mind, the letter combinations represent sounds unique to each dialect, not English phonics. Also, Romanizing Chinese dialects aside from Mandarin is not so standardized and is still in flux. This is why words are spelled in so many different ways on Chinatown's menus and signs. Another totally acceptable way of writing the Cantonese pronunciation is with numbers instead of diacritics. So those savory donuts, for instance, are jau4 zaa3 gwai2; but we opted for diacritics for easier reading. For the same reason, we dropped diacritics in some places, such as recipe titles, where words are clear enough from context. All this is to say that when dialect, script, or spelling was a hard call, we went with what we hope will be the most useful in our neighborhood.

1

Stocks, sauces, ferments, vinegars, and oils are the building blocks of our cooking. Condiments are diuh meih (調味), meaning they are notes for tuning and accenting flavor. You use them during cooking and also present them on the table as an integral part of the meal. At Mister Jiu's, we make many of the condiments in our pantry ourselves, the way it was done in days past, but there are also good products on the shelves in Chinatown, Asian markets, and the "ethnic foods" aisle at your supermarket or health food store.

Take note of some key raw ingredients that come up a lot in this book. Sunflower oil is our neutral oil. You can also use safflower or grapeseed oil. We use cold-pressed rice bran oil for frying, oil blanching, and any time we're dealing with very high heat, though unrefined peanut oil also works. Unrefined nut or seed oils such as sunflower, grapeseed, pumpkin seed, and walnut are good for cold dressings and baking. We also use Sicilian agrumato lemon or orange extra-virgin olive oils, the citrus and olives are pressed simultaneously, for finishing. For black vinegar, which is made from fermented rice and grains, look for Zhenjiang (a.k.a. Chinkiang) origin vinegar (镇江香醋, Zhènjiāng xiāngcù in Mandarin), preferably aged. We use Jacobsen sea salt (for cooking) and flake salt (for finishing). These recipes call for three kinds of soy sauce, light (meaning 生抽, sāng chāu), premium (meaning 頭抽, tàuh chāu), and dark (meaning 老抽, lóuh chāu). Avoid low-sodium options, which are sometimes also called "light." We use three different rice flours, sometimes in combination. For long-grain glutinous rice flour, we like the fine texture of Thai brand Erawan's water-milled flour (look for "水磨糯米粉" on the label). In savory applications, we often mix long-grain glutinous rice flour with a coarser short-grain glutinous rice flour such as Koda Farms organic Blue Star Mochiko. When plain rice flour is specified, we like Erawan (look for "粘米粉" on the label). Many called-for ingredients are within reach online.

STOCKS

We always have stocks bubbling on our stoves and chilling in the walk-in. We use them everywhere in stir-fries, braises, and soups to bring sīn flavor, depth, and sometimes richness. They are the backbone of our pantry.

SUPREME STOCK

Active Time — 30 minutes
Plan Ahead — You'll need 3 hours for simmering
Makes about 3 qt / 2.8L
Special Equipment — Cheesecloth (or coffee filter)

Supreme Stock doesn't get its name for nothing. Séuhng tōng (上湯) is Cantonese for "the G.O.A.T. of stocks." It is a sumptuous, deeply layered flavor-enhancer disguised as a clear stock. The stock should barely reach a simmer, so you never see more than a couple of little bubbles rising to the top. Collagen and fat need gentle heat to meld into the stock, so that the stock feels velvety rather than greasy on the tongue.

One 4-lb / 1.8kg whole chicken
2 lb / 900g pork bones, skin-on shanks, and trotters, split at the joints

8 oz / 225g salt pork or smoked ham
5 qt / 4.7L cold water
1½ lb / 680g yellow onions, coarsely chopped
8-inch piece ginger, peeled and coarsely chopped
2 large stalks celery, coarsely chopped
Kosher salt

Fill an 8-quart or larger pot halfway with tap water and bring to a vigorous boil over high heat. Add the chicken and blanch for 10 to 15 seconds, then remove to a colander set in the sink. Add the pork bones to the same water and blanch for 10 to 15 minutes, then transfer to the colander with the chicken. Discard the cooking water and wash out the pot.

Add the chicken, pork bones, salt pork, and 5 qt / 4.7L cold water to the pot and bring to a hard simmer over high heat. Skim off as much scum as possible from the surface. Add the onions, ginger, and celery; turn the heat to medium-low; and simmer gently, uncovered, skimming every 30 minutes as needed, for 3 hours. The stock should be deeply flavorful.

Line a fine-mesh strainer or colander with a double layer of cheesecloth (or a coffee filter) and fit it over a large bowl. Strain the stock and discard the solids. Skim the fat off the top of the stock, if desired. Taste, season with salt, and let cool.

Transfer the stock to an airtight container and store in the refrigerator for up to 5 days, or in the freezer for up to 2 months. When ready to use, warm to a gentle simmer over medium heat.

CHICKEN STOCK

Active Time — 30 minutes
Plan Ahead — You'll need 4 hours for simmering
Makes about 2½ qt / 2.4L
Special Equipment — Cheesecloth (or coffee filter)

The classic Chinese chicken stock is chicken, ginger, green onions, and peppercorns plus whatever dried herbs suit its purpose, but I wanted to layer in some strong, fresh herbs. Depending on the season, we use summer or winter savory, which tastes something like tarragon and thyme and something else entirely. This stock should be exceptionally clean and clear, so blanch the bones and skim often. This is my go-to base for soups and anything that needs a flavor boost without added richness.

2½ lb / 1.1kg chicken backbones
½ medium yellow onion, chopped

½ medium stalk celery, chopped

½ medium carrot, chopped

4 thyme sprigs

1 winter or summer savory sprig

2½ qt / 2.4L cold water

Fill a 6-quart or larger pot halfway with tap water and bring to a vigorous boil over high heat. Add the chicken bones and blanch for 10 to 15 seconds, then transfer to a colander set in the sink. Discard the cooking water and wash out the pot.

Add the chicken bones, onion, celery, carrot, thyme, savory, and 2½ qt / 2.4L cold water to the pot and bring to a hard simmer over high heat. Skim off as much scum as possible from the surface. Turn the heat to medium-low and simmer gently for about 4 hours, skimming every hour or as needed.

Line a fine-mesh strainer or colander with a double layer of cheesecloth (or a coffee filter) and fit it over a large bowl. Strain the stock, discard the solids, and let cool.

Transfer the stock to an airtight container and store in the refrigerator for up to 5 days, or in the freezer for up to 2 months. When ready to use, warm to a gentle simmer over medium heat.

Chef's Note: Stocking Up

Chinese stocks start with bones—ribs, marrow-rich leg bones, tails, feet, spines, whatever you've got will work.

BONE PREP

Fish and poultry bones make the lightest stocks, so you have to use a lot—generally about 2 lb / 900g per 1 qt / 950ml, give or take. You can open up thin bones to draw out more flavor and nutrients. The Chinese way is to use a heavy cleaver to crack pork ribs and chicken leg bones every couple inches. Or just chop straight through them to expose the marrow. Marrow can bring overpowering minerality, so balance that with plenty of aromatics and spice blends (see page 36).

Sometimes you need just a whisper of a stock, and one type of animal bone is enough. But when a rich stock such as Supreme Stock (facing page) is called for, you need a range of bones and sources of collagen, like the joints in between shanks, knuckles, spines, and tails. I always include some meaty bones in my poultry, pork, and beef stocks, leaving any skin and underlying fat those have intact. Skim away however much fat you wish later, once it has cooled.

BLANCHING IS KEY

Cantonese cooks insist on blanching bones before simmering, so that most of the impurities that muddy flavor and clarity are washed away at the start. Rinse fresh meats and bones for stock with a quick parboil, pour off the water, and then start the actual stock with fresh, cold water. Whether you blanch or not, whenever you see protein scum collecting during the simmer, skim it away.

ROASTING

You can deepen flavor by roasting bones before simmering. This works as well for vegetable stocks. Chinese cooks lightly roast dried, bony river fish before simmering to add the best kind of fishy flavor to many light stocks. Just watch out for overpowering flavor from deeply roasted beef bones.

SIMMERING

Simmer stock in an uncovered pot. Don't stir and don't let the stock boil. Turbulence emulsifies the fats into the water and breaks down big pieces, clouding everything. Adding ice cubes slows down the simmer and reduction, but you still need to keep an eye on the pot to ensure no more than a few bubbles.

Sometimes you *do* want a steady boil for a milk broth, a creamy white stock usually made from fish bones or pork feet. To keep everything emulsified, top off only with boiling water when needed. We use milk broths in our soups in the colder months.

SALTING

Salt in a stock is a matter of taste and also depends on what your dishes require. If you're making stock for a general use TBD, wait to add salt down the road.

STRAINING

We strain our stocks at the end through a cheesecloth-lined strainer for extra clarity.

FISH FUMET

Active Time — 15 minutes

Plan Ahead — You'll need overnight for soaking the fish bones, plus 1 hour for simmering

Makes about 5 cups / 1.2L

Special Equipment — Cheesecloth (or coffee filter)

Chinese fish stock is often milky, a result of churning the protein and animal fat enough that they emulsify into the broth. Look for a firm, white fleshy fish with a low fat content, like halibut and black bass carcasses (heads with gills removed are great). We soak the bones in cold water overnight to leach out any remaining blood for a super-clean, sīn, and sweet stock. Add ice cubes when cooking the stock, so that it takes even longer to come to a simmer and doesn't reduce. The result is crystal clear, the most subtle stock.

2 lb / 900g white fish bones and heads
2 medium stalks celery, chopped
1 small fennel bulb, thickly sliced
½ medium yellow onion, peeled and thickly sliced
1 cup / 170g ice cubes
6 cups / 1.4L cold water

Trim away and discard any guts and large blood vessels from the fish bones and remove and discard the gills from the head; rinse the bones. Place everything in a large bowl, cover with cold tap water, and let soak overnight in the refrigerator.

Drain the bones and place in a 5-quart or larger pot. Add the celery, fennel, onion, ice cubes, and 6 cups / 1.4L cold water and bring to a simmer over medium heat. Do not let it come to a boil. Skim off as much scum as possible from the surface. Turn the heat to medium-low and continue to simmer, uncovered, skimming occasionally as needed, until intensely flavored, about 1 hour.

Line a fine-mesh strainer or colander with a double layer of cheesecloth (or a coffee filter) and fit it over a large bowl. Strain the stock, discard the solids, and let cool.

Transfer the stock to an airtight container and store in the refrigerator for up to 2 days, or in the freezer for up to 1 month. When ready to use, warm to a gentle simmer over medium heat.

SPICES

Chinese spice blends got their start preserving meat, grew into a branch of Chinese medicine, and nowadays are on grocery store shelves. Like Ethiopian berbere, Indian garam masala, or Moroccan ras el hanout, the precise structure of Chinese spice blends is regional, down to the kitchen. White peppercorns are the foundation of many Chinese spice blends. Cumin means western China (see Xinjiang Spice, page 225). Sichuan peppercorn lands you in the central basin. I've found California bay leaves and fennel pollen fit right in.

SPICE BLENDS

Active Time — 40 minutes for Shrimp Salt, 10 minutes for everything else

Other than the peppercorns, each blend will make ⅓ to ½ cup / 40 to 60g

Special Equipment — Spice grinder or mortar and pestle

We use spice blends as meat rubs, as sachets for braises and soups, and as a finishing touch on everything from seafood to cocktails. Toasting spices right before use is the key to unleashing their maximum flavor.

5 SPICE — The classic Chinese blend

1 Tbsp white peppercorns
½ cup / 20g star anise
4 tsp fennel seeds
1 tsp whole cloves
Two 2½-inch Chinese cinnamon (cassia) sticks, broken into 2 or 3 pieces

10 SPICE — Works so well with all things roasted, we call it Duck Spice around here

1 Tbsp white peppercorns
½ cup / 20g star anise
4 tsp fennel seeds
1 tsp whole cloves
Two 2½-inch Chinese cinnamon (cassia) sticks, broken into 2 or 3 pieces
⅓ cup / 30g black cardamom pods (草果, chóu gwó)
2 Tbsp coriander seeds
2 Tbsp chopped dried licorice root or sassafras
1½ Tbsp allspice berries
1½ bay leaves

WOK SALT — A numbing blend good for finishing anything fried

2 Tbsp plus 1 tsp red Sichuan peppercorns
2 Tbsp black peppercorns
2 tsp white peppercorns
⅓ cup / 45g kosher salt

SHRIMP SALT — A textured savory, salty bump not unlike MSG crystals but tastier

1 large handful shrimp shells
Kosher salt (twice the weight of the toasted shrimp shells)

In a wok or a frying pan (large enough to hold the ingredients spread in an even layer) over medium heat, combine (if using) the white peppercorns, star anise, fennel seeds, cloves, cardamom pods, coriander seeds, allspice berries, and/or Sichuan peppercorns and black peppercorns and toast, tossing or stirring frequently, until fragrant, about 2 minutes. If you see or smell anything more than a wisp of smoke, it's probably best to start over.

Add (if using) the cinnamon, licorice, bay leaves, and salt and smash in the mortar or grind in the spice grinder, working in batches if necessary. If making Shrimp Salt, toast the shells on a baking sheet in a preheated 375°F oven until crisp and dry, about 30 minutes. Immediately transfer the toasted ingredients to a mortar and pestle, or let cool in a dish and add to a spice grinder. All of these blends, except the Wok Salt, work best as a very fine powder. Spice dust should float in the air if you breathe over it. Leave the Wok Salt coarse, like cracked pepper.

Transfer the spice blend to an airtight container; store in a cool, dry place; and use within a month or two.

SAUCES AND CHILE OILS

The first Chinese condiments to make it big overseas were likely soy sauce and ké tsiap (鮭汁, in Minnan), a fermented fish sauce blended with spices. English cooks tried to reproduce the sīn flavor with mushrooms and anchovies, eventually adding tomatoes in the early 1800s. When Americans were pouring on Chinese condiments at the turn of the nineteenth century, their cookbooks used the terms "soy sauce" and "ketchup" interchangeably. Both brought intense sīn flavor. There are many others to have on your table.

PEANUT BUTTER–HOISIN SAUCE

Active Time — 15 minutes
Makes 1½ cups / 950ml
Special Equipment — Food processor

Hoisin sauce (海鮮醬), or "sea-essence sauce," comes from the pantheon of aspirationally named flavorings in the Chinese pantry. Sometimes you hear someone call it plum sauce or duck sauce, which are also *not* what it is. Typically made from sweetened, fermented soybeans, chiles, and garlic, it is intensely sīn flavored. It's used most in barbecue marinades, but also as a dip. I added peanut butter and a little mustard powder, so this version is something like what you dab on your pancakes for mu shu and Beijing roast duck—but not quite. Sesame-Garlic Sauce (page 274) is a good alternative in case of allergies.

¼ cup / 30g fermented black beans
3 garlic cloves, thinly sliced
3 Tbsp packed light brown sugar
3 Tbsp brown rice syrup
3 Tbsp molasses (not blackstrap)
1½ Tbsp light soy sauce (生抽, sāng chāu)
1 Tbsp toasted sesame oil
1 Tbsp distilled white vinegar
2 tsp Chinese hot mustard powder
¼ tsp black peppercorns
⅓ cup plus 1 Tbsp / 95g natural unsalted smooth peanut butter
3 Tbsp water

Put the black beans and garlic in a small saucepan and cover with hot tap water. Soak for 5 minutes, then drain. Return the black beans and garlic to the saucepan and add the brown sugar, brown rice syrup, molasses, soy sauce, sesame oil, vinegar, mustard powder, and peppercorns. Warm over low heat, stirring occasionally, until the sugar is dissolved.

Transfer the contents of the pan to a food processor, add the peanut butter and water, and process until smooth, about 1½ minutes. The sauce should slowly run off a spoon like molasses.

Transfer the sauce to an airtight container and store in the refrigerator for up to 1 month.

Chef's Note: Chiles

You can buy the dried chiles needed for these recipes already stemmed and ground into flakes, but you'll get better results starting with whole varieties and breaking them down yourself. We use thin, 4-inch long èr jīngtiáo (二荊條) chiles, which are mild and fragrant, but we have also used dried, organic Sicilian chiles when necessary. You can find quality dried chiles online at Mala Market.

Chinatown markets also carry an abundance of options, from slender orange and red chiles from Yunnan to deep-red Mexican árbol, mild Korean gochugaru, and and all kinds of red chiles collectively labeled Tianjin, 天津, or tien tsin. You can use whatever flavorful dried chile you like; just keep in mind the general principle that the more seeds a chile has, the spicier it will be. Chiles on the tongue are meant to prolong the flavor of whatever you are using them in, not burn your palate. And each will bring its own flavor, ranging from smoky and sweet to bitter and ripping hot. Adjust the heat by removing some of the seeds and the membrane and ribs holding them in place, and upping the other aromatics and citrus. Or simply use fewer chiles.

Where fresh chiles are specified, the same principles apply for adjusting heat.

RED XO SAUCE

Active Time — 1½ hours
Plan Ahead — You'll need at least 1 day for brining, dehydrating, and then rehydrating the seafood (unless you buy it)
Makes about 2 cups / 480ml
Special Equipment — Food processor, spice grinder

XO at its core is an oil infused with dried seafood, salted meat, and aromatics. I like playing around within that framework. XO connoisseurs say that an XO should show off what's gone into it. You want to see morsels of shrimp or threads of scallop. So you have to take care when drying the seafood, then shredding it properly to retain the texture. Once you start cooking, work through each component in order, not cooking anything too long or at too high heat, or it will all turn to mush.

We dry our own seafood because I want to know how the animals were caught and treated afterward. To me, the ultimate luxury will always be using ingredients that have been cared for and thought about. But if you don't want to start from scratch, you can find quality dried seafood in Chinatown markets. Look for uniform scallops that are about the size of a quarter, and shrimp labeled "wild from Louisiana" about the size of a silver dollar. Keep in mind, when it comes to XO and everything that goes in it, price usually reflects quality.

1 cup / 240ml neutral oil
⅓ cup plus 1 Tbsp / 40g peeled and minced ginger
⅓ cup / 40g minced shallots
¼ cup / 30g thinly sliced (crosswise) green onions (white parts only)
¼ cup / 50g minced garlic
4 tsp tomato paste
1 Tbsp Chinese chile flakes

2 tsp shrimp paste (preferably Lee Kum Kee
    shrimp sauce)
4 oz / 115g Dried Shrimp or Dried Scallops
    (recipe follows)
½ cup / 60g small-diced spicy or
    fennel salami, casings removed
1¼ tsp coriander seeds
1 tsp red Sichuan peppercorns
¼ tsp anise seeds
1 tsp fennel pollen

In a small saucepan over medium heat, warm ¼ cup plus 1 Tbsp / 75ml of the neutral oil until shimmering. Stir in the ginger, shallots, green onions, and garlic; turn the heat to low; and cook until the aromatics are darkened in color, about 30 minutes.

Meanwhile, in a small frying pan over medium heat, warm 3 Tbsp oil until shimmering. Stir in the tomato paste and chile flakes, then stir in the shrimp paste. Turn the heat to low and cook until very aromatic, about 30 minutes. In a small bowl, cover the dried shrimp with warm water and let soak for 20 minutes. Drain the shrimp, then pulse in a food processor fitted with the blade attachment until shredded.

Stir the shrimp paste mixture into the garlic mixture. Add the remaining ½ cup / 120ml oil, the shredded shrimp, and salami and cook over low heat until the salami darkens in color and the oil is red, about 45 minutes.

Meanwhile, in a small frying pan over medium heat, combine the coriander seeds, peppercorns, and anise seeds and toast, tossing or stirring frequently, until lightly toasted and fragrant, about 2 minutes. Immediately transfer the contents of the pan to a dish and stir in the fennel pollen. Let cool, then transfer to a spice grinder and process until finely ground. Stir the ground spices into the sauce and cook for 5 minutes more. Remove from the heat and let cool.

Transfer the sauce to an airtight container and store in the refrigerator for up to 1 week.

Dried Shrimp or Dried Scallops

Makes about 4 oz / 115g
Special Equipment — Dehydrator

1½ cups / 360ml cold water
2 Tbsp kosher salt
1¼ lb / 570g peeled and cleaned large
    (21 to 25 count) shrimp

OR

1½ cups / 360ml cold water
2¼ tsp kosher salt
1¼ lb / 570g large sea scallops, preferably U-10 size

In a medium bowl, combine the water and salt and whisk until the salt is dissolved. Add the shrimp or scallops, then cover and refrigerate overnight.

Prepare a steamer in a wok or a large, lidded pot following the instructions on page 167 and bring the water to a boil over medium-high heat. Drain the seafood and place in the steamer in a single layer. Cover and steam the shrimp for 20 minutes or the scallops for 1 hour, adding additional water to the pot halfway through as needed.

If you have a dehydrator, use it set to 150°F for shrimp or 135°F for scallops. Otherwise, preheat the oven to 150°F and place the seafood on a wire roasting rack set over a baking sheet, arranging them so none is touching.

Dehydrate or bake until the seafood is dried but still pliable and a bit chewy in the middle, about 7 hours for shrimp or 9 hours for scallops, depending on the seafood size and your dehydrator or oven. Let cool, then transfer to an airtight container and store in the freezer for up to 2 months.

ON XO SAUCE

XO is short for "extra old" in the world of fine cognac and short for "baller" in the world of Chinese people. Depending on whom you ask, XO sauce got its start in Hong Kong, either at the posh Spring Moon restaurant or among the lively seafood restaurants around the harbor in the 1980s. It's a medley of dried seafood and ham that is intensely sīn with just a hint of heat, not so much a condiment but a side dish to eat by the spoonful.

Slapping a label on a chunky brown sauce was ingenious marketing. XO is packed with expensive dried seafood and prized Jinhua ham, and sometimes goes for $160 a jar.

Despite its price, XO is now a pantry staple that's gone way beyond the realm of Chinese cuisine. It's paired with everything from bacon to unagi, toast, and prime rib, a fashionable flavor ambassador trying on new styles.

BASIC CHILE OIL

Active Time — 10 minutes

Plan Ahead — You'll need at least 2 days for infusing the chiles

Makes 1¾ cups / 415ml

Special Equipment — Deep-fry thermometer

This is our play on the delicious, bright-orange chile oil you drizzle over wontons, dumplings, and noodles. It's floral, citrusy, and not-so-spicy, so it works for finishing pretty much anything that needs a kick without messing with texture. We usually use finely chopped Yunnan chiles or árbol for the chile flakes, and Aleppo or gochugaru chile for color (see Chef's Note: Chiles, page 38). To bring out all these flavors, you have to first heat the oil to smoking; to the edge of catching fire, really. Keep the spices and cold oil nearby, so things don't get out of hand. Once the oil is made, don't reheat it. Add a dash to the wok at the very end of cooking or drizzle over a dish at the table.

> One 2½ × ¾-inch strip fresh orange peel
> 2 Tbsp Chinese chile flakes
> 4 tsp red Sichuan peppercorns
> ½ tsp Aleppo chile or ground Korean chile (gochugaru)
> ½ star anise pod
> 2 cups / 480ml neutral oil

Put the orange peel, chile flakes, peppercorns, Aleppo chile, and star anise in a heatproof bowl or 1-quart jar. Fill a small saucepan with 1½ cups / 360ml of the neutral oil and secure a deep-fry thermometer on the side. Place over medium-high heat and warm the oil to 300°F. Pour the oil over the chile mixture, then immediately top with the remaining ½ cup / 120ml oil. Let cool, then cover and infuse at cool room temperature for 2 to 3 days.

Strain the chile oil through a fine-mesh strainer into an airtight container and discard the solids. Store in the refrigerator for up to 3 months.

LANZHOU CHILE OIL

Active Time — 20 minutes

Plan Ahead — You'll need overnight for steeping

Makes a scant 1 cup / 240ml

Special Equipment — Deep-fry thermometer, cheesecloth, kitchen twine

This easy-to-savor chile oil usually goes into bowls of Lanzhou beef–noodle soup. Lánzhōu lā miàn (蘭州拉麵, in Mandarin) is a Hui dish with an official standard, like the Bolognese people with their tagliatelle. The rules dictate how each component must be made, from the miàn, which has to be pulled to order by hand into strands that measure so many millimeters wide, to the chile oil, which should use a specific chile, èr jīngtiáo (二荆條, in Mandarin). We've also used organic Sicilian crushed red pepper, which is spicier and lends a smoky sweetness (see Chef's Note: Chiles, page 38). Sometimes we add Potato Crisps (see page 143) for a Cali-Guizhou chile crisp, which definitely is not in the rulebook.

> 1 cup / 240ml neutral oil
> ⅛ medium yellow onion, coarsely chopped
> 1 green onion, coarsely chopped
> ½-inch piece fresh ginger, peeled and thinly sliced
> ½ small cinnamon stick
> 1 black cardamom pod (草果, chóu gwó)
> 1 star anise pod
> ½ tsp fennel seeds
> ½ tsp red Sichuan peppercorns
> ¼ cup / 25g Chinese chile flakes

1 Tbsp raw white sesame seeds

1 Tbsp raw black sesame seeds

1 dash dark soy sauce (老抽, lóuh chāu)

Fill a wok or small saucepan with the neutral oil and secure a deep-fry thermometer on the side. Add the yellow onion, green onion, ginger, cinnamon, cardamom, star anise, fennel seeds, and peppercorns. Place the pan over medium heat and warm the oil until it reaches 300°F (no higher, or the oil will taste burnt) and the onions begin to caramelize at the edges, 12 to 14 minutes. Remove from the heat.

Line a fine-mesh strainer with a double layer of cheesecloth and set over a heatproof bowl. Pour the oil mixture through the strainer, then gather up the sides of the cheesecloth and tie closed with kitchen twine to form a sachet. Add the sachet, chile flakes, white and black sesame seeds, and soy sauce to the oil and stir to combine. Let cool to lukewarm, then cover and let sit overnight at room temperature. Remove the sachet and gently squeeze any oil in it back into the bowl. Discard the sachet.

Transfer the chile oil to an airtight container and store in the refrigerator for up to 3 months.

SPICY BEEF CHILE OIL

Active Time — 10 minutes

Makes about 1½ cups / 360ml

This is the most flavorful of chile oils you will ever meet. It calls for beef fat, which we all know is magic. This spicy oil is what makes Chongqing hot pot great. It's the intensity behind mapo doufu that's so often missing. Get your tallow from a butcher or online. We use dried Yunnan chiles (see Chef's Note: Chiles, page 38), stem and remove some seeds, and then finely chop the flesh for the Chinese chile flakes used here.

1 cup / 200g beef tallow or rendered beef fat

⅓ cup / 60g minced garlic

¼ cup / 25g Chinese chile flakes

½ tsp red Sichuan peppercorns

In a small saucepan over medium heat, warm the tallow until melted. Add the garlic and cook until fragrant and starting to turn light golden brown, 1 to 2 minutes. Stir in the chile flakes and peppercorns and continue to cook until the garlic is golden brown and very fragrant, 2 to 3 minutes more. Remove from the heat, cover, and set aside to cool.

Transfer the chile oil to an airtight container and store in the refrigerator for up to 1 week, or in the freezer up to 3 months.

FERMENTS AND PICKLES

Drying, smoking, adding salt or sugar, and fermentation were the first ways humans preserved food. Above everything else, fermentation created new flavors and made things easier to eat by breaking proteins down into amino acids such as glutamic acid, which our brains are hardwired to recognize as digestible and thus delicious. This is why soy sauce is so much more flavorful than straight salt, and fermented greens are so much more interesting than greens dressed with vinegar.

FERMENTED MUSTARD GREENS

Active Time — 25 minutes

Plan Ahead — You'll need at least 1 week or up to 1 month for fermenting, depending on the texture and intensity you desire

Makes about 1 qt / 500g

I started fermenting mustard greens in a Chinese way at Bar Agricole, which technically serves California cuisine with Mediterranean sensibilities. The sharp tang of suān cài (酸菜, in Mandarin) went perfectly with a dish of spot prawns, rendered bacon, chiles, olive oil, and crusty bread. You can't go wrong with the flavor trifecta of fresh, salt-cured, and fermented. That combo feels distinctly Chinese to me, though there are echoes of it across every ancient cuisine. You can eat fermented vegetables straight as a condiment or garnish, or use them in smaller doses to bring the acid you need to balance richness. The same method works for fermenting greens as for hefty stem vegetables and roots. Look for leafy, mature peppery Chinese mustard, not the kind with big stems or flowers. Spicy gai choy or sweet napa work wonderfully too. How long you ferment is mostly up to you (see Chef's Note: Fermentation, page 43). If you wait a month as we tend to do, the vegetables develop a deep, intensely sour flavor and feel effervescent on the tongue.

2 bunches leafy Chinese mustard greens
Kosher salt
Seeded and minced red Fresno chiles
Minced garlic

Trim the mustard greens, cut into 2-inch pieces, and then weigh the pieces. Calculate the amounts of the remaining ingredients based on that weight (this can be easily scaled to a smaller or larger batch): 3 percent kosher salt, 5 percent Fresno chiles, and 2 percent garlic.

Put the mustard greens in a large bowl and sprinkle with the salt. Massage the salt gently into the greens, taking care not to tear them, until they are limp and most of their juices have been coaxed out, about 10 minutes. Mix in the chiles and garlic.

Tightly pack the greens with their juices into a nonreactive 1½-quart container. If the greens are not completely submerged, make a 3 percent brine by whisking ½ cup / 120ml water with 1¼ tsp kosher salt and add what you need.

Press a sheet of plastic wrap directly onto the surface of the greens and secure with a lid or a cloth and rubber band. Let ferment at cool room temperature (65° to 75°F) out of direct sunlight for 1 month. Burp regularly. The ferment is ready to eat once the brine has turned yellow-green and the leaves have developed a bright sourness.

Store the ferment in the refrigerator for up to 2 months, though the flavor and texture will change over time.

VARIATION: FERMENTED CABBAGE

Quarter and core 1 medium head green cabbage, then thinly slice and weigh it. Add 4 percent kosher salt based on that weight and then massage, pack, and brine as described in the method.

FERMENTED TOKYO TURNIPS

Active Time — 25 minutes
Plan Ahead — You'll need at least 1 week or up to 1 month for fermenting, depending on the texture and intensity you desire
Makes about 1 qt / 500g

These are delicious as is, or do them up by quartering and tossing with equal parts lemon juice and agrumato lemon extra-virgin olive oil and topping with threads of lemon peel.

3 bunches Tokyo turnips
2 cups / 480ml water
2 Tbsp kosher salt

Trim the greens from the turnips. Scrub and then pack the turnips into a nonreactive 1-quart container.

In a medium bowl, whisk together the water and salt until the salt is dissolved. Pour enough of the resulting brine over the turnips so that they are completely submerged. Press a sheet of plastic wrap directly onto the surface of the turnips and secure with a lid or a cloth and rubber band. Let ferment at cool room temperature (65° to 75°F) out of direct sunlight for 1 month. Burp regularly.

Store the ferment in the refrigerator for up to 2 months, though the flavor and texture will change over time.

FERMENTED KOHLRABI

Active Time — 25 minutes
Plan Ahead — You'll need at least 1 week or up to 1 month for fermenting, depending on the texture and intensity you desire
Makes about 1 qt / 500g

Eat these straight, or dry them slightly (see variation) to give them a nice chew.

1 lb / 450g medium kohlrabi bulbs
2 Tbsp kosher salt
½ lemongrass stalk, smashed and coarsely chopped
6 thin slices jalapeño chile

Peel and halve the kohlrabi and then cut into 1-inch wedges. In a large bowl, toss the kohlrabi with the salt, lemongrass, and jalapeño until the salt is dissolved.

Tightly pack the vegetables with their juices into a nonreactive 1½-quart container. If the vegetables are not completely submerged, make a 3 percent brine by whisking ½ cup / 120ml water with 1¼ tsp kosher salt and add what you need.

Press a sheet of plastic wrap directly onto the surface of the vegetables and secure with a lid or a cloth and rubber band. Let ferment at cool room temperature (65° to 75°F) out of direct sunlight for 1 month. Burp regularly.

Store the ferment in the refrigerator for up to 2 months, though the flavor and texture will change over time.

VARIATION: DEHYDRATED FERMENTED KOHLRABI

To dehydrate the fermented kohlrabi, cut into small dice. Set a dehydrator to 135°F and use the dehydrator's fruit leather/roll or flexible screen so the kohlrabi doesn't fall through, or preheat the oven to 150°F and arrange the dice on a baking sheet so that none is touching. Dehydrate or bake for 1 to 1½ hours. Store in the refrigerator up to 3 days.

FERMENTED CHILE PASTE

Active Time — 20 minutes
Plan Ahead — You'll need 3 to 4 weeks for fermenting
Makes about 1½ cups / 310g
Special Equipment — Blender

Lacto-fermented chiles are the foundation of hot sauces from Tabasco to Sriracha and the jars of all-purpose chile paste on every table at your local Chinese, Vietnamese, and Thai restaurants. We use this paste as both a base heat and acid accent. If you can't find Fresno chiles, sub in the same proportions of jalapeños and green bell peppers for a bright green variation.

> 8 oz / 225g red Fresno chiles, stems trimmed, halved
> 8 oz / 225g red bell peppers, stems trimmed, halved
> Kosher salt

Remove and discard some or all of the chiles' seeds to adjust the heat of the resulting sauce as desired. Remove all the seeds from the bell peppers. Roughly chop the chiles and bell peppers, put them in a large bowl, and sprinkle with 4 tsp salt. Massage the salt into the chiles and peppers (you may want to wear gloves) until they feel tender and have released most of their juices, about 5 minutes.

Tightly pack the chiles and bell peppers with their juices into a nonreactive 1-pint container. If they are not completely submerged, make a 4 percent brine by whisking ½ cup / 120ml water with 1½ tsp kosher salt and add what you need.

Press a sheet of plastic wrap directly onto the surface of the chiles and peppers and secure with a lid or a cloth and rubber band. Let ferment at cool room temperature (65° to 75°F) out of direct sunlight for 3 weeks to 1 month. Burp regularly. Once it has developed a fruity, fiery flavor, process in a blender into a paste.

Transfer the chile paste to an airtight container and store in the refrigerator for up to 2 months.

Chef's Note: Fermentation

Chinese cooking integrated fermentation methods into all levels of cuisine, from home cooking to imperial banquets. Some ground rules when you're fermenting:

1. Start with clean hands, utensils, containers, and ingredients. Fermenting safely is about promoting lactic acid bacteria growth to the exclusion of spoilage microbes from the air and on surfaces.

2. Use a nonreactive container, ideally glass or ceramic, that can be covered with a lid or a cloth secured with a rubber band. If using an airtight lid, open to burp regularly. Use a plate, ceramic or glass weights, or a cabbage leaf to press down anything that isn't submerged.

3. The process tends to go faster in warmer months. A best practice is to check that the ferment measures below a pH of 4.6 before tasting. Once it's in the safe zone, taste until the flavors and textures you want have developed.

4. While the bacteria do their work, the ferment will bubble. Foam or a veiny, white skin may form on the top and is generally a sign of healthy fermentation. This is kahm yeast, which is a catch-all for several yeast types. Kahm is benign but not very tasty, so skim. Mold, on the other hand, is more likely to be toxic. It tends to grow fuzzy and hairy and presents colors other than white. If you see molds of black, blue, or green, scraping them away may not get to their hyphae, which reach deep like roots, so it's probably best to start again.

PICKLED SHIITAKE MUSHROOMS

Active Time — 10 minutes

Plan Ahead — You'll need 2 days for pickling

Makes 1 qt / 340g

Special Equipment — Cheesecloth, kitchen twine

These super-versatile mushroom pickles are loaded with sīn flavor and have a delicious anise finish. I always have them in my refrigerator.

½-inch piece ginger, peeled, thinly sliced, and smashed
½ garlic clove, peeled and smashed
1½ tsp coriander seeds
2 petals from a star anise pod
1 cup / 240ml rice vinegar
⅔ cup / 160ml water
⅓ cup / 65g granulated sugar
1 Tbsp kosher salt, plus 1 tsp
8 oz / 225g fresh shiitake or wild mushrooms, stems removed
1 Tbsp neutral oil

Preheat the oven to 425°F.

Meanwhile, place the ginger, garlic, coriander seeds, and star anise on a double layer of cheesecloth and tie closed with kitchen twine to make a sachet. Place the sachet in a small saucepan with the vinegar, water, sugar, and 1 Tbsp salt. Bring to a boil over medium-high heat, stirring to dissolve the sugar and salt, then remove from the heat and set this pickling liquid aside.

On a rimmed baking sheet, toss the mushrooms with the neutral oil and remaining 1 tsp salt until evenly coated. Flip the caps gill-side up and roast until cooked through, the gills take on a dark golden color, and the mushrooms are not too crisp, about 20 minutes.

Transfer the mushrooms to a 1-quart container with a lid. Add the pickling liquid and sachet, making sure the mushrooms and sachet are completely submerged. Let cool, then seal and refrigerate for at least 2 days or up to 1 month. (We like them best at 2 weeks.)

To use, strain off the juice and slice up thinly or dice.

HOT MUSTARD

Active Time — 10 minutes

Plan Ahead — You'll need 2 days for mellowing the mustard

Makes a scant 1 cup / 225g

There are the white mustard seeds that go into ballpark mustard, which is sometimes fermented and mixed with vinegar and other things that neutralize their intensity. And then there's Chinese hot mustard, which is made with uncut black or brown ground mustard seeds. The darker the mustard seed, the more potent. Once mixed with water, Chinese mustard releases a burst of sulfur that shoots up the sinuses. This is my mellow but still pungent in-between that goes with everything from bao to roast pork.

2 Tbsp rice vinegar
5 tsp water
1 tsp kosher salt
½ tsp granulated sugar
¼ cup plus 2 Tbsp / 90ml Chinese lager beer (preferably Tsingtao)
⅔ cup / 60g Chinese hot mustard powder
Finely grated zest of 2 navel oranges

In a ½-pint container with a lid, whisk together the vinegar, water, salt, and sugar until the salt and sugar are dissolved. Stir in the beer, mustard powder, and orange zest. Seal and let sit at cool room temperature for 1 to 2 days for the mustard powder to mellow slightly.

Store the mustard in the refrigerator for up to 2 weeks. Stir before using.

CHARCUTERIE

Cured meats have been local specialties in Chinese cuisine since at least 350 BCE, when nobles kept a designated jerky master on staff (along with masters of sausages, pickles, condiments, and salt). In Chinatown, specialists still sometimes post signs reading "臘味" (laahp meih), which often gets translated as "wax flavor" but actually refers to the flavor of the hunting season, since curing was about keeping the spoils of autumn delectable into spring.

CURED BEEF HEART

Active Time — 15 minutes

Plan Ahead — You'll need 3 days for curing and dehydrating

Makes about 2¾ lb / 625g

Special Equipment — Dehydrator

Because meat was viewed as a luxury, Chinese chefs mastered using every part to its most delicious extent. This usually came hand in hand with how to also keep meat and its by-products shelf stable for longer periods of time. This method works for most any meat (*not* seafood) of your choice, since the curing spices are determined by weight, though dehydrating time will vary depending on size and shape. You can eat this beef heart straight as a carnivore's dream snack, or shred or shave it wherever a hit of salty sīn flavor would hit the spot.

> One 4½-lb / 2.2kg beef heart
> Coriander seeds
> Green peppercorns
> Red Sichuan peppercorns
> Kosher salt
> Granulated sugar
> Pink curing salt No. 2

Trim the beef heart of hard surface fat and arteries, cut into ½- to ¾-inch-thick slices, and then weigh the slices. Calculate the amounts of the remaining ingredients based on that weight (this can be easily scaled to a smaller or larger batch): 0.05 percent coriander seeds, 0.05 percent green peppercorns, 0.05 percent red Sichuan peppercorns, 3 percent kosher salt, 1 percent granulated sugar, and 0.16 percent pink curing salt No. 2.

Warm a wok or small frying pan over high heat. Add the coriander seeds, green peppercorns, and Sichuan peppercorns and toast, stirring (or tossing) frequently, until fragrant and just making popping sounds, about 2 minutes. Let cool, then transfer to a mortar and pestle and coarsely grind.

Place the beef heart slices in a large bowl; sprinkle with the ground spices, kosher salt, sugar, and curing salt; and toss until evenly coated. Cover and place in the refrigerator to cure for 2 days.

Set a dehydrator to 135°F, or preheat the oven to 150°F. Arrange the slices, on a wire roasting rack set over a baking sheet if necessary, so that none is touching. Dehydrate or bake until the outside is dry to the touch. It should be just slightly pliable, like beef jerky, 12 to 16 hours depending on thickness and your dehydrator or oven. Let cool.

Transfer the beef heart to an airtight container and store in the refrigerator for up to 2 months.

LAP CHEONG

Active Time — 1 hour

Plan Ahead — You'll need 3 to 5 days for curing plus time to make 10 Spice

Makes about twenty-four 5-inch sausages

Special Equipment — Meat grinder, sausage stuffer

There's a reason why Mow Lee Shing Kee on Commercial Street in Chinatown has been making lap cheong for more than 160 years: Everyone loves the sweet and savory sausages, but few know how to make them. Whenever recipes for fried rice, stir-fried vegetables, and noh mái gāi call for lap cheong (臘腸), they tell you to buy it. It took a while, but I pieced together a recipe based on what I tasted and my knowledge of Italian charcuterie, which I picked up largely from Mike Tusk at Quince and Jon Smulewitz at Adesso, both disciples of Paul Bertolli, who knows how to make a sausage. Lap cheong depends foremost on achieving the right texture of meat and plump morsels of fat that explode with flavor in your mouth. In the beginning, we hand-diced everything, but fortunately I eventually found we could compromise by hand-dicing just the fat. Don't compromise any further, though, or you might as well buy from a good specialist (choose varieties without pork or duck liver to be most like this recipe). Rose wine was the last piece of the puzzle (see Chef's Note: Curing Meats, opposite).

A classic way to serve lap cheong is to steam some rice and add a few links in the last 5 minutes in the pot. You can stop there, though I like to crisp them up with a little oil in a pan for a few minutes more, or slice on the diagonal and stir-fry with vegetables. Don't fry without steaming first, or you'll render out all the fat. However you do it, cook before eating.

About 10 feet sheep sausage casings
1½ lb / 680g boneless pork shoulder, trimmed of sinew
1 lb / 450g pork back fat
¼ cup / 50g granulated sugar
¼ cup / 60ml light soy sauce (生抽, sāng chāu)
2 Tbsp Chinese rose wine
2 tsp kosher salt
1 tsp ground white pepper
½ tsp pink curing salt No. 2
½ tsp 10 Spice (see page 36)

Brine
½ cup / 120ml water, at room temperature
1 Tbsp kosher salt

Rinse the casings under running water, then set aside in a bowl of lukewarm water to soak.

Cut the pork shoulder into 1½-inch pieces, trimming off any large chunks of fat and setting them aside. Arrange the pork shoulder pieces in a single layer on a baking sheet and put in the freezer.

Working quickly, cut the reserved pork shoulder fat and back fat into ½-inch dice. Add to the baking sheet in the freezer in a single layer and freeze until the surface of the fat is frozen but the center is still soft enough to be ground, about 15 minutes.

Using a meat grinder, grind the pork shoulder through a coarse grinding plate (¼-inch / 6mm holes) into a large bowl. Add the pork fat, sugar, soy sauce, rose wine, kosher salt, pepper, curing salt, and 10 Spice and, working quickly, stir with a wooden spoon until well-combined and sticky. Place in the refrigerator for 15 minutes.

Meanwhile, run warm water through the casings to flush them out, being careful not to tangle them, then drain. Set up a sausage stuffer with a stuffing tube that's ½-inch / 1.3cm wide. (We do not recommend the KitchenAid stuffer, as it tends to heat things up too much and the fat will get stuck. If you don't have an alternative, do it like the OGs and use a funnel and chopsticks to stuff by hand instead.) Slide 3 to 4 feet of casing onto the stuffing tube. Tie a double knot at the end of the casing.

Tightly stuff the casing with the meat mixture. Avoid air pockets; but don't worry too much about perfection, as you can readjust the stuffing as you make links. Starting about 5 inches from the knot, pinch off a length of sausage, squeezing from both sides to pack the stuffing tighter. Twist the link toward you a few times. As you form more links, alternate the direction of twists, until you run out of casing or filling. Tie off with another double knot.

To make the brine: In a medium bowl, stir together the water and salt until the salt is dissolved.

Dip a paper towel in the brine and give each link a sponge bath, making sure to wipe off any filling left on the outside. If there are any air bubbles, prick each sausage with a needle that has been sterilized over a flame (hold a few seconds until it glows red).

Hang the lap cheong to cure on a rack (plastic clothes hangers will do), making sure the links are not touching, in a cool (about 65°F), dry spot out of direct sunlight. The lap cheong will shrivel slightly into firm, sweet-smelling links in 3 to 5 days. Check their aroma and color daily. A powdery, white mold may develop on their surface. You can leave it as is, but if you see any *fuzzy* white growth, make more brine and wipe off the mold. Unfortunately, molds of any other color probably mean a spoiled batch that should be discarded. Once cured, transfer the links to an airtight container.

Store the lap cheong in the refrigerator for up to 3 weeks or in the freezer for up to 3 months.

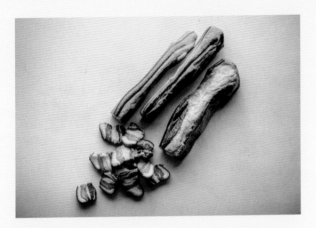

LAP YUK

Active Time — 20 minutes

Plan Ahead — You'll need about 1 week for marinating and curing

Makes about 6 strips (enough for a few dishes)

Special Equipment — Kitchen twine, skewer

In a Chinese family, you know winter's coming when there's bacon dangling from coat hangers in every dark corner of the house. It makes me smile whenever I catch, through the restaurant's dining-room windows, one of our neighbors hanging theirs on the fire escape. Lap yuk (臘肉) is one of the easiest cured meats to make. Just marinate and hang until the flavor has intensified and the color has turned a dark mahogany cream. Lap yuk should feel dry and preserved but still pliable. Ask your local Chinese butcher for a boneless cut of pork belly called ńgh fā yuhk (五花肉), which has two layers of meat sandwiched between three layers of fat and is topped with pork skin. For the baijiu, we use Ming River Sichuan Baijiu, but any floral, younger baijiu (generally 二曲酒 grade) works well for this. If you buy lap yuk, you'll have the choice of smoked, which is delicious when stir-fried with leeks but probably too strong for the recipes in this book.

Steam lap yuk for about 5 minutes before using to soften it, then use however you would any bacon or lap cheong. Slice it thinly, then sauté with crunchy vegetables, like gai lan, broccoli, or cauliflower, or add to rice in a clay pot. The rendered fat is great for cooking.

> ½ cup plus 1 Tbsp / 135ml light soy sauce (生抽, sāng chāu)
> ¼ cup / 50g granulated sugar
> ¼ cup plus 3 Tbsp / 105ml Chinese rose wine
> ¼ cup / 60ml baijiu
> 3 Tbsp dark soy sauce (老抽, lóuh chāu)
> 1 lb / 450g skin-on pork belly, cut lengthwise into 1-inch-thick slices

In a small saucepan over low heat, warm the light soy sauce and sugar, not letting it reach a simmer, stirring until the sugar is dissolved. Remove from the heat and let cool to room temperature. Pour the mixture, the rose wine, baijiu, and dark soy sauce into a large zip-top bag. Add the pork belly, seal the bag, and massage to coat the slices with the marinade. Refrigerate the pork belly in the bag overnight, making sure that the slices are lying flat in a single layer. The next day, remove the pork belly from the marinade and pat dry with towels.

Tie a 12-inch piece of kitchen twine onto the end of a skewer. Push the skewer through the fatty part of a pork slice about 1 inch from an end and pull the twine through. Tie a knot to keep the slice hanging on the twine. String all the slices together this way.

Hang the pork to cure on a rack (plastic clothes hangers will do), making sure the slices are not touching, in a cool (about 65°F), dry spot out of direct sunlight. The pork will shrivel slightly and is ready when the surface feels completely dry but the inside is still soft, 4 to 6 days. Once cured, cut from the twine to use. The lap yuk keeps pretty much indefinitely in a cool, dry place; but to prevent it from drying out over longer periods, store in a zip-top bag in the refrigerator for up to 3 weeks or in the freezer for up to 3 months.

BREADS, BAO, AND BING

From soft and squishy to chewy with a crust, steamed, fried, leavened and not, Chinese breads run the gamut.

Tangzhong (湯種) is a hot-water dough method that results in a squishy, light, and moist crumb. *Tangzhong* translates roughly to "roux starter." Basically, you are seeding dough with a gel made by heating flour and water (or some other liquid, like milk) to at least 149°F (we go up to 194°F). Precooking starch with liquid in this way creates a super-hydrated dough structure. Flour seeded this way holds on to more moisture through kneading, baking, and sitting on a shelf waiting to be eaten. Super-hydrated dough also does wonders for keeping steamed or fried doughs airy and soft. When you add tangzhong to wheat doughs, its structure slows down the formation of the gluten.

We make tangzhong in different ways. Sometimes it entails boiling a ball of rice dough, as we do with our Jin Deui (page 103) and Pig Trotter Ham Sui Gok (page 100). Other times we add boiling water to un-yeasted wheat flour, stirring to ensure every starch grain hydrates and cooks evenly. Add tangzhong to dry flour before it cools past warm room temperature and it should still feel smooth and jiggly, not solid, when you mix it into the rest.

We use this technique when we want something to have a tender crumb instead of tooth, or when we want steamed or fried doughs to be especially airy and soft.

We recommend using the metric measures for these recipes.

MILK BREAD

Active Time — 40 minutes

Plan Ahead — You'll need about 2 hours for rising

Makes one 16-inch loaf, two 8-inch loaves, or forty 2½-inch buns

Special Equipment — Stand mixer; 16 × 4-inch Pullman pan with lid, or two 8½ × 4½-inch loaf pans and a baking sheet; large, heavy ovenproof pan

This is our basic bread recipe, and the start to many of our soft baked buns and toasts. Melissa Chou, our pastry chef, uses the tangzhong technique to keep them light and airy. It's a bit on the sweet side, so it pairs really well with savory things. To eat on its own, top a toasted slice with a sprinkling of pork floss (see page 221). It also makes incredible French toast. You can bake a single loaf if you have a Pullman pan, or two loaves in regular loaf pans.

> **Tangzhong**
> ½ cup / 120ml water
> ½ cup / 120ml whole milk
> ¼ cup / 35g bread flour
>
> 3¼ cups / 455g bread flour
> ⅓ cup / 65g granulated sugar
> 1 Tbsp instant dry yeast
> 2 tsp kosher salt
> 1 egg, at room temperature
> ⅔ cup plus 1 Tbsp / 175ml whole milk, at room temperature, plus more for brushing
> 6 Tbsp / 85g unsalted butter, cut into 6 pieces and at room temperature, plus more for greasing

To make the tangzhong: In a small saucepan, combine the water, milk, and flour and whisk until smooth. Place over medium heat and cook, whisking constantly, until bubbling and thickened to a pudding consistency, 4 to

5 minutes. Remove from the heat and set aside to cool to lukewarm, whisking every few minutes to prevent lumps, about 15 minutes.

Meanwhile, in the bowl of a stand mixer fitted with the dough hook attachment, combine the flour, sugar, yeast, and salt and whisk to combine. Add the lukewarm tangzhong and mix on low speed until moist clumps form, about 2 minutes. Add the egg and mix until combined. Slowly pour in the milk and mix until a very wet dough forms, about 1 minute.

Increase the speed to medium and mix in the butter, one piece at a time, letting each fully incorporate before adding the next, about 5 minutes. Continue mixing until a smooth, sticky dough forms that clears the sides of the bowl, about 10 minutes more.

Stop the mixer and scrape down the dough hook and sides of the bowl. Cover with a kitchen towel and let the dough rise in a warm place until doubled in size, about 45 minutes.

Punch down the dough and transfer to a lightly floured work surface. (If making buns, refer to the directions on page 220.)

Position a rack in the lower third of the oven, remove any racks above it, and preheat the oven to 375°F. Grease the loaf pan(s) and lid (or baking sheet) with butter.

For a single loaf, using floured hands, pat and stretch the dough into a 17 × 11-inch rectangle about ½ inch thick; for two loaves, pat and stretch into two 10-inch squares about ½ inch thick. Roll the dough tightly (start from a long end for the single loaf), then pinch the seam and ends closed. Position the loaf seam-side down, then tuck the ends in under it. Place seam-side down in the prepared pan(s).

Cover the dough loosely with a kitchen towel and set aside to proof to about ½ inch from the top of the pan, which should take about 15 minutes. (If the dough does overproof, turn it out of the pan, reshape, and proof again, keeping in mind it will rise faster than before.)

Uncover the dough and brush lightly with milk. For a large loaf, slide on the prepared cover before baking. For two loaves, place side by side on the oven rack, cover with the prepared baking sheet, buttered-side down, and place a large, heavy ovenproof pan on the baking sheet to weigh it down.

Bake for 30 minutes, then uncover and continue baking until the bread is golden brown and registers 200°F in the center, about 15 minutes more. Immediately flip the bread onto a wire rack, let cool completely, and then wrap in plastic wrap.

Store the bread at room temperature for up to 5 days, or in the freezer for up to 3 months.

MANTOU AND BAO

Active Time — 15 minutes
Plan Ahead — You'll need about 1½ hours for rising
Makes about 1 lb / 450g dough or 13 mantou buns
Special Equipment — Stand mixer, steamer

Mantou are plain soft steamed breads, and bao are stuffed. We add milk and cream, which cut through the gluten, giving an even more tender crumb than the classic versions. This recipe is calibrated for the fluffy, low-gluten flour we source from Hong Kong that's milled for just these types of steamed applications. You can substitute cake flour, like King Arthur's unbleached, but you may need a few spoons more of it if the dough feels too wet.

1¾ cups / 250g Hong Kong flour or cake flour,
    sifted, plus more as needed
¼ cup plus 1 Tbsp / 60g granulated sugar
1¾ tsp instant yeast
1¼ tsp baking powder
¼ cup plus 1 Tbsp / 75ml water
¼ cup / 60ml whole milk, at room temperature
4 tsp heavy cream, at room temperature

In the bowl of a stand mixer fitted with the dough hook attachment, whisk together the flour, sugar, yeast, and baking powder. In a liquid measuring cup, combine the water, milk, and cream. While mixing on low speed, slowly pour in the liquid and mix until the dough forms a ball, then continue mixing until the dough is very smooth, about 10 minutes total. If the dough has not formed a ball after 2 minutes, gradually add more flour 1 tsp at a time until it does. Alternatively, place the flour mixture in a medium bowl and, with a spoon or your hands, mix in the liquid until a shaggy, loose dough forms. Knead on a work surface until smooth and shiny, about 10 minutes.

Cover the dough with a damp kitchen towel and let rest until slightly risen and puffed, 30 minutes to 1 hour. (At this point, this dough is ready to be used in Wild Mushroom Bao, page 93, or Chicken in a Space Suit, page 89.)

Meanwhile, cut out thirteen 3-inch squares of parchment paper. (If you have perforated pans and a Combi oven set up like we do, you can use one parchment paper, as pictured on page 50.)

Portion and form the dough into thirteen pieces, each about 1¾ inches in diameter. Form each into an 8-inch-long rope. Tie a knot in the center of each rope. Tuck the end that came up through the knot underneath the bun. Tuck the other end over into the center, then place on a parchment square.

MANTOU

CHINESE PANCAKES

Cover the dough loosely with a damp, clean kitchen towel, and let rise in a warm place until slightly puffed and marshmallow-y in texture, 30 to 45 minutes.

Prepare a steamer in a wok or a large, lidded pot following the instructions on page 167 and bring the water to a boil over medium-high heat. Place as many dough pieces as will fit in the steamer with about 2 inches of room around each one (we can get five in a 12-inch steamer). Cover and steam until the dough is cooked through, about 8 minutes. Remove the mantou from the steamer. Add water to the pot between batches as needed.

Steamed mantou can be frozen on a baking sheet until solid and then transferred to a zip-top bag and stored in the freezer for up to 2 months. Thaw in the refrigerator overnight and then re-steam for 3 minutes to heat through. Serve warm.

CHINESE PANCAKES

Active Time — 45 minutes
Makes 10 pancakes

These delicate, savory pancakes, bǐng (餅, in Mandarin), are as simple as it gets—flour, salt, and boiling water. Pancakes for wrapping mu shu (see page 145) or roast duck (see page 203) are often thin enough to read a newspaper through, but we like ours more substantial. Pancake duty used to take six hours every day, but eventually, I saw an automated pancake machine in Guangzhou and it changed our lives. Fortunately, you just need two or three pancakes per guest.

> 1 cup plus 2 Tbsp / 170g bread flour,
>   plus more for dusting
> ½ tsp kosher salt
> ⅓ cup plus 1 Tbsp / 95ml boiling water
> Neutral oil for brushing

In a medium bowl, mix together the flour and salt. Slowly stir in the boiling water and mix until a dough forms in moist clumps. Scrape the dough onto the counter and knead by hand until smooth, about 5 minutes. Form the dough into a ball, cover with a damp kitchen towel, and set aside for 10 minutes.

Divide the dough into ten pieces and roll into smooth balls; flatten each into a 2-inch round. Dust the tops with a light coating of flour and then brush with a thin film of neutral oil. Stack one round on top of a second so that the oiled sides touch. Repeat until you have five stacks. Using a dowel or rolling pin, from the center out, roll each stack into a 6-inch round.

Warm a small frying pan over medium heat. Add one pancake stack at a time and cook until just set and dry but not browned on the bottom, about 1½ minutes. Flip and cook the second side, about 1½ minutes more. Remove from the pan and let cool for just 1 minute, then pull apart into two pancakes (don't wait too long, or they will stick together forever).

Pile the pancakes on a plate and cover with a kitchen towel to keep warm for serving; reheat in a steamer for a few minutes, if needed. Or wrap tightly in plastic wrap and store in the freezer for up to 1 month; thaw and steam briefly to warm through before serving.

2

When I was still a very young cook, I heard about a chef on the edge of Chinatown who created dishes to go along with lines of classical Chinese poetry. I saved for months for the prix fixe at Jai Yun, a one-room restaurant behind a folding metal gate on Pacific Avenue. I walked in and Chef Chia Ji Nei presented twelve dishes to the table immediately, each with its own distinctive character—crispy bitter melon slivers, a sweet doufu skin salad, a crackling bite of smoky fish, some spicy fermented cabbage—all these little things to introduce himself. You could see his skill and care, the surgical knife-cuts in each dish. It blew me away. These were glimpses of a chef with something to say. (Legend has it, Chef Nei still cooks pop-ups in Chinatown, if you can track him down.)

Not long after, when I was about to turn thirty, I took a trip with my buddy Danny Bowien to the heartland of decadent dining, mounds of butter, and piles of foie gras—Paris. This was before Mister Jiu's and Mission Chinese (Danny's restaurant). We both were cooks executing other people's visions, and we had only enough money between us to eat for a few days. Lunch was at the prix-fixe places (we couldn't afford their dinners), where they served either three courses or a three-hour performance of plate and silverware changes. Everything was beautiful, delicate, and, to be honest, not always delicious. When it was incredible, I had to lie down after. It's a cliché, haute cuisine being too precious and too rich. But my favorite meals were our dinners in the brasseries, where I wore jeans and a T-shirt and the dishes were all over the table. A plate of offal, another of foie gras, a multitude of terrines, a simple vegetable dish, and not a drop of pretense. They were meals about the sum of their parts rather than a single showstopper. Danny and I both came back feeling done with conventional fine dining and proceeded to quit our jobs.

I knew I had to cook the way I wanted to eat. I enjoyed the spectacle and precision of fine dining, but I didn't want to spend my days in it. I wanted an abundance of little dishes filled with different flavors and textures, a tablescape of experiences to share with the people beside me.

In Chinese cuisine, you often get a bunch of small dishes to share at the start. These are dishes to nibble and mix and match. You graze and drink in everything and everyone at the table while the plates swirl. The American paradigm is three courses per person—an appetizer, an entree, and dessert—in increasing size and richness. But there's a different flow to a Chinese meal, where a lot will come at once, but everything will be different in intensity, texture, color, and temperature. Flavors weave together, like the heat of chile oil followed by the cool crunch of cucumber. You experience salty and sweet, fried and then boiled, and tastes and textures that come in peaks and lulls, shouts and whispers. There is a rhythm to it all.

When we serve the first course at the restaurant, we try to get every dish on the table at once, accompanied by a bunch of little condiments and sauces. We call them *xiao chi*, meaning many "little bites." It's in the tradition of dim sum, the banquet spread of a billion splendid dishes, and the Chinese family table loaded with pickles and sauces and cold things. It's the way I love to eat and the way I love to cook.

CHERRY MUI

Active Time — 15 minutes

Plan Ahead — You'll need 2 to 3 days for brining and then 6 to 16 hours for drying the cherries

Makes about 2 cups / 250mg

Special Equipment — Dehydrator

1½ cups / 360ml water

2 Tbsp plus 2 tsp kosher salt

1 Tbsp plus ½ tsp granulated sugar

1 lb / 450g sweet cherries (such as Bing or Rainier), stems removed

1 Tbsp chopped dried licorice root

3-inch cinnamon stick

½ tsp whole cloves

2 black cardamom pods (草果, chóu gwó)

My mom keeps salty, tart dried plums in the glove compartment of her car to tuck in her cheek on long drives. *Léuih hàhng múi* (旅行梅) means "traveling plum," because they keep well and their salty-sourness hits the spot. Chinese have carried them everywhere. In Hawaii, you put "li hing mui" powder on shave ice. In Mexico, "chamoy" goes on fruit or the rim of a Michelada. Our version is more mouth-watering than puckering and calls for more licorice flavor. We leave the fruit still a little moist and tender. This recipe works in warm months with many small stone fruits, but I like Bing cherries in late spring, for their flavor and story. Bing cherries are named for a man his employers knew only by his last name, a 6'2" emigrant from northern China who became the foreman at an Oregon orchard where he cared for new varieties of trees, including the now famous Bing. While visiting family in China, the Chinese Exclusion Act was passed and Bing could not return to America or continue growing his namesake fruit.

In a 1-quart jar, whisk together the water, salt, and sugar until the salt and sugar are dissolved. Stir in the cherries, licorice, cinnamon, cloves, and cardamom and make sure the cherries are submerged. Cover, transfer to the refrigerator, and let soak for at least 2 days but not more than 3 days.

If you have a dehydrator, set it to 135°F. Remove the cherries from the brine and space them out on the dehydrator racks so none is touching. Otherwise, preheat the oven to 150°F and arrange the cherries on a wire roasting rack set over a baking sheet.

Dehydrate or bake until the cherries are wrinkled all over and no longer squishy. Be patient, as this can take 6 to 16 hours depending on the size of the cherries and parameters of whatever you're drying them with. Let cool and then either eat immediately or transfer to an airtight container and store in the refrigerator for up to 1 week.

SMOKED OYSTER YOU TIAO

After a morning at the Chinatown markets, my grandma Ying Ying would take me for a bowl of jook (see page 231) and yóu tiáo (油條, in Mandarin) at Hing Lung on Broadway, which for decades was the city's busiest jook joint. I loved watching the line of sifu, master cooks, ladling out porridge from behind a curtain of steam. There was a wooden counter where one sifu made their famous yóu tiáo. He would stretch pieces of ammonium bicarbonate–risen wheat dough, divide the dough (with a flick of a moistened chopstick) into two strips just barely joined, and drop them in the fryer until they floated up crisp and golden. They're known around Chinatown as yàuh ja gwái (油炸鬼), Cantonese for "oil-fried devils" after a traitorous couple, who are still shamed a thousand years later every time someone eats these with gusto. I decided to introduce Chinese savory donuts, by way of a New Orleans–style beignet, with this recipe. We mix the batter with green onions and oysters smoked in the wok and let the dough proof until it bubbles from the yeast. These aren't what Ying Ying would recognize immediately as oil-fried devils; but when I take a bite, I can hear her calling me to our table over the din of the breakfast rush. To get the right crispy and fluffy ratio, plan to double fry.

Active Time — 45 minutes

Plan Ahead — You'll need 1½ hours for smoking

Makes 6 servings

Special Equipment — 1 cup apple-wood smoking chips, soaked in water about 1 hour; kitchen torch; deep-fry thermometer; wok with a rack and lid

6 oz / 170g shucked large oysters with juices

1½ cups / 220g cake flour

2 tsp granulated sugar

1½ tsp kosher salt

1½ tsp instant yeast

1 cup / 240ml whole milk, warmed to 110°F

¼ cup / 15g thinly sliced (crosswise) green onions

1½ tsp oyster sauce

1½ qt / 1. 4L neutral oil

Green Onion Powder (see page 66) for dusting

Rig your wok as a smoker following the directions on page 59.

Put the oysters and their juices in a small, shallow heatproof bowl (wide enough that the oysters snuggle in a single layer—you want the smoke to touch as much surface area as possible but not have the oysters dry out too fast). Set the bowl on the rack in the smoker. Check that the wok lid fits tightly, then remove the rack and bowl of oysters.

With the lid off, ignite the wood chips with a kitchen torch, turn the heat to high, and leave until the wood chips start smoking, about 5 minutes. Place the rack and oysters back in the wok. Cover, turn the heat to medium, and smoke for 10 minutes. Without opening the lid, turn off the heat and let the oysters steep in the smoke for another 20 minutes.

Uncover the wok. Return the heat to medium, cover, and smoke for another 10 minutes. Let steep off the heat for 20 minutes twice more, for a total of three rounds of smoking. The oysters should be light golden brown on the surface with plenty of liquid still in the bowl. Let cool. (At this point, the oysters can be transferred to an airtight container and stored in the refrigerator for up to 3 days.) Drain and cut the oysters into small dice.

In a large bowl, combine the flour, sugar, salt, and yeast and whisk together. Pour in the milk and stir until a smooth, wet batter just forms. Stir in the smoked oysters, green onions, and oyster sauce. Cover with a damp kitchen towel and set aside in a warm place for 15 minutes. The batter should grow to about a third larger and be speckled with bubbles. (This batter can be finicky, and it is better to underproof. Overproofed batter is watery and deflated and will fry up like hockey pucks.)

Meanwhile, preheat the oven to 200°F. Fit a wire rack over a rimmed baking sheet. Set up a holding station by fitting another wire roasting rack over a second baking sheet and placing it in the oven.

CONTINUED

Fill a wok or Dutch oven with the neutral oil and secure a deep-fry thermometer on the side. Set over medium-high heat and warm the oil to 325°F, being careful to maintain this temperature as you fry. Frying in batches of six (max!), gently drop 2-Tbsp portions (or use a 1-oz scoop) of the batter into the hot oil. They should sink first and then float up. Stir gently after 1 minute in case any are stuck on the bottom, otherwise leave them alone until they have turned barely golden, about 3 minutes total. Transfer to the prepared rack to drain. (At this point, the yóu tiáo can wait at room temperature up to 1 hour, or be transferred to a zip-top bag and stored in the freezer for up to 2 months. Thaw in the refrigerator before the final fry.)

Over medium-high heat, rewarm the oil to 350°F. Again, fry the yóu tiáo in batches of no more than six until dark golden brown, 2 to 2½ minutes. Transfer to the holding station as you fry each batch.

Serve hot, dusted with green onion powder.

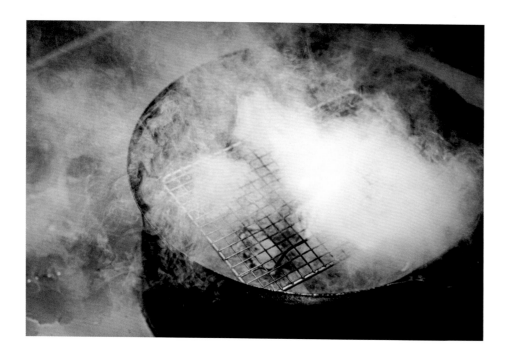

Chef's Note: Smoking

When it comes to smoking, it matters how hard and fast you burn. You have to control smoke just like any other part of cooking. You need just enough smoke to complement the flavors of a brisket, an oily fish, the fat, and the seasonings. Keep smoke in the background, everywhere, but quiet.

You can smoke anything—proteins, vegetables, grains, and oils. We often smoke our salt. Smoke adds undertones of caramel, flowers, bread, and vanilla, depending on the ingredient, and triggers a part of our primal brains that remembers cooking over an open fire. With just smoke, you can build complex flavor without adding fat or basting with a sauce.

In terms of what to burn, I like almond wood with most seafood, and cherry wood with duck. A classic Chinese pairing is sweet lychee wood with pork (apple wood or maple are decent substitutes), and brown rock sugar and tea leaves with oily fish or game birds. I skip the sugar but throw in a handful of flavorful tea leaves, like an oolong or lapsang souchong, and black cardamom (草果, chóu gwó), which is dried over an open flame, to add depth to all kinds of meats.

You can rig your wok, a deep pan such as a Dutch oven, or a roasting pan for large birds (like duck) into a stove-top smoker by doing the following:

1. Find a heatproof rack that fits inside the wok and a tight-fitting domed lid that will help the smoke to circulate. If you don't have a rack or lid that fits all the requirements, aluminum foil is your friend. Use it to make a rack, to seal the lid edges, or to construct a tent over the wok. Check that your ingredients will sit a couple inches above the bottom of the wok (elevate with a foil coil, if needed).

2. Submerge 1 to 2 cups wood chips of choice in water for about an hour. Drain well.

3. In the meantime, unless you have a dedicated wok for smoking, tightly line a wok with widely overlapping sheets of foil, leaving no surface bare other than where the wok touches the burner. Line the lid the same way.

4. Spread the wood chips evenly on the bottom of your wok and use a kitchen torch to blitz them until they are smoldering. If you don't have a torch, set your chips on a roasting rack over a burner flame, then add to your wok once they are smoking. The chips shouldn't actually ignite. If they do, they need more time to soak.

5. Time to turn on your exhaust fan and open your windows. Set the burner to high and let the wok heat up until the wood chips are continuously sending off white wisps of smoke, about 5 minutes.

6. Replace the rack and set whatever you're smoking in the center of the wok. Cover tightly, making sure nothing is touching the ingredients, so that smoke can circulate.

7. For most of the recipes in this book, smoke the ingredient with the wok on the flame for 10 minutes before turning off the heat and leaving to smoke for another 20 minutes. (See the exception for Liberty Roast Duck, page 203.)

8. Uncover the wok, remove whatever you're smoking, and repeat steps 5 through 7 twice more. The ingredients will darken in color. Three rounds should be enough for everything from oysters to whole duck, but your ingredients may require fewer or more rounds. The best way to know if you've smoked an ingredient long enough is to taste, but wok-smoking does not cook raw proteins. Finish by stir-frying, grilling, roasting, or as specified in the recipe.

BRINED CELTUCE

This is a play on a classic, small cold dish but with a hit of citrus instead of rice wine. "Celtuce" is a play on words for a "lettuce stalk," what Chinatown grocers call wō séun (萵筍). When Burpee first imported the seeds from western China in 1938, people decided that it sounded better for a vegetable with a CELery-letTUCE flavor, rather than "asparagus lettuce," which someone had already tried in the 1890s. Despite all the marketing, until fairly recently, I could still only find it in Chinatown. I couldn't get it certified organic anywhere until, after a few years of experimenting, Annabelle Lenderink at Star Route Farms figured out how to grow them juicy and dense with flavor reminiscent of heart of palm. This preparation is a bit like a reverse pickle. Brining first, then adding acid, keeps the chlorophyll bright green.

Active Time — 15 minutes

Plan Ahead — You'll need about 2 days for brining

Makes 8 servings

5 cups / 1.2L water

3 Tbsp plus 1 tsp kosher salt

2 cups / 40g fresh lemon verbena leaves

1 Tbsp slivered southern Chinese almonds (南杏, nàahm hahng; see page 133)

1½ lb / 680g celtuce

2 Tbsp agrumato lemon extra-virgin olive oil

2 Tbsp fresh lemon juice

In a large saucepan over high heat, combine the water and salt and bring to a boil. Stir in the lemon verbena and almonds, remove from the heat, and set this brine aside to steep until cooled to room temperature, about 1½ hours.

Peel the celtuce well, making sure you peel until you get to the green parts. Any parts thicker than 1¾ inches need to be cut in half lengthwise. Slice with a roll cut into 1-inch-long pieces and place in a 2-quart container. Add the brine (do not strain), cover, and transfer to the refrigerator for 2 to 3 days before serving. Store in the brine, refrigerated, up to 1 week.

Remove the celtuce from the brine and place in a serving bowl. Drizzle with the olive oil and lemon juice and toss to combine. Eat immediately.

SPICY CRISPY PEANUTS

It all began when friends from Shanghai brought bags of Huang Fei Hong crispy anchovies, chile, and peanuts and I could not stop eating them, nobody could. Inspired by the combination of spicy and sīn, I decided to make my own version. You can eat this by the handful, or sprinkled on rice or wherever you want a crunchy kick. There are many peanut snack variations across Asia, ranging from sweet and spicy to briny and green with seaweed. Our peanuts are candy-coated with numbing peppercorns and chiles (use more or less depending on your heat preference), and go great with a cold beer. Use very small, dried whole anchovies (less than 1 inch in length), like the kind you find frozen in Korean grocery stores. If you forget to pick up gochugaru while you're there, any mild chile flake will do (see Chef's Note: Chiles, page 38).

Active Time — 50 minutes

Makes 10 to 12 servings

Special Equipment —
Deep-fry thermometer

2 cups / 480ml neutral oil or unrefined peanut oil

8 to 10 dried árbol chiles

½ cup / 30g very small dried whole anchovies

2 Tbsp plus 1 tsp Korean chile flakes (gochugaru)

2 tsp kosher salt

2 tsp red Sichuan peppercorns, crushed with a mortar and pestle

2 cups / 250g roasted, unsalted peanuts

½ cup / 100g granulated sugar

2 Tbsp water

Line a large plate with paper towels. Line a baking sheet with a silicone baking mat or parchment paper.

Pour the neutral oil into a medium saucepan and secure a deep-fry thermometer on the side. Set over medium-high heat and warm the oil to 325°F, being careful to maintain this temperature as you fry.

Carefully add the árbol chiles and fry, ladling oil over them constantly, until crisp, darkened in color, and shiny, 20 to 30 seconds. Using a slotted spoon, transfer the chiles to one side of the prepared plate. Add the anchovies to the pan and fry, stirring occasionally, until light golden brown and crispy, about 30 seconds. Transfer with a slotted spoon to the other side of the plate. Set aside and let cool.

Pinch the stems off the chiles and then, over a medium bowl, crush the chiles with your hands into pieces ⅓ inch or smaller. Add the chile flakes, salt, and peppercorns and mix to combine.

In a large saucepan over medium heat, combine the peanuts, sugar, and water and cook, stirring occasionally with a wooden spoon. The water will evaporate and the sugar will seize and become powdery and grainy, 10 to 12 minutes. At that moment, turn the heat to medium-low and keep cooking, stirring every minute or so, until the sugar melts and caramelizes to a dark blonde and the peanuts are evenly coated, 8 to 10 minutes more. If the mixture smokes at any point, take it off the heat for a few seconds and lower the heat before continuing. Remove from the heat and stir in the chile mixture.

Transfer the caramelized peanuts to the prepared baking sheet, spread into a single layer, and let cool, then break up pieces that are stuck together. Transfer the fried anchovies and caramelized peanuts to separate airtight containers and store at room temperature for up to 2 weeks. Serve the peanuts with the fried anchovies on top.

ON PRAWN TOAST

The height of American dinner-party shtick had to be the 1960s to '70s, when fondue, ham cooked in Coca-Cola, and the exotic pu-pu platter were all the rage. Pu-pu were a very loose interpretation of Hawaiian ceremonial platters. In tiki-themed restaurants, it was an assortment of Oriental exoticisms, like crab rangoon (crab and cream cheese fried in a wonton wrapper), rumaki (water chestnut and chicken liver wrapped in bacon), teriyaki chicken wings, char siu pork, ribs, satay, and prawn toast. Tiki pioneer Trader Vic's capitalized on the nostalgia of GIs back from the Pacific. Trader Vic's management were regulars on Grant Avenue in Chinatown, recruiting staff to cook what founder Victor Bergeron called Cantonese-Polynesian food. Tiki and pu-pu were, in essence, a mash-up of Chinese American cooks' creativity and GI wives' whimsy.

Recipes for prawn toast, as we know it, bounced between both sides of the Pacific. A recipe for "Shrimp Straws"—minced shrimp, onion, and ginger bound with egg white on strips of sliced bread—appeared in the 1938 American *Epicure in China* cookbook as part of a "typical Cantonese menu" for seven. In Hong Kong, "ice box diners," bīng sāt (冰室), served milk teas and snacks such as har tohsie (蝦多士, *tohsie* being the Cantonese transliteration of "toast"). They were triangular, hot pockets stuffed with a mince of bay shrimp, ham, green onion, and béchamel. Southern Chinese dim sum parlors served gold-coin shrimp cakes on round toasts of mantou. Prawn toast in its American incarnation reached mainstream China when its first domestic fast-food joint opened in Beijing in 1984. Yili (伊利, "righteousness and profit") introduced Western exoticisms such as elevator music, disposable plates, and typical American "dry" bread, which it used for its hamburgers, hot dogs, and the priciest item on the menu, prawn toast.

PRAWN TOAST

Active Time — 45 minutes

Plan Ahead — You'll need time to make the Milk Bread and Shrimp Salt

Makes 4 servings

Special Equipment — Food processor

Lemon Aioli

1 egg yolk

1 garlic clove, finely grated

Finely grated zest of ½ lemon, plus 2 tsp fresh lemon juice

½ tsp kosher salt

½ cup / 120ml grapeseed oil

Prawn Mousse

2 garlic cloves, peeled

8 oz / 225g peeled and cleaned large shrimp

2 Tbsp egg white (whisked before measuring)

½ tsp toasted sesame oil

¼ tsp light soy sauce (生抽, sāng chāu)

½ tsp cornstarch

2 Tbsp finely diced uncooked bacon

2 Tbsp finely diced jicama

2 Tbsp thinly sliced (crosswise) green onions

2 tsp peeled and minced ginger

¼ cup / 30g raw white sesame seeds

Four 1-inch-thick slices Milk Bread (page 48)

2 Tbsp rendered pork or duck fat

Shrimp Salt (see page 37) for dusting

1 Tbsp cured trout roe or caviar

Edible marigold flower petals or soft herbs (such as tarragon, parsley, or chervil) for garnishing (optional)

Every Chinese cookbook written for Americans that I've ever seen includes a recipe for prawn toast. It's become as American as the sliced sandwich bread with which it's made. I love the kitsch but also the mixing of cultures. I usually serve one toast per person, but once you've got them sizzling in the pan, everyone will congregate in the kitchen, so prepare for seconds.

To make the aioli: In a medium bowl, whisk together the egg yolk, garlic, lemon zest, lemon juice, and salt. While whisking, slowly stream in the grapeseed oil a little bit a time until thick and emulsified. Transfer to an airtight container and store in the refrigerator for up to 5 days.

To make the mousse: Bring a small saucepan of water to a boil. Add the garlic and boil until just knife-tender, about 2 minutes. Drain the garlic, finely chop, and place in a medium bowl.

Butterfly half of the shrimp, then cut into medium dice. Add to the garlic.

In a food processor fitted with the blade attachment, pulse the remaining shrimp until coarsely chopped. With the motor running, pour in the egg white, sesame oil, and soy sauce and process into a smooth paste, stopping and scraping down the sides of the bowl occasionally. Don't pulse further or the emulsion will break. Add the cornstarch and process briefly until just combined. Alternatively, hand mince the shrimp with a cleaver to a smooth paste, then stir in the egg white, sesame oil, soy sauce, and cornstarch.

Add the shrimp paste to the chopped shrimp. Then add the bacon, jicama, green onions, and ginger and stir to combine.

Put the sesame seeds in a small dish. Using a round cutter, cut each slice of bread into a 2½-inch circle (or just trim into a square) with no crust. Spread the prawn mousse onto the bread slices in a thick, even layer to the edges. Dip each toast, mousse-side down, in the sesame seeds to coat well.

In a medium nonstick frying pan over medium heat, warm the rendered fat until shimmering. Place the toasts seed-side down in the pan and cook until the sesame seeds are dark golden brown and the mousse is firm and cooked through, about 10 minutes. Flip the toasts, slide them around the pan a little so that the bread soaks up some of the fat, and cook until the bottom of the bread is golden brown and toasted, about 3 minutes more. Transfer the toasts to a serving plate.

Garnish the toasts with a dollop of lemon aioli, a light dusting of shrimp salt, some trout roe, and flower petals, if desired. Serve immediately.

SOURDOUGH GREEN ONION PANCAKES

Active Time — 3 hours

Plan Ahead — Make the green onion powder and soubise the day before. The morning of serving, make the poolish. Start resting and folding the dough 4 to 6 hours before you want to eat.

Makes six 5-inch pancakes; 12 servings

Special Equipment — Dehydrator, deep-fry thermometer, spice grinder, blender

When I wanted to incorporate something truly San Franciscan into this classic Chinese snack, our pastry chef Melissa Chou turned immediately to sourdough. Yeast and bacteria, like *L. Sanfranciscensis*, thrive in our foggy sea air and give our breads a distinctive sourness. Chinese cooks working in the '49er camps tucked jars of sourdough starter in their jackets to keep the starter warm and happy. If you want your pancakes light and less on the vinegary side, watch that your leaven and poolish do not overproof. This recipe calls for dropping the batter into the oil like you would fry bread. If you don't have a live starter (or a baker friend who can share some), you can find buy it (or find a recipe) online.

Green Onion Powder

1 bunch green onions,
   trimmed of roots and
   thinly sliced crosswise

Sauce Soubise

1 lb / 450g yellow or white
   onions, thinly sliced
Kosher salt
Scant ¼ cup / 55g
   crème fraîche
2 Tbsp buttermilk

Leaven

1½ Tbsp active sourdough
   starter (see headnote)
½ cup / 120ml water
¼ cup plus 1 Tbsp / 45g
   whole-wheat flour
¼ cup plus 1½ tsp / 45g
   bread flour

Poolish

⅓ cup / 50g whole-wheat flour
¼ cup / 60ml water
¼ tsp active dry yeast

1¾ cups / 250g bread flour,
   plus more for dusting
½ cup / 120ml water
1½ cups / 120g thinly sliced
   (crosswise) green onions
1 Tbsp kosher or flake salt

To make the green onion powder: If you have a dehydrator, set it to 135°F. Place the green onions on the fruit leather/roll or flexible screen so they don't fall through. Otherwise, preheat the oven to 150°F and arrange the green onions on a baking sheet so they aren't touching.

Dehydrate or bake the green onions, checking every hour, until dried and crisp, 2 to 3 hours total. Let cool.

Place the green onions into a spice grinder and grind into a fine powder. Transfer to an airtight container and store at room temperature for up to 1 month.

To make the soubise: In a medium saucepan over medium heat, cook the onions with a pinch of salt until just turning translucent but not browned, about 10 minutes. Cover, turn the heat to low, and continue cooking, stirring every few minutes, until the onions are completely soft but still not browned, about 25 minutes more. Drain off any remaining liquid and let cool.

Transfer the onions to a blender, add the crème fraîche and buttermilk, and blend until smooth. Taste and season with salt. Transfer to an airtight container and store in the refrigerator for up to 3 days.

To make the leaven: In a medium bowl, combine the starter, water, and both flours and stir until combined and smooth. Cover the bowl with a damp kitchen towel and leave in a warm place until bubbly, 3 to 4 hours. The leaven is ready when a small pinch floats in water.

To make the poolish: Meanwhile, in a medium bowl, combine the flour, water, and yeast and stir until combined and smooth. Cover the bowl with a damp kitchen towel and leave in a warm place (ideally, around 80°F) until it looks spongy with tiny bubbles, 3 to 4 hours. Don't let it go too far. If it rises and collapses or it gets too warm and develops a flavor and aroma of alcohol, discard and start over.

When the leaven is ready, give it a stir, then measure out ½ cup / 120g into a large bowl. Add the poolish, bread flour, and water to the leaven and stir with your hands to work out any lumps, until you have a very loose, shaggy dough (well-mixed with no dry spots but still lumpy and layered). Cover with a kitchen towel and set aside in a warm place for 20 minutes.

Fried Shallots

1½ qt / 1.4L neutral oil
4 medium shallots, thinly sliced
    into rings
¼ cup / 35g bread flour
Kosher salt

1 cup / 140g bread flour
Minced chives for serving
    (optional)

Lightly coat a baking sheet with cooking spray.

Uncover the dough, add the green onions and salt, and knead with your hands until everything is evenly incorporated. The dough should be sticky but manageable. Don't worry about overworking it. Cover the bowl with the towel.

Rest the dough at warm room temperature (75° to 80°F) for 3 hours, but every 30 minutes, lift one side of the dough and fold it over on itself, giving the bowl a quarter turn after each fold until all the dough has been folded. Cover with the towel after each session. The dough will start out still very loose and shaggy but will gradually smooth out and tighten as you continue folding. Cover with the towel and let rest at room temperature for 1 hour more.

Transfer the dough to a lightly floured work surface. Divide into six portions and dust the tops with flour. Using lightly floured hands, gently knead and roll each portion into a smooth-ish ball (it won't look perfect and will still be sticky). Place the dough balls on the prepared baking sheet, spacing evenly apart. Cover with oiled plastic wrap and refrigerate at least 1 hour or up to 3 hours.

To make the shallots: Fill a wok or Dutch oven with the neutral oil and secure a deep-fry thermometer on the side. Set over medium-high heat and warm the oil to 300°F, being careful to maintain this temperature as you fry. Meanwhile, in a medium bowl, toss together the shallots and bread flour, separating the rings with your hands. Transfer to a fine-mesh strainer and shake to remove excess flour.

Line a plate with a double layer of paper towels.

When the oil is ready, add half the shallots and fry, stirring occasionally, until golden brown, 2½ to 3 minutes. Using a slotted spoon, transfer to the prepared plate and season lightly with salt. Repeat with the remaining shallots. Save the oil to fry the pancakes.

Preheat the oven to 200°F and fit a wire roasting rack over a baking sheet. In the same wok or Dutch oven over medium-high heat, rewarm the oil to 375°F. Spread out the 1 cup / 140 g flour in a pie plate or wide bowl.

Set a dough ball in the plate to coat the bottom with flour, then flip the dough over. Using your fingers, gently press the dough into a 5-inch round about ⅓ inch thick. Make sure the center is no thinner than the edges.

Slide the pancake into the oil and fry until cooked through, 3 to 4 minutes per side. It should puff up and turn golden brown. Transfer to the prepared rack and keep warm in the oven as you fry the other pancakes.

Lightly dust the pancakes with green onion powder. Serve hot with bowls of the sauce soubise, fried shallots, and chives, if desired, to slather and sprinkle on each bite.

ORANGE CHICKEN WINGS

In certain fancy restaurants, you'll see "gastrique" or "agrodolce" on the menu, which are just other ways to say "sweet and sour." All are a viscous sauce made with a sugar (sucrose most of the time, but you can also use honey, agave, or anything else sweet) that can carry an acid, like a vinegar. As you reduce the sugar, you concentrate its sweetness until it is a perfect balance to the abrasiveness of vinegar. They bring out the best in each other. However you come at it, sweet and sour is most delicious when you get that first bite of crispiness followed by a hit of tangy, mouthwatering sweetness. To make that crispiness last, you need a batter built from three starches. Short-grain glutinous rice flour (such as mochiko) makes the batter stick, while water-milled, long-grain glutinous rice flour (look for "水磨糯米粉" on the label) holds the crunch. Cornstarch walls in the juices from the chicken as it cooks. For the glaze, instead of straight sugar, this recipe calls for orange juice cooked down for a couple hours with some honey, brown rice syrup, and Shaoxing. There's a little tingle and kick, too, from garlic, ginger, and chile. I kept these as wings, not nuggets, for that extra flavor, as the Chinese say, that comes from eating the meat closest to the bone, right off the bone. The wings will be double-fried, first in a dry dredge and then a wet batter, so plan to dredge and fry in batches.

Active Time — 1 hour, 15 minutes

Plan Ahead — You'll need at least 2 hours for brining the wings and simmering the sauce, and time to make the Wok Salt

Makes about 30 wings; 6 to 8 servings

Special Equipment — Deep-fry thermometer

Brined Chicken Wings

3 lb / 1.4kg chicken wings
2 qt / 1.9L water
⅓ cup / 45g kosher salt
1 Tbsp granulated sugar
1 Tbsp coriander seeds
1½ tsp fennel seeds
2 star anise pods

Orange Sauce

1 qt / 950ml rice vinegar
2 cups / 480ml Shaoxing wine
1 cup / 240ml fresh
    orange juice, strained
1 cup / 240ml brown rice syrup
¾ cup / 255g honey
⅓ cup / 40g peeled and
    coarsely chopped ginger
¼ cup / 40g coarsely chopped
    garlic
2 habanero chiles, halved
    and seeded

To make the wings: Cut the wings at both joints. Keep the drumettes and flats; discard the wing tips (or save for chicken stock, see page 34).

Fit a fine-mesh strainer over a large bowl. In a large saucepan over high heat, combine the water, salt, sugar, coriander seeds, fennel seeds, and star anise and bring to a boil, stirring to dissolve the salt and sugar. Strain this brine into the prepared bowl and discard the solids. Let cool to room temperature and then add the chicken wings, making sure they are submerged. Cover and refrigerate at least 2 hours or up to 3 days.

To make the sauce: In a large saucepan over medium heat, combine the vinegar, wine, orange juice, brown rice syrup, honey, ginger, garlic, and chiles and simmer until reduced to the consistency and color of warm molasses, about 2 hours.

When the sauce is reduced, fit a fine-mesh strainer over a small bowl. Strain the sauce, discard the solids, and let cool. Transfer to an airtight container and store in the refrigerator for up to 1 week, or in the freezer for up to 2 months.

To make the vinaigrette: Set a medium frying pan over medium-high heat. Add the orange slices and sear until charred, about 2 minutes per side. Transfer the slices to a cutting board, let cool, and then mince. Transfer to a small bowl. Add the vinegar, orange juice, neutral oil, fennel seeds, and salt and whisk together. Transfer to an airtight container and store in the refrigerator for up to 3 days. Re-whisk before using.

CONTINUED

ORANGE CHICKEN WINGS continued

Charred Orange Vinaigrette

Two ¼-inch-thick round
    slices navel orange, skin on,
    seeds removed
¼ cup / 60ml rice vinegar
1 Tbsp fresh orange juice
2 tsp neutral oil
¼ tsp crushed fennel seeds
¼ tsp kosher salt

1½ qt / 1.4L neutral oil
1 cup / 150g short-grain
    glutinous rice flour (such
    as mochiko)
⅔ cup / 75g long-grain
    glutinous rice flour (糯米粉,
    noh máih fán)
½ cup / 70g cornstarch
1½ cups / 360ml water
4 tsp Wok Salt (see page 37)
2 Tbsp chopped fennel fronds,
    plus 4 cups / 280g thinly
    shaved fennel bulb
¼ cup / 15g thinly sliced
    (crosswise) green onions
1 medium jalapeño chile,
    thinly sliced into rounds
    and seeded

Preheat the oven to 200°F. Fit two wire roasting racks over two rimmed baking sheets.

Fill a wok or Dutch oven with the neutral oil and secure a deep-fry thermometer on the side. Set over medium-high heat and warm the oil to 375°F, being careful to maintain this temperature as you fry. Meanwhile, in a large bowl, whisk together both glutinous flours and the cornstarch. Drain the wings.

Toss about one-third of the wings in the flour mixture. Transfer to a colander and shake off the excess flour back into the bowl. Place the wings in the oil and fry, stirring occasionally, to set the coating, 3 to 4 minutes (they will not be cooked through or look browned yet). Transfer to a prepared rack. Repeat with the remaining wings in two more batches.

Measure 1⅔ cups / 200g of the flour mixture into a large bowl and discard the rest. Add the water, wok salt, and fennel fronds and whisk until a smooth, thin batter forms.

Toss about one-third of the wings in the batter. Pick them out of the batter one at a time, allowing excess batter to drain into the bowl, then slide into the oil and fry until light golden brown, crisp, and cooked through, 5 to 6 minutes. Transfer to the second prepared rack and keep warm in the oven as you fry the rest. Whisk the batter between each batch. Rewarm the orange sauce over low heat while the last batch is frying.

Place the wings in a large bowl, drizzle with the orange sauce, and toss to coat. (Toss in batches if your bowl isn't big enough for the wings to really move.) Transfer to a serving platter and sprinkle with the green onion and jalapeño. Dress the shaved fennel with ⅓ cup / 80ml of the vinaigrette, taste, and add more as needed. Serve the wings hot with the fennel salad on the side.

ON SWEET AND SOUR

In Sichuan, the ingredient that defines sweet and sour is fermented tangerine peel, chén pí (陳皮 in Mandarin). The best is so prized that fights break out over who will inherit the priceless family stash. Kumquats and Chinese haw, which look like tiny red apples and bring bright orange color and acidity to match, are other classic ways to bring sweet and sour to a dish.

Not having the usual ingredients for a sweet and sour recipe in the United States left it open to reinterpretation. In Chinatown, variations on the sweet and sour theme were made possible by blends of ingredients such as sugar, honey, vinegar, fresh orange juice, canned pineapple, and ketchup. In his 1963 cookbook, Johnny Kan included Hong Kong Lemon Chicken, which called for a whole deep-fried chicken with chén pí, warm spices, and a sweet and sour gravy of fresh lemon juice and zest, making the classical approach a good dose of California sunshine.

All those who shaped orange chicken into the now-ubiquitous tangy orange nuggets are impossible to know, but according to airport/mall juggernaut Panda Express, in 1987, while opening a Hawaiian franchise, chef Andy Kao decided an existing sweet and sour chicken dish could sell better without bones. He tossed the nuggets prepped for General Tso's with a fresh orange-based sauce, and a bestseller was born. Panda locked down "The Original Orange Chicken" with a copyright, hired PR to share the story, and now sells eighty million pounds of it each year. That's about as American as you can get.

FOUR SEASONS OF POT STICKERS

Making pot stickers is the fastest way to understanding what Chinese mean when they talk about the flavor of skillful hands. Pot stickers require gung fu, which is a term that also applies to round-kicking a wooden board, meditating, and driving a taxi in Shanghai—anything that takes technique, practice, and patience. Few other foods take as much time, I'm talking years, to build muscle memory and grandma wisdom to get them just right. We make hundreds of pot stickers at a time at Mister Jiu's, so we've developed wrapper doughs that work well whether rolled with a pasta machine or by hand. But there are no shortcuts when it comes down to wrapping. The process for cooking is in two phases, first steaming and then pan-frying until crisp and browned on the bottom, ideally without you touching the pan lid. They will stick to the pan in the middle of the process, so don't try to remove them too soon. We've laid out four of our seasonal variations here, which all get the same treatment. You can always swap the juice in the colorful wrappers for water if you want to keep things simple (or maintain some mystery). Grinding your own pork blend works best, but you can substitute the equivalent amount of fatty ground pork in a pinch.

Active Time — 2 hours

Plan Ahead — You'll need 30 minutes for resting the dough. Winter pot stickers require at least an additional 1 hour for salting the cabbage.

Makes about 40 pot stickers; 6 servings

Special Equipment — Juicer or blender, stand mixer, pasta roller, meat grinder, 3½-inch round cutter

Pot Sticker Wrappers

1¼ cups / 300ml Seasonal Juice (see table, page 78) or water

3 cups / 420g all-purpose flour

1½ tsp kosher salt

Pot Sticker Filling

12 oz / 340g pork shoulder, cut into 1-inch pieces

3 oz / 85g pork back fat, cut into 1-inch pieces

Seasonal Vegetable (see table, page 78)

¾ cup / 45g thinly sliced (crosswise) green onions

2 Tbsp plus 1 tsp peeled and finely chopped ginger

1 Tbsp toasted sesame oil

1 Tbsp kosher salt

1 tsp ground white pepper

½ cup / 120ml neutral oil

Water as needed

Fresh sorrel leaves for garnishing (optional)

Chinese black vinegar for dipping

Thread-cut peeled young ginger for dipping

To make the wrappers: Set a fine-mesh strainer over a small saucepan. Pour the juice through, pressing on the solids with a spoon to extract as much juice as possible; discard the solids. Set the strained juice over medium heat and bring to a simmer.

In the bowl of a stand mixer fitted with the dough hook attachment, combine the flour and salt. With the mixer on low speed, slowly pour in 1 cup plus 2 Tbsp / 265ml of the juice and mix until a dough forms into a fairly smooth ball around the hook, about 10 minutes. If the flour is not completely incorporated after 2 minutes, add more juice, ½ Tbsp at a time. If mixing by hand, mix together the flour and salt in a bowl and add the juice a little at a time, kneading the dough until smooth.

Form the dough into a smooth ball and let rest in the bowl, covered with a damp kitchen towel, for 30 minutes. The dough should now look super-smooth, feel soft, and slowly spring back when you poke it.

Divide the dough into six pieces of roughly the same size. If using a pasta roller, roll one piece at a time (keep the rest covered), starting at the thickest setting and moving down incrementally until slightly more than 1⁄16 inch thick (setting 4 on a KitchenAid pasta roller), doing your best to roll out a wide sheet. Roll the dough through twice on this final setting. If rolling by hand, lightly flour a rolling pin and roll each piece out to 1⁄16 inch thick.

Using a 3½-inch round cutter, cut out circles of dough, layering the rounds between sheets of parchment paper and covering the top layer with a damp kitchen towel. Gather up the dough scraps, reroll, and cut until you have about forty wrappers. Leave covered with a damp kitchen towel and refrigerate until ready to use, up to 2 days.

CONTINUED

ON POT STICKERS

Pot stickers are so much a part of American culture now that you can get them at The Cheesecake Factory and frozen as Lean Cuisine. In 1945, physician and writer Buwei Yang Chao coined the term "pot stickers," a pretty literal translation of guōtiē (鍋貼, in Mandarin), in her seminal book *How to Cook and Eat in Chinese*. But a decade later, Joyce Chen still couldn't sell them in her Cambridge restaurant until she called them "Peking ravioli," which you still hear around New England. Chen knew TV could work wonders opening up more minds to Chinese food, and eventually she got a show, sharing a set with Julia Child at WGBH. *Joyce Chen Cooks* was the first nationally broadcast program to teach Chinese cooking, and the first to feature a woman of color. In 1967, she demonstrated slowly wrapping dumplings in five different ways for the camera. Each time, the dough seemed to form itself, as happens with masterful hands. Her dumplings stood with a paunch at the back. "Like an armchair," she said. "This is the first time for you to cook these. I don't expect you make right away that way."

To make the filling: In a medium bowl, using your hands, roughly mix together the pork shoulder and back fat. Using a meat grinder, grind the pork and fat through a coarse grinding plate (¼-inch / 6mm holes) into the medium bowl. Grind again through a fine grinding plate (⅛-inch / 3mm holes) into the bowl of a stand mixer.

Place the bowl in a stand mixer fitted with the paddle attachment; add the vegetable, green onions, ginger, sesame oil, salt, and pepper; and mix on medium-low speed until the mixture forms a sticky paste (don't worry too much about overworking), about 2 minutes. If mixing by hand, vigorously mix the ground pork and the rest of the ingredients together in a large bowl with a wooden spoon until it comes together as a sticky paste.

Line a rimmed baking sheet with parchment paper. Uncover six of the wrappers at a time (keep the rest under a damp kitchen towel while working). Spoon 1 Tbsp filling in the center of a wrapper and flatten a bit. Fold the wrapper in half by bringing the bottom up to the top, but don't yet seal firmly. Starting at one end, pleat the front edge of the wrapper and then pinch the pleat with the back edge until completely sealed, about eight pleats (see Chef's Note: Dumplings, page 80). Hold the pot sticker by the pleats and gently plop it down on the baking sheet to form a flat bottom. Repeat until all the filling is used up. If at any point the wrappers start to dry out and stop sealing when pinched together, trace the edges of the wrapper with a water-dampened finger. (If not cooking right away, refrigerate the pot stickers on the baking sheet, covered with a damp kitchen towel, for up to 1 day. You can also freeze them solid, uncovered on the baking sheet, then transfer to a freezer bag and store in the freezer for up to 2 months. Cook from frozen; do not thaw first.)

Preheat the oven to 200°F.

In a large nonstick frying pan over medium-high heat, warm 2 Tbsp of the neutral oil until shimmering. Add the pot stickers in batches of about a dozen. (The exact number depends on the size of your pan and dumplings. To get the dumplings to stick, they need to entirely fill the pan without touching.) Leave in the oil for about 1 minute; get the lid ready as you carefully add ¼ cup / 60ml water to the bottom of the pan (the water should barely cover the bottom of the dumplings). Cover immediately and leave to steam for about 4 minutes. (If the pot stickers are frozen, steam for 5 to 6 minutes.) Try not to check on them by lifting the cover or moving them around. This is where a glass lid is handy—when the steam clears, you have just a few minutes of cooking to go.

Uncover the pot stickers and continue to leave them alone (let them stick to the pan; it should feel like you're taking them to the edge of burnt) until they have developed a golden brown crust on the bottom, 2 to 3 minutes more. Using a thin spatula, release the pot stickers and transfer to a platter and place in the oven. If burnt bits form, wipe out the pan before adding more oil for the next round.

Let the pot stickers cool for a minute or two before serving, crowned with a sorrel leaf, if desired, and shallow dishes of black vinegar with a small pile of ginger threads for dipping.

POT STICKERS SEASONAL JUICE AND VEGETABLE

	SPRING	SUMMER	FALL	WINTER
	Juice 12 oz / 340g baby spinach 1½ cups / 360ml water **Vegetable** 1 lb / 450g fava leaves or pea shoots 1 Tbsp neutral oil Kosher salt	**Juice** 1¼ cups / 300ml freshly pressed beet juice, or 1½ lb / 680g loose red beets **Vegetable** 1 lb / 450g rainbow Swiss chard 1 Tbsp neutral oil Kosher salt	**Juice / Vegetable** 6½ lb / 2.9kg butternut squash	**Juice / Vegetable** 2½ lb / 1.1kg red cabbage 1½ tsp kosher salt
TO MAKE THE JUICE	Bring a large pot of water to a boil over high heat. Meanwhile, prepare an ice bath in a large bowl by filling it with ice and a little water. Add the spinach to the boiling water and cook until just wilted, about 1 minute. Drain, then transfer to the ice bath. Once cool, drain again. Squeeze as much moisture as possible from the spinach with your hands. Place the spinach in a blender with the water and blend until smooth.	Skip starting from scratch if you can buy high-quality beet juice. Otherwise, scrub the beets well; no need to peel them. Cut into 1½-inch chunks, then juice with a juicer.	Peel the squash and remove the seeds. Set aside 8 oz / 225g. Cut the remainder into 1½-inch chunks, then juice with a juicer.	Cut the core from the cabbage, then cut the cabbage into 1½-inch-wide wedges. Set aside 8 oz / 225g. Juice the remaining cabbage with a juicer.
TO PREPARE THE VEGETABLE	Separate the fava leaves from the thicker stems. Warm a wok or large frying pan over medium heat. Add the neutral oil and the stems, season with salt, and cook until just tender, 3 to 4 minutes. Add the leaves a few handfuls at a time and cook until wilted, about 5 minutes more. Remove from the heat, let cool, and then squeeze as much moisture as possible from the greens with your hands. Transfer the greens to a cutting board and finely chop.	Tear the chard leaves from the stems and keep them separate. Finely chop the stems. Working with a few leaves at a time, stack them and chop into fine shreds. Warm a wok or large frying pan over medium heat. Add the neutral oil and the stems, season with salt, and cook until just tender, about 3 minutes. Add the leaves a few handfuls at a time and cook until wilted, about 5 minutes more. Remove from the heat, let cool, and then squeeze as much moisture from the greens as possible with your hands. Transfer the greens to a cutting board and finely chop.	Grate the reserved 8 oz / 225g squash on the large holes of a box grater.	Cut the reserved 8 oz / 225g cabbage into fine shreds. In a colander, toss with the salt and leave to drain in the sink for 1 hour. Squeeze as much moisture from the cabbage as possible with your hands.

TEA AND DUMPLINGS: YUM CHA

Dumplings are the great uniter, bringing together Chinese families on weekend mornings at the dim sum parlors and banquet houses in Chinatown for yum cha (飲茶). *Yum cha* means "to drink tea," but implies so much more. Dim sum are the dishes. Yum cha is the act and the spectacle, the organized chaos of grandparents in their silky pajamas sharing gossip and reading the paper, parents slurping jook and stacking rib bones on the table, and kids scrambling for mango pudding. Strangers seated together at a table start chatting like old friends, all while servers breeze by pushing carts and refilling tea.

Dumplings connect us beyond the borders of Chinatown too. Yum cha extravaganzas came from southern China, while dumpling banquets and jiaozi parties came from the north. Xiao long bao and its ilk are from the east, and momos stuffed with yak meat from the west. In Nepal, there are momos, too; in Turkey, there are manti; Russia has pelmeni; Sweden, pitepalt. Poland offers pierogi. Israel serves kreplach. Not that long ago, you'd see some of these terms pop up on Chinese restaurant menus, because what easier way to connect than by sharing an appreciation for good dumplings, in whatever name.

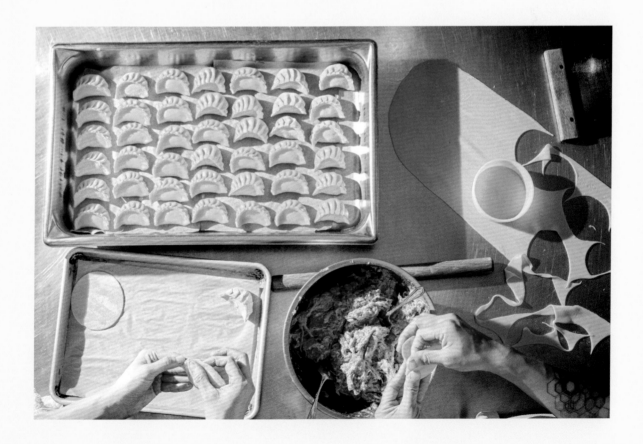

Chef's Note: Dumplings

Every family has its own dim sum order from which it does not deviate. Ours was har gow, siu mai, ham sui gok (see page 100), turnip cake (see page 95), and jook with yóu tiáo (see page 56). We'd go off menu and add some chow fan and greens.

Cooking a full dim sum spread is for the pros, but our family, like many Chinese families, made some dumplings such wontons, shui jiao, and pot stickers in our own way at home. Their shapes speak of family heritage. For instance, triangles, rectangles, little fish, ingots, nurse's caps, and round purses are all wonton canon, each with their own regional origins. If your family makes wàhn tān (雲吞) resembling birds with scissored tails, you probably have southern roots. If you make chāo shǒu (抄手), triangles with the corners crossed loosely like arms, you may have ancestors from Sichuan. If your family's wontons are pleasing blobs formed with a quick squeeze in one hand, it's hard to say, though the form is no less legit. The ancient root word for "wonton" is hùn dùn (混沌), which basically means "chaos."

A few keys to wrapping dumplings:

- If using frozen wrappers (homemade or store-bought), defrost overnight in the refrigerator. Keep wrappers covered with a damp kitchen towel as you work. If your previously frozen wrappers are cracking, wrap them in a warm, damp towel for 10 minutes and then try again.

- If rolling out your own wrappers, you shouldn't need to add much, if any, flour and only a few drops of water. The doughs in this book are forgiving and won't tend to stick, whether you use a mixer and pasta machine, or do every step by hand. Roll wrappers as thinly as possible. If using a dowel, make them thinnest at the edges. In our kitchen, wonton wrappers are thinnest. Pot sticker wrappers are thickest by a hair.

- When filling, think plump but not overstuffed.

- Completely seal the edges before cooking or the insides will spill out. Dab a little water on the edges if using store-bought wrappers to help seal tight.

❶ Wontons—Seal first, then join the corners; or seal just the top corner, then join the bottom corners before sealing all the edges.

❷ Shuijiao—Seal first, then pleat.

❸ Pot stickers—Pleat the front edge of the wrapper first, then seal.

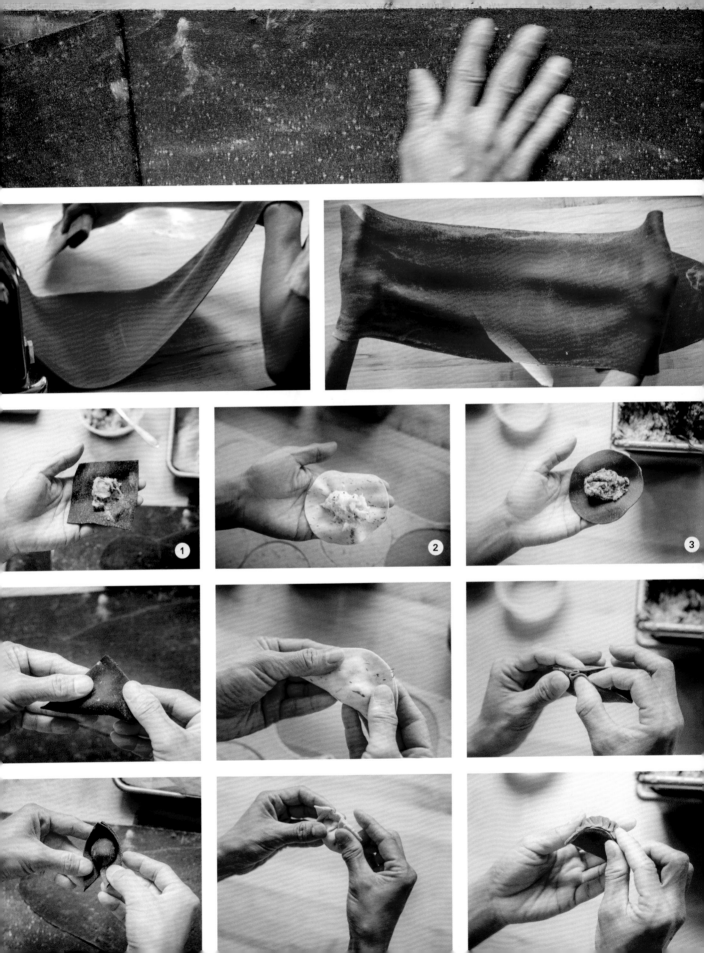

SEAFOOD SHUI JIAO

Active Time — 2 hours, 15 minutes

Plan Ahead — You'll need time to make Basic Chile Oil and Lanzhou Chile Oil. You can make the wrappers ahead of time and freeze.

Makes about 36 shui jiao; 6 to 8 servings

Special Equipment — Stand mixer, pasta roller, meat grinder, 3½-inch round cutter

Shui Jiao Wrappers

2¾ cups plus 3 Tbsp / 400g all-purpose flour

1 Tbsp finely chopped dill fronds

1½ tsp kosher salt

¾ cup plus 2 Tbsp / 205ml hot water, just boiled, plus more as needed

Seafood Filling

1 tsp neutral oil

4 cups / 290g cored and finely shredded Savoy cabbage

12 oz / 340g boneless, skinless rock cod or other lean white fish fillets, cut into 2-inch pieces

6 oz / 170g cleaned and peeled shrimp

4 oz / 115g sea scallops

3 Tbsp wheat starch (look for "澄麵粉" [chìhng mihn fán] or sometimes "wheaten cornflour" or "non-glutinous flour")

1½ Tbsp cornstarch

⅓ cup / 15g finely chopped chives

1½ Tbsp kosher salt

Florence Lin showed me the depth of Chinese cuisine beginning with starches. In her *Complete Book of Chinese Noodles, Dumplings and Breads*, she explains the importance of water temperature for achieving the right spring and bite in Chinese doughs. You need very hot water to hydrate the flour most efficiently for shui jiao (水餃) wrappers and other boiled dumplings. I had learned with Italian pasta to use egg yolk to give flour elasticity, but Florence revealed how to achieve it with just the right temperature water in the right proportion. Florence wasn't a purist. She was okay with substituting sauerkraut and Tabasco when needed, but she believed in technique. Through it, she showed that Chinese cuisine wasn't a monolith but a world of diverse cuisines. I never got to meet her, but I carried her *Chinese Regional Cookbook* around with me everywhere for a long time.

To make the wrappers: In the bowl of a stand mixer fitted with the dough hook attachment, combine the flour, dill fronds, and salt. With the mixer on low speed, slowly pour in the hot water and mix until a dough forms a fairly smooth ball around the hook, about 10 minutes. If the flour is not completely incorporated after 2 minutes, add more water, 1 tsp at a time, until all the flour is moistened. If mixing by hand, in a bowl, mix together the flour, dill, and salt and then, with a pair of chopsticks, stir in the hot water a little at a time until the flour is damp enough that it begins binding together. Knead the dough for a couple minutes in the bowl until smooth and combined.

Form the dough into a smooth ball and let rest in the bowl, covered with a damp kitchen towel, for 30 minutes. The dough should now look perfectly smooth, feel soft, and slowly spring back when you press it.

Divide the dough into six pieces of roughly the same size. If using a pasta roller, roll one piece at a time (keep the rest covered), starting at the thickest setting and moving down incrementally until slightly more than 1/16 inch thick (setting 4 on a KitchenAid pasta roller), doing your best to roll out a wide sheet. Roll the dough through twice on this final setting. If rolling by hand, lightly flour a rolling pin and roll each piece out to 1/16 inch thick.

Using a 3½-inch round cutter, cut out circles of dough, layering the rounds between sheets of parchment paper and covering the top layer with a damp kitchen towel. Gather up the dough scraps, re-roll, and cut until you have about thirty-six wrappers. Leave covered with a damp kitchen towel and refrigerate until ready to use, up to 1 day.

To make the filling: Warm a wok or large frying pan over medium heat. Add the neutral oil and let it heat up a few seconds. Add the cabbage and cook until completely tender, about 10 minutes. Transfer the cabbage to a bowl and put in the refrigerator until chilled, about 30 minutes.

CONTINUED

SEAFOOD SHUI JIAO continued

½ cup / 120ml Chinese
   black vinegar
½ cup / 120ml Basic Chile Oil
   (page 40)
½ cup / 120ml Lanzhou
   Chile Oil (page 40)
⅓ cup / 80ml light soy sauce
   (生抽, sāng chāu)
2 Tbsp plus 1 tsp toasted
   sesame oil
Dill fronds for garnishing

Meanwhile, using a meat grinder, pass the fish, shrimp, and scallops through a coarse grinding plate (¼-inch / 6mm holes) into a medium bowl. Or hand chop each component with a cleaver until a rough dice, then combine and continue to chop until an even, fine mince. Transfer to a bowl and put in the refrigerator.

When the cabbage is cool, use your hands to squeeze as much moisture from it as possible and add to the bowl of seafood. Add the wheat starch, cornstarch, chives, and salt and vigorously mix with a wooden spoon until a sticky paste forms.

Line a rimmed baking sheet with parchment paper. Uncover six of the wrappers at a time (keep the rest under a damp kitchen towel while working). Spoon 1 Tbsp filling in the center of a wrapper and flatten a bit. Fold the wrapper in half by bringing the bottom up to the top, then pinch the edges together to seal. Starting at one end, make about six pleats along the sealed edge (see Chef's Note: Dumplings, page 80). Hold the shui jiao by the pleats and gently plop it down on the baking sheet to form a flat bottom. Repeat until all the filling is used up. If at any point the wrappers start to dry out and stop sealing when pinched together, trace the edges of the wrapper with a water-dampened finger. (If not cooking right away, refrigerate the shui jiao on the baking sheet, covered with a damp kitchen towel, for up to 1 day. You can also freeze them solid, uncovered on the baking sheet, then transfer to a freezer bag and store in the freezer for up to 2 months. Cook from frozen; do not thaw first.)

In a medium bowl, stir together the vinegar, both chile oils, soy sauce, and sesame oil. Set this sauce aside.

Bring a large saucepan of heavily salted water (it should remind you of seawater) to a boil over high heat. Add one-third of the shui jiao and boil until cooked through, 5 minutes if fresh, or 6 minutes if frozen. Using a slotted spoon, transfer the shui jiao to a plate. Repeat with the remaining shui jiao.

Spoon a generous amount of the reserved sauce into individual serving bowls and add five or six shui jiao to each bowl. Garnish with dill fronds and serve immediately.

SQUID INK WONTONS

You can watch the wontons through the window at Hon's Wun-Tun House on Kearny Street, floating up like clouds from the depths of a huge pot of boiling water. Wontons are easy to make, but there are nuances known only to those who have made thousands. The cooks at Hon's fold them with one pinch—signed, sealed, delivered and then on to the next in a flash. It takes time to build that muscle memory; but once you get into a rhythm, it's meditative. When my mom wanted a heart-to-heart, she'd call me into the kitchen to wrap wontons. We'd talk about school or my ninety-nine problems, while I was distracted by the task of getting our wontons to look like birds with scissor tails. Whatever form you make them, aim for a 30/70 ratio of filling to silky skin. This recipe draws from the Sichuan (pork with chile) and Guangdong (shrimp with green onions) styles, and the squid-ink mezzaluna stuffed with guanciale that I loved in Italy. You can often find squid ink—technically, it's from cuttlefish—frozen or jarred in Asian and Mediterranean grocery stores.

Active Time — 1 hour, 15 minutes

Plan Ahead — You'll need 30 minutes for resting the dough, plus time to make Basic Chile Oil and Fermented Chile Paste

Makes about 30 wontons; 6 servings

Special Equipment — Stand mixer, pasta roller, meat grinder

Wonton Wrappers

⅓ cup / 80ml boiling water, plus more as needed

1 Tbsp squid ink or cuttlefish ink

1¼ cups / 175g all-purpose flour

Wonton Filling

4 oz / 115g skinless pork belly, cut into 1-inch chunks

4 oz / 115g peeled and cleaned shrimp

2 Tbsp beaten egg

2 Tbsp thinly sliced Chinese chives

2 tsp light soy sauce (生抽, sāng chāu)

½ tsp minced garlic

⅛ tsp cayenne pepper

Wonton Vinegar

¼ cup plus 2 Tbsp / 90ml Basic Chile Oil (page 40)

1½ Tbsp Chinese black vinegar

1 Tbsp light soy sauce (生抽, sāng chāu)

1½ tsp toasted sesame oil

To make the wrappers: In a small bowl, stir together the boiling water and squid ink. Place the flour in the bowl of a stand mixer fitted with the dough hook attachment. With the mixer on low speed, slowly pour in the diluted ink and mix until a smooth dough forms a ball around the hook, about 5 minutes, adding more water a tiny bit at a time if it needs help coming together. If mixing by hand, drizzle the diluted ink into the flour while stirring with a fork or your fingers. Using your hands, knead to incorporate all the flour into the dough, adding a little more water at a time, if required. Knead the dough on a clean work surface until smooth, about 5 minutes.

Form the dough into a ball by tucking the sides of the dough under itself, turning the ball as you go. Cover with a damp kitchen towel and let rest for 30 minutes.

Line a rimmed baking sheet with parchment paper.

The dough should now look smooth; divide it into three pieces. Roll one piece of the dough at a time (keep the rest covered with a damp kitchen towel) through the pasta roller, starting at the thickest setting and moving down incrementally until slightly less than ¹⁄₁₆ inch thick (setting 5 on a KitchenAid pasta roller). Roll the dough through twice on this final setting. If the dough gets too long to handle, cut it in half before continuing to roll. You can also use a rolling pin to make scant-¹⁄₁₆-inch-thick sheets (no need to flour).

Using a knife or pizza cutter, trim and cut the dough sheets into 2½-inch squares. Arrange the squares on the prepared baking sheet so none is touching, layering parchment paper between the squares and covering with damp kitchen towels, until you have thirty wrappers. Leave covered and refrigerate until ready to use, up to 3 hours.

CONTINUED

SQUID INK WONTONS continued

1 Tbsp neutral oil

8 oz / 225g cleaned squid, tentacles whole, bodies cut into ½-inch rings

½ cup / 15g sliced green onions (1-inch pieces; greens only)

2 Tbsp Fermented Chile Paste (page 43) or sambal oelek

Mico-celery for garnishing (optional)

To make the filling: Using a meat grinder, pass the pork belly through a coarse grinding plate (¼-inch / 6mm holes) into the bowl of a stand mixer. Repeat with the shrimp. Add the egg, chives, soy sauce, garlic, and cayenne to the bowl. Set the bowl in the stand mixer fitted with the paddle attachment and mix on medium-low speed into a sticky paste (don't worry too much about overworking), about 1 minute.

Line a rimmed baking sheet with parchment paper. Uncover six of the wrappers (keep the rest under the towel while working). Spoon about 1½ tsp filling in the center of a wrapper. Fold the wrapper in half to form a triangle and seal, pressing hard enough that the edges thin slightly. Holding the stuffed triangle flat, pull the two lower corners to meet and overlap slightly (there should be some tension so that the stuffed part pooches), and press together, forming a wonton in the shape of a little swallow (see Chef's Note: Dumplings, page 80). (I find it easier to seal just the top of the triangle, then join the two lower corners, before sealing the entire edge.) Repeat until all the filling is used up. If at any point the wrappers start to dry out and stop sealing when pinched together, trace the edges of the wrapper with a water-dampened finger. (If not cooking right away, refrigerate the wontons on the baking sheet, covered with a damp kitchen towel, for up to 3 hours. You can also freeze them solid, uncovered, on the baking sheet, then transfer to a freezer bag and store in the freezer for up to 2 months. Cook from frozen; do not thaw first.)

To make the vinegar: In a small bowl, whisk together the chile oil, vinegar, soy sauce, and sesame oil until combined. Set aside.

Bring a large saucepan of heavily salted water (it should remind you of seawater) to a boil over high heat. Add the wontons and boil until cooked through, 3 minutes if fresh, or 4 minutes if frozen.

Meanwhile, warm a large frying pan or wok over high heat. Add the neutral oil and let it heat up for a few seconds. Add the squid and green onions and then don't touch until they char in spots, about 30 seconds. Stir-fry until the squid is just cooked through, about 30 seconds more. Remove from the heat and toss with the chile paste.

When the wontons are ready, use a slotted spoon to transfer them to a large bowl. Toss with ⅓ cup of the wonton vinegar. Transfer to a serving dish and top with the squid and micro-celery, if desired. Serve with the remaining wonton vinegar for dipping.

CHICKEN IN A SPACE SUIT

Active Time — 1 hour,
10 minutes

Plan Ahead — You'll need
1 hour for rising, plus time to
make Bao Dough, Lemon Aioli,
and Fermented Cabbage

Makes 8 servings

Special Equipment —
Steamer, meat grinder, food
processor, sausage stuffer,
kitchen twine, deep-fry
thermometer

1 recipe Bao dough
   (see page 49)
8 small Chicken Boudin Blanc
   (page 90)
2 tsp raw white sesame seeds
1 green onion, thinly sliced
   crosswise (white part only)
1 Tbsp sweet potato vinegar
   or red wine vinegar
3 Tbsp neutral oil
Lemon Aioli (see page 65)
   for serving
Coarsely chopped Fermented
   Cabbage (see variation,
   page 42) for serving
Fresh tarragon leaves
   for serving

Many Chinese dishes are poetic. There are dishes named for powerful women, fallen heroes, and beloved artists. Pork and shrimp meatballs are "Peaches of Immortality." Dumplings stuffed with late-fall ingredients are "Frosted Willow Leaves." A soup of a few dozen different seafoods and meats is so delicious, even "Buddha Jumps over the Wall" for it. Which brings me to Chicken in a Space Suit and my dad. He didn't cook much when I was growing up. I'll give him credit for well-built salami sandwiches and spaghetti with red sauce from the jar. But his greatest work was his variation, if you will, on the standard sausage in a bun/pig in a blanket/lap cheong wrapped in bao. He'd wrap a hot dog in Wonder Bread, encase it all in foil, and throw it in my lunch bag. Although I did feel a little funny unwrapping them in the middle of the cafeteria with everyone eating sandwiches, I loved them. Chicken in a Space Suit is my tribute.

Cut eight 2 × 4-inch rectangles of parchment paper. Portion the bao dough into eight pieces and roll into 12-inch-long, ⅔-inch-wide ropes. Spiral-wrap each rope around a sausage, leaving ¼ to ½ inch of both ends of the sausage bare. Make sure there are no overlaps or gaps in the spacesuit. Place each space chicken on a parchment rectangle.

Brush the tops of the dough very lightly with water, then sprinkle with the sesame seeds. Cover loosely with a damp, clean kitchen towel and let rise in a warm place until slightly puffed like svelte Michelin men, 30 to 45 minutes.

Meanwhile, in a small bowl, combine the green onion and vinegar and set aside.

Prepare a steamer in a wok or a large, lidded pot following the instructions on page 167 and bring the water to a boil over medium-high heat. Pick the rolls up by the sausage ends and arrange in the steamer, leaving enough room around each for them to double in size (we squeeze four into a 12-inch steamer). Cover and steam until the dough is cooked through, about 8 minutes. (If you want to save some for later, freeze on a baking sheet until solid, transfer to a freezer bag, and store in the freezer for up to 2 months. Thaw in the refrigerator and then steam for 5 minutes to heat through.)

In a large frying pan over medium heat, warm 2 Tbsp of the neutral oil until shimmering. Remove the papers from the space suits. Add four suits to the pan at a time, making sure they don't touch. Leave them alone until a dark golden brown, crispy crust forms, about 3 minutes. Flip and cook for 3 minutes more. Using tongs, transfer to a plate. Add 1 Tbsp of the oil to the pan before the second batch.

Serve your Chicken in a Space Suit hot, topped with lemon aioli, fermented cabbage, vinegared green onions, and tarragon leaves.

VARIATION: PORKONAUTS
If you would prefer a porky version, cut Lap Cheong (page 45) into eight 6-inch pieces and roll the bao dough into 16-inch-long, ½-inch-wide ropes. Once wrapped, place the Porkonauts on eight 2 × 5-inch rectangles of parchment paper. Steam and fry as directed and serve with Red XO Sauce (page 38).

CHICKEN BOUDIN BLANC

Makes about 20 small sausages or 7 large sausages

Note — If using water chestnut flour, which tends to clump, pound in a mortar and pestle into a fine powder before measuring.

One 3½-lb / 1.5kg whole chicken

4 oz / 115g pork back fat

¼ cup / 20g chestnut flour, or 2 Tbsp plus 1 tsp water chestnut flour

5 tsp milk powder

1½ Tbsp kosher salt

2 tsp ground ginger

½ tsp ground star anise

½ tsp ground cloves

10 feet natural sheep casings (for small sausages) or hog casings (for large sausages)

Ice cubes as needed

Keeping the skin attached, cut the chicken breast meat from the breastbones, cut off the legs, cut through the joint between the leg and thigh to separate, and then cut the bones out of the thighs. Weigh the breast meat and thigh meat—you want 1½ lb / 680g; if you need more meat, trim some meat from the drumsticks to make up the difference. (Do as I do and roast the drumsticks and wings as a cook's snack or save for another meal, and reserve the carcass for making chicken stock, see page 34.)

Cut the breast and thigh meat with the skin attached into 1-inch pieces. Cut the pork fat into 1-inch pieces.

In a large bowl, stir together the chestnut flour, milk powder, salt, ginger, star anise, and cloves until lump-free. Add the chicken meat and pork fat and toss until no powdery bits remain. Cover and refrigerate overnight.

Using a meat grinder, grind the seasoned meat and fat through a coarse grinding plate (¼-inch / 6mm holes) into a medium bowl. Switch to a fine grinding plate (⅛-inch / 3mm holes), then regrind everything back into the original bowl. Chill the meat mixture while you prepare the casings.

Rinse the salt from the casings under running water, then soak in a bowl of lukewarm water.

Weigh the meat mixture. You will need 14 percent of the meat mixture weight in ice, so calculate accordingly. Working quickly to keep the meat mixture as cold as possible, place the mixture in a food processor fitted with the blade attachment and add the ice cubes. Process for 30 seconds, then scrape down the sides of the bowl. Continue to process until the mixture is emulsified into a sticky, smooth paste, about 30 seconds more. Transfer back to the bowl and refrigerate for 30 minutes.

Run warm water through the casings to flush them out, being careful not to tangle them, and then drain. Set up a sausage stuffer with a stuffing tube that's ½ inch / 12mm wide for sheep casings, or 1 inch / 25mm wide for hog casings. Slide 3 to 4 feet of casing onto the stuffing tube and tie a double knot at one end of the casing. Fill a large baking dish with ice cubes. Set the bowl of filling in the ice.

Stuff the casings tightly with the meat mixture. You want to avoid air pockets, but don't worry too much about perfection as you can readjust the stuffing while you make links. (If you expect to need a lot of boudin blanc at once, like we do, making links is optional.) Starting about 3½ inches from the knot, pinch off a length of sausage, squeezing from both sides to pack the stuffing tighter. Twist the link toward you a few times. Pinch off another link, alternating the direction of twists, until you run out of casing or filling. Tie off with a knot. To release any air bubbles, prick each sausage once or twice with a needle that was sterilized over a flame (hold a few seconds until it glows red).

Set a large pot of heavily salted water (it should remind you of seawater) over medium-high heat and secure a deep-fry thermometer on the side. Bring to 150° to 175°F (it should not be simmering). Add the sausages and poach, never letting the water temperature go above 175°F, until cooked through, about 5 minutes for sheep casings and 8 minutes for hog casings. Using tongs, transfer to a baking sheet, pat dry with paper towels, arrange into a single layer, and let cool. (At this point, the hog-casing sausage is ready to be used in Moo Goo Gai Pan, page 149.) Transfer to an airtight container and store in the refrigerator for up to 1 week, or in the freezer for up to 2 months.

WILD MUSHROOM BAO

Active Time — 2 hours

Plan Ahead — You'll need time to make Bao Dough, and an additional 1½ hours for portioning and rising

Makes 18 bao; 6 to 8 servings

Special Equipment — Steamer

Mushroom Filling

6 tsp neutral oil

1½ cups / 75g halved and very thinly sliced fresh shiitake mushrooms

1½ tsp minced garlic

Kosher salt

1½ cups / 75g very thinly sliced fresh wild mushrooms, such as chanterelle or black trumpet

1½ cups / 75g very thinly sliced leeks (white and light green parts)

2 cups / 75g very finely shredded green cabbage

1 Tbsp light soy sauce (生抽, sāng chāu)

1 tsp toasted sesame oil

Finely grated zest of ½ medium lemon

1 recipe Bao dough (see page 49)

1 Tbsp raw white or black sesame seeds

4 Tbsp neutral oil

These bao are one example of the versatility of mantou dough. When filled, they can still be light, airy, and pillowy. Then you roll the tops in sesame seeds and pan-fry to give them even more textural elements. I like that this bao looks really simple from the outside and doesn't give away its complexity until you bite into it. Since it is meant to have a smooth sheen, it's especially important to round the dough properly into a tight ball with a taut outer skin to avoid it splitting in the steamer.

To make the filling: Warm a wok or large frying pan over medium-high heat. Add 1½ tsp of the neutral oil, then add the shiitakes and garlic, season with ½ tsp salt, and cook until tender, about 1½ minutes. Transfer to a medium bowl. Add the wild mushrooms to the pan with another 1½ tsp oil and stir-fry until tender, about 1½ mintues. Transfer to the bowl. Repeat with the leeks and cabbage in separate batches in the same pan until tender, about 1½ minutes each, adding more oil to the pan between each round, as needed.

Return all the vegetables to the pan, add the soy sauce and sesame oil, and stir to combine. Remove from the heat, let cool to room temperature, and then stir in the lemon zest. Place the mushroom filling in a strainer for 30 minutes to drain off any excess liquid. (At this point you can transfer to an airtight container and store in the refrigerator for up to 1 week.)

Make sure the mushroom filling is not sitting in any excess liquid; if so, drain again. Now taste the filling, it should be slightly over-seasoned to balance with the bao dough, so season with salt.

Cut out eighteen 2-inch squares of parchment paper. Portion the bao dough into eighteen balls, each about 1½ inches in diameter (the size of a Ping-Pong ball). Working with one piece at a time, cup your hand over the dough, keeping the sides of your palm on the work surface. Round the dough by pressing with your palm while moving the dough in a circular motion on the work surface until a tight ball with a taut skin is formed.

Flatten each dough ball in your palms and stretch and press into a 3-inch-wide round, doing your best to make the edges slightly thinner than the center. Place a heaping 1 Tbsp filling in the middle. Gently gather the edges of the dough around the filling, then pinch together at the middle to seal completely. Place seam-side down on a parchment square. Repeat with the remaining filling and dough balls.

Place the sesame seeds in a small bowl. Brush the top of each bao very lightly with water, then gently dip into the seeds so there is about a 1-inch round of sesame seeds on top. Cover the bao loosely with a damp, clean kitchen towel and let rise in a warm place until slightly puffed and marshmallow-y in texture, 30 to 45 minutes.

CONTINUED

WILD MUSHROOM BAO continued

Prepare a steamer in a wok or a large, lidded pot following the instructions on page 167 and bring the water to a boil over medium-high heat. Place as many bao as will fit in the steamer (six in a 12-inch steamer) with about 2 inches of room around each. Cover and steam until the dough is cooked through, about 10 minutes. Add water to the pot between batches as needed. (The steamed bao can be frozen on a baking sheet until solid, transferred to a freezer bag, and then stored in the freezer for up to 2 months. Thaw in the refrigerator and then re-steam for 5 minutes to heat through.)

In a large frying pan over medium heat, warm 2 Tbsp of the neutral oil until shimmering. Remove the papers from the bao. Add the bao in batches of six, making sure they don't touch, and pan-fry until a dark golden brown, crispy crust forms on the bottom, about 3 minutes. Flip the bao and pan-fry to create a crust on top, about 3 minutes more. Add 1 Tbsp oil to the pan between each batch. Serve hot.

CRISPY SCARLET TURNIP CAKES

Like many Chinese Americans, my family referred to lòh baahk gōu (蘿蔔糕) as "turnip cakes" in English, but this is one of those instances where something got lost in translation. Turnip cakes are made with lòh baahk, a radish; specifically, the long white ones we call "daikon" in the United States. But I didn't know that when I first put in orders for my favorite turnip, the Scarlet Queen, from Full Belly Farm and Riverdog Farm. The Scarlet Queen has a beautiful green top and a bright fuchsia skin surrounding a snow-white heart; and as it turns out, works beautifully in this recipe. It takes on the varying textures that this cake needs, from creamy (when grated or cut thinly, it steams into a soft paste) to chunky (when medium diced, it retains its bite even after a lot of heat). The classic lòh baahk gōu has dried shrimp and sausage bits, but I like these vegetarian to really let the turnips shine. If you deep-fry them, you'll get a crunchy, hash-brown texture all the way through, while pan-frying results in a soft interior with crispy edges.

Active Time — 2 hours, 15 minutes

Plan Ahead — You'll need about 2 hours for steaming, and overnight for chilling

Makes forty 2-inch cakes; 20 servings

Special Equipment — Steamer, deep-fry thermometer

Turnip Cake

1½ lb / 680g scarlet turnips or peeled daikon

2 Tbsp neutral oil

6 medium shallots, cut into small dice

2 Tbsp minced garlic

10 oz / 285g fresh shiitake mushrooms, stemmed and cut into small dice

1 lb / 450g rice flour (粘米粉, jīm máih fán)

1½ Tbsp kosher salt

1½ tsp cornstarch

½ tsp ground white pepper

1 qt / 950ml neutral oil

1 recipe Pickled Shiitake Mushrooms (page 44), drained and cut into small dice

⅓ cup / 50g black olives (preferably dry-cured), pitted and finely chopped

Kosher salt

½ cup / 120ml light soy sauce (生抽, sāng chāu)

¼ cup / 60ml hot water

5 red radishes, cut into ⅛-inch-thick matchsticks

To make the cake: Coat an 8-inch-square (2-inch-high) baking pan (make sure it fits in your steamer) with cooking spray. Line the pan with parchment paper, then coat the paper with more cooking spray.

Grate half of the turnips on the large holes of a box grater (no need to peel). Cut the remaining turnips into small dice.

Place the grated turnips in a large frying pan and add enough water to cover the turnips halfway. Place over high heat and bring to a boil. Continue cooking, stirring occasionally, until just softening but not mushy, about 5 minutes more. Pour into a colander set in the sink and leave there to drain.

Wipe out the frying pan, add the diced turnips, and cover halfway with water. Place over high heat and bring to a boil. Continue cooking, stirring occasionally, until just softening, about 4 minutes more. Pour into the colander with the grated turnips and leave there to drain.

Wipe the frying pan dry, add the neutral oil, and set over medium heat until the oil is shimmering. Add the shallots and garlic and cook until softened, about 2 minutes. Add the mushrooms and cook until softened, about 5 minutes more. Pour into the colander with the turnips and let drain.

In a large, wide pot or Dutch oven, whisk together 2⅔ cups / 630ml water, the rice flour, salt, cornstarch, and white pepper until smooth. Add the contents of the colander and cook over medium heat, stirring and scraping the bottom of the pot frequently with a wooden spoon, until starting to bubble, about 4 minutes. Continue to cook, still stirring and scraping frequently, until the mixture forms a thick paste that sticks to the spoon, about 3 minutes more. Transfer to the prepared baking pan and smooth into an even layer.

CONTINUED

Prepare a steamer in a wok or a large, lidded pot following the instructions on page 167 and bring the water to a boil over medium-high heat. Place the pan in the steamer and steam until the turnip cake is set, about 2 hours (the top may still be a little wet). Check every 30 minutes or so to see if you need to add more water to the pot.

Set the cake aside to cool slightly, about 30 minutes. Press a sheet of plastic wrap directly onto the surface to keep it from drying out. Refrigerate overnight in the pan to fully set.

Fill a wok or Dutch oven with the neutral oil and secure a deep-fry thermometer on the side. Set over medium-high heat and warm the oil to 350°F, being careful to maintain this temperature as you fry.

Meanwhile, in a medium bowl, stir together the pickled mushrooms and olives.

Turn the turnip cake onto a cutting board and discard the parchment. Using a damp knife, cut the cake into four 2-inch wide strips. Then cut each strip crosswise into ten pieces; forty cakes total.

Preheat the oven to 200°F. Fit a wire roasting rack over a baking sheet.

Add the turnip cakes to the wok in batches of six, so they don't stick together, and fry until golden brown and crisp all over, about 4 minutes. Transfer to the prepared rack, sprinkle lightly with salt, and keep warm in the oven as you fry the other batches.

In a small bowl, stir together the soy sauce and hot water.

Sprinkle each turnip cake with a small spoonful of mushroom-olive mixture and some radish pieces. Drizzle the diluted soy sauce generously around (not over) the turnip cakes. Serve immediately.

SEA URCHIN CHEUNG FAN

Active Time — 1 hour

Makes eleven 9 × 1-inch rice rolls; 6 to 8 servings

Special Equipment — Steamer, 9-inch round cake pan or ⅛ sheet pan (6½ by 9½ inches)

Cheung Fan Batter

1 qt / 950ml water, at room temperature

2 cups / 250g rice flour (粘米粉, jīm máih fán)

½ cup plus 1 Tbsp / 80g tapioca flour or tapioca starch

¼ cup / 60ml neutral oil

¼ cup plus 1½ tsp / 40g cornstarch

2 Tbsp small dried shrimp

Cheung Fan Sauce

3 Tbsp light soy sauce (生抽, sāng chāu)

3 Tbsp hot water

2 Tbsp rice vinegar

1 Tbsp toasted sesame oil

1 Tbsp agrumato orange extra-virgin olive oil

4 green onions, thinly sliced crosswise

Sea urchin (3 pieces per cheung fan), cooked crab (3 Tbsp per cheung fan), or trout roe (1 Tbsp per cheung fan) for garnishing

Toasted white sesame seeds for garnishing

Micro-cilantro, torn red shiso leaves, or thinly sliced (crosswise) green onions for garnishing

Cheung fan (腸粉) are the silky, wide rice noodles riding the carts at dim sum houses. Servers drop them on the table, whip out scissors to portion them up, drizzle generously with sweetened soy, and move on. You can find them plain or stuffed with shrimp, pork, yóu tiáo, or tender greens. I always thought they'd be happy doing the work of sushi rice or a blini, being the soft pillow for the freshest raw seafood, like the briny Santa Barbara sea urchin in this recipe. Move fast, like our servers: Cheung fan are best hot, right out of the steamer, when you can still smell the sweetness of the rice.

To make the batter: In a large bowl, whisk together the room-temperature water, rice flour, tapioca, neutral oil, and cornstarch until completely smooth. Let rest for at least 30 minutes or up to 3 hours.

In a small saucepan over high heat, bring ½ cup / 120ml water to a boil. Add the dried shrimp, remove from the heat, and let soak until the batter is ready.

To make the sauce: In a small bowl, stir together the soy sauce, water, vinegar, sesame oil, and olive oil. Set aside.

Prepare a steamer in a wok or a large, lidded pot following the instructions on page 167 and bring the water to a boil over medium-high heat. Meanwhile, drain and finely chop the shrimp.

Generously coat a 9-inch round cake pan or ⅛ sheet pan with cooking spray. Re-whisk the batter.

Scoop ½ cup / 120ml of the batter into the prepared pan and tilt slightly if needed so that it evenly coats the bottom. Sprinkle with ½ tsp shrimp and a generous 1 tsp green onion. Steam until the top is firm and set, about 2½ minutes. Let cool for about 30 seconds.

Starting at one end (the short one if using the sheet pan), use a heatproof rubber spatula and your fingers to gently nudge and flip the edge of the noodle onto itself to start a ¾-inch-wide roll; continue rolling it up tightly. In between cooking each cheung fan, coat the pan with more cooking spray (no need to cool the pan) and re-whisk the batter well.

Serve straight out of the steamer, placing seam-side down on a small serving plate. Top with a few pieces of urchin, sprinkle with sesame seeds, and drizzle with about 1 Tbsp of the sauce. Garnish with cilantro, shiso, or green onions.

PIG TROTTER HAM SUI GOK

Active Time — 3½ hours

Plan Ahead — You'll need the day before for braising the pork trotter, and time to make 5 Spice

Makes about 35 puffs; 18 servings

Special Equipment — Cheesecloth, kitchen twine, deep-fry thermometer, stand mixer

These fried pork puffs (鹹水角) are a study of contrasts. They start with a crispy but then chewy bite and lead into a warm, savory interior. The texture comes from the Chinese technique of a wet dough starter (see "Breads, Bao, and Bing," page 48), plus two starches—glutinous rice, which gives it a stretchy stickiness, and wheat starch, which has nearly no gluten and makes the outer layer of dough crisp and light. Rendered leaf lard, the clean, dense fat cushion around a pig's kidneys, amps up the savoriness. You can find it in butcher shops and Asian or Italian markets.

Braised Pork Trotter

¼ cup / 20g red Sichuan peppercorns

6 star anise pods

3-inch cinnamon stick

6 whole cloves

2 small black cardamom pods (草果, chóu gwó)

1 Tbsp neutral oil

½ cup / 50g peeled and small-diced ginger

16 garlic cloves, peeled and crushed

⅓ cup / 40g diced shallots

2 green onions, cut into 1-inch pieces

¾ cup / 150g granulated sugar

½ cup / 120ml Shaoxing wine

2½ cups / 590ml water

1 cup / 240ml light soy sauce (生抽, sāng chāu)

3 Tbsp dark soy sauce (老抽, lóuh chāu)

2 Tbsp Chinese black vinegar

One 4½- to 5-lb / 2 to 2.3kg split pork trotter

2 Tbsp neutral oil

1 cup / 75g small-diced fresh shiitake mushrooms

¾ cup / 90g peeled and small-diced jicama

1 Tbsp thinly sliced (crosswise) green onion

Preheat the oven to 325°F.

To make the trotter: In a large saucepan over medium heat, combine the peppercorns, star anise, cinnamon, cloves, and cardamom in an even layer. Toast, tossing or stirring frequently, until fragrant, about 2 minutes. Transfer the spices to a double layer of cheesecloth. Gather up the sides of the cheesecloth and tie closed with kitchen twine to form a sachet.

In the same saucepan over medium heat, warm the neutral oil for a few seconds. Add the ginger, garlic, shallots, and green onions and cook until the shallots are softened, about 3 minutes. Stir in the sugar and cook until it melts, darkens in color, and thickens and coats the aromatics, about 15 minutes. Add the wine, turn the heat to medium-high, and cook until mostly evaporated, about 8 minutes. Add the water, both soy sauces, and vinegar and bring this braising liquid to a simmer, scraping up anything stuck to the bottom of the pan with a wooden spoon.

Place the trotter halves skin-side up in a roasting pan. Add the sachet and pour the braising liquid over the trotters and cover the pan tightly with aluminum foil. Braise in the oven for 2 hours, then uncover the pan and flip the trotters. Cover again with foil and continue braising until the trotters are knife-tender and falling off the bone, about 2 hours more.

Uncover the trotters and discard the sachet. Once cool enough to handle but while still warm, remove the trotters from the braising liquid. Remove the bones, then cut the meat and skin (including all the gelatinous bits!) into small dice. Measure out 1¾ cups / 275g for the filling and refrigerate for up to 1 day; freeze the rest for future batches.

Set a fine-mesh strainer into a bowl and pour the braising liquid through; discard the solids. Refrigerate the liquid until the fat rises to the top and hardens. Scrape off and discard the fat. Measure out ⅓ cup / 75g of the gelatinous braising liquid and refrigerate; freeze the rest for future batches.

Warm a wok or large frying pan over medium heat. Add the neutral oil, then the mushrooms and jicama, and cook until the mushrooms are softened, about 3 minutes. Add the green onion, ginger, and garlic and cook, stirring, until fragrant, about 30 seconds.

Add the trotter meat to the pan and break up any large clumps by smashing them with a wooden spoon. Add the braising liquid, oyster sauce,

CONTINUED

1½ tsp peeled and
    minced ginger

¾ tsp minced garlic

5½ tsp oyster sauce

¾ tsp fish sauce

¾ tsp toasted sesame oil

¾ tsp cornstarch

1 tsp water

¾ tsp ground white pepper

Ham Sui Gok Dough

½ cup plus 1½ tsp / 80g
    wheat starch (look for
    "澄麵粉" [chìhng mihn fán],
    or sometimes "wheaten
    cornflour" or "non-glutinous
    flour")

¼ cup / 60ml boiling water, plus
    1 cup plus 1 Tbsp / 255ml
    room-temperature water

2¾ cups / 340g long-grain
    glutinous rice flour (糯米粉,
    noh máih fán)

½ cup / 100g granulated sugar

⅓ cup plus 1 Tbsp / 80g cold,
    rendered pork leaf lard

2 qt / 1.9L neutral oil

5 Spice (see page 36)
    for dusting

fish sauce, and sesame oil and bring to a simmer, stirring occasionally, until the liquid is mostly evaporated, about 5 minutes.

Meanwhile, in a small bowl, stir together the cornstarch and water to make a slurry.

Add the pepper and cornstarch slurry to the pan and cook until the liquid thickens, about 30 seconds. Transfer to a bowl and set aside to cool to room temperature. Once cooled, drop 2-tsp scoops of this filling onto a baking sheet or plate to make it easier for wrapping up later. Refrigerate for at least 30 minutes or up to 1 day.

To make the dough: Place the wheat starch in a medium bowl. Slowly pour in the boiling water and stir with chopsticks until the starch is hydrated, then mix with your hands until a very smooth dough forms. Cover with a damp cloth and let sit for 5 minutes to hydrate.

In the bowl of a stand mixer fitted with the paddle attachment, combine the rice flour and sugar. With the mixer on low speed, slowly pour in the room-temperature water and mix until a dough comes together and is a bit shaggy, about 1 minute. With the mixer still running, drop in the hydrated wheat starch a little at a time and mix until combined, about 1 minute. Drop in the leaf lard a little at a time and mix until the dough clears the side of the bowl, is smooth, and has the texture of soft taffy, about 2 minutes more. Cover the dough and refrigerate until chilled, about 2 hours.

Line a baking sheet with parchment paper. Portion and form the dough into thirty-five smooth balls, each about 1½ inches in diameter (the size of a Ping-Pong ball). Working with one at a time, using your fingertips, flatten each dough ball into a 3-inch-long oval. Hold the dough in the palm of one hand, use your other hand to drop a prepared scoop of filling in the middle of the dough. Gently cup the dough as you pull the edges up and around the filling and tightly pinch together at the center. (No fancy folding here, you just want it completely sealed.) Form into a smooth football shape and place on the prepared baking sheet. If the filling breaks through the dough in spots, patch with additional dough. If the dough gets too soft at any point, chill it for 15 minutes before trying again. Cover and refrigerate for 1 hour. (At this point, you can freeze the ham sui gok solid on the baking sheet, transfer to a freezer bag, and store in the freezer for up to 2 months. Fry straight out of the freezer.)

Fit a wire rack over a baking sheet. Fill the wok or Dutch oven with the neutral oil and secure a deep-fry thermometer to the side. Set over medium-high heat and warm the oil to 375°F, being careful to maintain this temperature as you fry. Add the ham sui gok in batches of six and fry until light golden brown, about 5 minutes (or 6 to 7 minutes if frozen). They will sink to the bottom at first, so use a metal spatula to release gently after 15 to 30 seconds. As they fry, stir occasionally and make sure they don't stick together. Transfer to the prepared rack.

Place 5 Spice in a fine-mesh sieve and dust over the tops of the ham sui gok. Let cool for 10 minutes before serving, as the filling stays extremely hot, or snip them in half with scissors at the table, dim sum cart–style, so they will cool faster.

JIN DEUI

Active Time — 1¼ hours

Plan Ahead — You'll need about 1 hour for resting the dough. If using Red Bean Paste, make it the day before.

Makes fifteen 2-inch jīn dēui; 15 servings

Special Equipment — Stand mixer, deep-fry thermometer

1¾ cups / 210g long-grain glutinous rice flour (糯米粉, noh máih fán), plus 3 Tbsp

⅓ cup / 65g granulated sugar

⅔ cup / 200g chunky fruit jam

¼ cup / 30g raw black sesame seeds

¼ cup / 30g raw white sesame seeds

2½ qt / 2.4L neutral oil

These crispy, chewy sesame balls are my favorite fried dim sum staple. My grandmother Ying Ying was famous for her jīn dēui (煎堆) in her village in Toisan, and was undoubtedly faithful to the classic red bean, black bean, or lotus paste fillings. Our pastry chef Melissa uses whatever California fruit is currently at its peak, like quince, apricot, or salted plums, and since she always liked the fried part best, she makes them smaller than usual to pack in more crust per bite. If you choose to go the bean paste route, swap in ½ cup / 130g Red Bean Paste (see page 257) for the frozen fruit jam here.

In the bowl of a stand mixer fitted with the paddle attachment, combine the 1¾ cups / 210g rice flour and sugar. Place the remaining 3 Tbsp rice flour in a small bowl.

Fill a small saucepan with 3 cups / 720ml water and bring to a boil over medium-high heat. Drizzle 1½ Tbsp of the boiling water into the small bowl of flour. Stir with a spoon until the flour is moistened and then use your fingers to squeeze it into a rough ball. Knead the dough into a smooth ball (if the dough is very dry, lightly dampen your hands).

Add the dough ball to the boiling water and boil until it is glossy and floats, about 3 minutes. Using a slotted spoon, transfer the dough ball to the stand mixer. Mix on low speed until the dough ball breaks up into flaky pieces, about 1 minute. If making by hand, use your fingers to break up the dough ball into the flour.

Add ½ cup plus 1 Tbsp / 135ml of the boiling water to the mixer bowl. Mix on low speed until a dough forms, about 1 minute. Increase the speed to medium-high and mix until the dough sticks to the sides of the bowl but not the paddle, about 1 minute more. If making by hand, stir with a spoon until the dough is evenly moistened, then knead on the counter into a sticky paste (the dough will remain very soft and messy). Scrape the dough onto a sheet of plastic wrap, wrap tightly, and let rest for 1 hour at room temperature.

Meanwhile, in a small saucepan over medium heat, cook the jam, stirring occasionally, until it is reduced to a sticky paste that no longer jiggles and measures ½ cup / 120ml, about 10 minutes. Scrape into a small heatproof bowl and refrigerate until set, about 10 minutes.

Line a plate with plastic wrap.

Portion the jam into fifteen dollops, about 1½ tsp each, on the prepared plate (or in an airtight container) and freeze for at least 1 hour or up to 4 months.

Line a rimmed baking sheet with parchment paper or plastic wrap and fill a small bowl with water for dampening your hands to prevent sticking. In a wide, shallow bowl, combine the black and white sesame seeds and stir together.

CONTINUED

Dip your fingers in the water bowl, then portion and form the room-temperature dough into fifteen smooth balls, each about 1½ inches in diameter (the size of a Ping-Pong ball). Place the balls on the prepared baking sheet and cover with a damp kitchen towel or plastic wrap to keep them moist.

Working one at a time, use your fingertips to flatten each dough ball into a 3-inch round, leaving the center slightly thicker than the sides. Drop a piece of frozen jam in the middle. Gently pull the edges of the dough up and around the filling and tightly pinch together at the center. (No fancy folding here, you just want it completely sealed.) Form a round ball and then roll the ball in the sesame seeds until completely covered (if the seeds don't stick, dampen your hands and lightly moisten the dough ball). Return to the baking sheet. Repeat with the rest of the dough and filling. If the jam gets too soft and starts to run, put it back in the freezer for a few minutes.

Place the jīn dēui in the freezer, not the refrigerator, while you heat the frying oil. (At this point, you can freeze them solid on the baking sheet, transfer to a freezer bag, and store in the freezer for up to 2 months.) Always fry jīn dēui straight out of the freezer, otherwise the filling will run.

Fit a wire rack over a baking sheet.

Fill a wok or Dutch oven with the neutral oil and secure a deep-fry thermometer to the side. Set over medium-high heat and warm the oil to 350°F, being careful to maintain this temperature as you fry. Add one-third of the jīn dēui and fry until golden brown all over. They will sink to the bottom at first, so use a metal spatula to gently release them. When they float on their own, after 1½ to 2 minutes, use the spatula to continuously turn them so they color evenly, 6 to 7 minutes. Transfer to the prepared rack. Repeat with the remaining jīn dēui.

Let cool for 30 minutes before serving, as the filling stays extremely hot, or snip them in half with scissors at the table, dim sum cart–style, so they will cool faster.

DRINK GOOD TEA

You still get a free pot of oolong most places in Chinatown. Tea is hospitality. For the tea at our restaurant, I went to Peter Luong. He's not interested in the kinds of rituals that require you to hold your tea cup balanced on your thumb and forefinger, or so-called prestigious tea fields, but he is all about what's delicious. He works closely with tea farmers who take the time to do everything right and don't balk when he asks them to buck tradition.

Peter grew up in Chinatown. He and his family are ethnic Chinese and escaped from impossible circumstances in Vietnam by crossing the Pacific on a boat packed with twenty people. After they landed, the Luongs opened an apothecary on Grant Avenue. In the 1980s, Peter was the kid folding paper packets of raisins for his dad's patients every day after school. The Luongs turned their focus to tea in 2005; and in 2013, Peter went out on his own, opening Song Tea & Ceramics in another part of town to work solely with small producers willing to experiment. Peter's sister Alice still runs Red Blossom Tea Company in that same storefront in Chinatown.

Peter believes that tea doesn't have to be a certain way, so keeping that in mind, here are his suggestions for good tea.

1 — Start with tea that smells good. A green tea should smell fresh and vegetal. Oolongs and other fermented teas will smell very sweet. Bad smelling or artificially perfumed tea are low quality and impossible to fix. If you like how a tea smells, look at the leaves as its steeps. An oolong should unfurl as whole clusters of leaves with a nice sheen, not disintegrate into broken leaves or dust. Green tea leaves should look green, shiny, and whole. Now taste. Do you like it? You're all set.

2 — If you really want to get into it, you can think about a tea's aroma, texture, and taste. People consider the balance of flavor notes such as "grassy," "fruity," "woody," and "earthy" in the same way that they do with wine and spirits. But with tea, it's even more important to consider texture (how viscous it feels on the tongue) and finish. There should be no astringency; and if there is any bitterness, it should only be on the back of the tongue as it goes down. Tea shouldn't catch in your throat. You're looking for an elusive quality that will become clearer as you drink a lot of tea.

3 — Water matters, but maybe not as much as connoisseurs say. Chinese tea people still quote ancient books that describe drawing the water from the center of a very particular swift mountain stream and transporting the water, without shaking it, in a jar filled with some of the stream's stones. This translates into modern terms as using water with a neutral pH and total dissolved solids of 10 to 30 parts per million, free of chlorine and fluoride. Achieving the proper, neutral-tasting water generally requires just a charcoal filter.

4 — To bring out a tea's character, you want to steep it for only as long as it needs in the highest-temperature water possible without tipping the flavor to bitter. The more water you use, the longer tea needs to steep. Here is where a scale and a kettle with a thermometer helps. When getting to know a tea, I start at the low range of temperature at first and increase incrementally each time I brew a new batch of leaves until I've found its sweet spot.

5 — Steep more than once. With oolongs, in fact, the first steep is not as revealing as the second steep. Pu'ers last through many rounds. The flavors and aromas will change each time. And consider that someone had to pluck three hundred buds to make that one cup of green tea. Let it show off more than once.

6 — In terms of tea ware, you'll want different pots for different types of teas to avoid muddling flavor. But you don't need a designated teacup. I like drinking from a Gibraltar glass.

7 — Store tea in a cool, dry place. Absorbing water makes teas go stale. Generally, the lighter and less oxidized the tea, the shorter the shelf life. Drink green teas and white teas within a year of harvest, though some white teas age surprisingly well. Everything else should last as long as they stay perfectly dry.

Whole Leaves	Amount per ⅔ cup / 150ml water	Water Temperature	Time
Green	3 to 4 grams	180° to 185°F	Just under 1 minute
White	3 to 4 grams	200° to 208°F	1 minute
Oolong	5 to 7 grams	205° to 208°F	2 minutes
Red	5 to 7 grams	205° to 208°F	2 minutes
Black (including pu'er)	3 to 5 grams	212°F	2 minutes

3

My parents were blue collar, a cop and a dental hygienist. On the rare nights we went out to eat, the choices were McDonald's, Sizzler, and Chinese. The service at American fast-food and all-you-can-eat places was basically nonexistent. Mom-and-pop Chinese restaurants were my idea of fancy service.

Every Saturday-night dinner at a Chinese restaurant started with soup. The server would take down our order and a minute later appear pushing a cart stacked with clattering bowls and spoons and a huge tureen. You never knew what it would be. Egg drop with orange flecks of fake crab, or a clear chicken consommé with slivers of carrot and ginger. Or maybe West Lake Soup, pork broth with swirls of egg and green herbs. Whatever it was didn't matter so much compared to what happened next.

The server would arrange the bowls in a semicircle on the lazy Susan, a million bowls for our family and the friends we called family, and then ladle out the gold. He would serve the elders first, using one hand to rotate the platter with precision. Spin, stop, spin again, until finally my little brother had his. He knew exactly how much to serve to each of us so that the tureen would be empty when the last bowl was full. It was all service and ceremony, a gesture centered around something for which the restaurant didn't even charge.

Soup is always part of a proper Chinese meal. There are different kinds of soup for different occasions, seasons, and ailments. There are savory soups to open a meal, sweet soups to close it, and light soups to cleanse after a fried dish. There are hearty soups thickened with starch that you see most in Chinatown, like chicken corn or hot and sour. There are steamed soups, braised soups, soups built on stocks that have been boiling and compounding for years. Each form is so varied that there are entire banquets that are, basically, a parade of soups.

My maternal grandma, we called her Ball Ball (the traditional is Poh Po [婆婆], which shows how freestyle my family is), always kept a pot of soup, made with bags of dried herbs she picked up in Chinatown, bubbling on the back burner. Ball Ball lived on her own, and had been an independent woman even before her husband, my Gung Gung (公公), passed. I never knew him but Gung Gung had been a military man, cooked professionally all around the city, and was so resourceful that he turned those earnings into real estate. Ball Ball was deep into Chinese medicine. She would greet us with kisses at the door and then disappear to the kitchen, reemerging with a bowl of soup for each of us. That was the order of things. Nothing else could happen at her house until you finished your soup.

Hers was always the same—carrots, ginger, chicken and pork bones, gelatinous fungi, and bitter roots. It was no cake and ice cream, but it was delicious. Ball Ball was happy to lose our admiration temporarily rather than miss a chance to nourish us. She served it so hot, we had to slow down, take small sips, and savor.

"This is how to care for yourself," she was telling us.

She knew what she was talking about. She passed away at one hundred years old, her pantry still stocked for a hundred years more.

ON LAZY SUSANS

The lazy Susan, as we know it, was created in Chinatown in 1954. Johnny Kan wanted a sleek show of service at his eponymous Kan's restaurant, so he asked one of his partners, George Hall, to tinker. Hall had made his fortune bottling Wing Nien, the first naturally fermented soy sauce in the mainland United States, starting in a basement in Chinatown. This time, in his garage on Jackson Street, he came up with a black-lacquered table set on ball bearings. Hall's "revolving table" design took off and became one of the trademarks of Chinese American restaurant service, along with Kan's other touches—pressed linens, hand towels spritzed with a signature scent, equal billing for English and Chinese on the menu, lettuce cups, roast duck, and fortune cookies to finish. Kan continued to revolutionize Chinese American fine dining with an unmatched attention to detail until he died suddenly in 1972. The restaurant closed in 2014, but I still get inspired looking out at Kan's awning from our dining room.

SIZZLING RICE SOUP

Active Time — 1 hour

Plan Ahead — You'll need 1 hour oven-drying the rice, and time to make the stock

Makes 8 servings

Special Equipment — Deep-fry thermometer

Rice Cakes

2⅔ cups / 385g cooked, warm jasmine rice (see page 229)

Spring Vegetables and Shrimp

24 sugar snap peas, halved crosswise

½ cup / 60g shelled English peas, preferably young and small

8 asparagus spears, trimmed and cut into ½-inch pieces

8 fresh water chestnuts, peeled and cut into ¼-inch-thick rounds

2 Tbsp chicken fat or schmaltz

8 large, peeled shrimp (16 to 30 count), each butterflied into 2 pieces

1 stalk green garlic, very thinly sliced on a slight diagonal

1 qt / 950ml neutral oil

1½ qt / 1.4L Supreme Stock (page 34)

½ cup / 70g small-diced smoked ham

3 Tbsp minced fresh chives, or chive flowers

You learn early in cooking to never mix oil and water, but sizzling rice soup is all about that violent reaction. The sooner the rice cakes go from frying oil to hot broth, the louder the thunderclap. It's a controlled collision, done tableside. Getting it all doled out quickly is also a practical requirement, so that the toasted rice can impart as much flavor as possible into the broth before getting soggy. Serving it to eight people in less than a minute is the true mic drop. We usually serve this soup in the spring when all kinds of peas (we use English, snap, and snow) are crisp and sweet. I love that such an elegant soup probably came from needing a way to loosen up the toasty crust stuck to the bottom of the rice pot. If only cleaning pans were always so delicious.

To make the rice cakes: Preheat the oven to 300°F.

With wet hands, gently pack the rice into an even layer in an 8-inch-square baking dish. Flip the rice cake out onto a sheet of parchment paper. Cut into nine squares but do not separate them (you'll have one extra). Slide the parchment with the rice cake onto a baking sheet.

Bake the rice cake until firm and dried on the top and sides but still damp in the middle, about 1 hour. When cool enough to handle, break the squares apart. Set aside.

To make the spring vegetables and shrimp: Bring a large saucepan of heavily salted water (it should remind you of seawater) to a boil over high heat. Meanwhile, prepare an ice bath in a large bowl by filling it with ice cubes and a little water. Line a baking sheet with a double layer of paper towels.

Drop the snap peas into the boiling water and blanch until crisp-tender; 10 to 30 seconds. Use a slotted spoon to transfer to the ice bath, then blanch the English peas for 10 to 30 seconds before transferring to the ice bath. Add the asparagus to the boiling water for up to 1 minute and then transfer to the ice bath. Finally, blanch the water chestnuts (they cloud up the water) for about 30 seconds; they just need to lose their starchiness, and transfer to the ice bath. When each vegetable is cool, transfer to the prepared baking sheet.

In a wok or large frying pan over high heat, melt the chicken fat. Add the shrimp, spread into a single layer, and sear for 30 seconds. Add the green garlic, asparagus, and snap peas and stir-fry until charred in spots, 1 to 2 minutes more. Set aside.

Timing really matters here, so don't start this part until you're ready to go.

Fill a wok or Dutch oven over medium-high heat with the neutral oil and secure a deep-fry thermometer on the side. Heat the oil to 400°F, being careful to maintain this temperature as you fry. Meanwhile, bring the stock to a boil and keep very hot. Divide the vegetables, shrimp, water chestnuts, and ham among eight individual bowls.

Add the rice cakes to the oil and fry until crisp and puffed, 1 to 2 minutes.

Meanwhile, top the bowls with hot stock and the chives. Make sure your guests are seated and bring the bowls to the table. Transfer the fried rice cakes to a plate, but do not drain off excess oil. Use chopsticks or tongs (something other than your bare hands!) to drop the hot rice cakes into each bowl to serve. Sizzle sizzle!

YELLOW CORN AND SQUASH BLOSSOM EGG DROP SOUP

Active Time — 1 hour

Plan Ahead — You'll need 3 hours for simmering

Makes 4 to 6 servings

Special Equipment — Blender

4 large ears fresh yellow corn, husked

2½ qt / 2.4L water, plus more as needed

1 Tbsp neutral oil, plus a few drops

¼ medium yellow onion, cut into medium dice

Kosher salt

6 large cilantro sprigs

½ cup / 10g packed baby spinach

1 medium squash blossom (optional)

1 egg

One of the more clever techniques in Chinese cooking is egg dropping. In order to achieve cirrus egg clouds, not cumulus or stratus, you need the soup to have the right viscosity. The starch in the kernels and cobs of summer corn will slow the pace of the egg as it drops to the bottom of the gently simmering pot and the rate that the egg proteins clump. Swirling the soup to create a whirlpool helps keep the egg moving, ensuring the softest wisps. Since our version is vegetarian, we like a generous dose of herb oil on top.

Cut the corn kernels off the cobs, place in a bowl, and transfer to the refrigerator. Cut the cobs into 2- to 3-inch-long pieces.

Put the cobs and water in a large pot and bring to a boil over high heat. Turn the heat to medium and simmer, uncovered, until the broth is reduced by about a third, about 2 hours. Remove and discard the cobs. Pour the broth into a large bowl.

In the same pot over medium heat, add the 1 Tbsp neutral oil, then the onion, and cook until translucent but not browned, about 4 minutes. Add the corn kernels and 1 Tbsp salt and cook, stirring occasionally, until heated through, about 5 minutes. Add the broth, turn the heat to high, and bring to a boil. Then turn the heat to low and simmer until the corn is tender and the broth is very deeply flavored, stirring and skimming foam from the surface occasionally, about 1 hour.

In batches, transfer the soup to a blender and blend until smooth. Strain the soup through a fine-mesh strainer fitted over a large saucepan, using a spoon to push as many bits through as possible. Discard any solids and then season with salt.

Bring a small saucepan of water to a boil over high heat. Prepare an ice bath by filling a medium bowl with ice cubes and a little water.

Add the cilantro to the boiling water and blanch for 1 minute. Add the spinach and continue to blanch until both are wilted and tender, about 1 minute more. Transfer the greens to the ice bath. After 2 minutes, use your hands to squeeze as much water as possible out of the greens and transfer the greens to a cutting board. Chop into a fine paste, transfer to a small bowl, and then mix with a few drops of oil and a pinch of salt.

Brush any dust from the squash blossom (if using) and then pinch off the tough stem and greenish sepals at the base. Pluck out the stamen and pistil. Cut the blossom in half lengthwise and thinly slice crosswise.

In a liquid measuring cup, whisk the egg with enough water to get to ½ cup / 120ml of liquid.

Bring the soup back to a simmer over medium-low heat. Stir the soup so that it swirls in a whirlpool, then slowly drizzle in the egg mixture, just off center, and immediately remove from the heat. Stir gently as the residual heat sets the egg into long strands.

Ladle the soup into bowls and garnish with a spoonful of the spinach-cilantro paste and a scattering of squash blossoms. Serve immediately.

PORK RIBS AND WINTER MELON SOUP

Active Time — 45 minutes

Plan Ahead — You'll need at least 3 hours for marinating and steaming the ribs and pickling the melon, plus time to make the Supreme Stock

Makes 8 servings

Special Equipment — Blender, cheesecloth, steamer, juicer

This homey soup is a Chinese family's winter standard. Here in San Francisco, it feels just right to eat around July and August; when everyone else seems to be enjoying sunny weather, we are getting our infamous cold start of summer. Winter melon (冬瓜) ripens under the summer sun, but its frosted, waxy exterior (its other name is wax gourd) allows it to last for months without refrigeration. Some varieties grow to thirty pounds and are sold in chunks. I like the smaller ones, whole. This soup has a refreshing quality, as the mild grassiness of winter melon lightens the rich, clear pork broth.

Pork Riblets

One 1½-lb / 680g rack pork baby back ribs, cut into individual 2-inch-wide riblets (have the butcher do this)

1 tsp kosher salt

5 pieces white fermented doufu (白腐乳, baahk fuh yúh)

1½ Tbsp Shaoxing wine

1 Tbsp light soy sauce (生抽, sāng chāu)

Winter Melon Pickle

One 12-oz / 340g chunk winter melon

⅓ cup / 80ml apple juice

2 Tbsp celery juice

1½ qt / 1.4L Supreme Stock (page 34)

Kosher salt

3 Tbsp minced chives

Finely grated zest from 1 lemon

Chrysanthemum Oil (page 118) for serving (optional)

To make the riblets: In a medium bowl, toss the riblets with the salt and let sit for 20 minutes. Meanwhile, in a blender, combine the doufu, wine, and soy sauce and blend until smooth.

Pour the doufu marinade over the riblets and toss together. Transfer to the refrigerator and let marinate for at least 2 hours or, ideally, up to overnight.

Prepare a steamer in a wok or a large, lidded pot following the instructions on page 167 and bring the water to a boil over medium-high heat. Arrange the riblets in a single layer in the steamer, cover, and steam until tender but not falling apart, about 45 minutes, adding more water halfway through if needed. (At this point, you can let cool, transfer to an airtight container, and store in the refrigerator for up to 2 days.)

To make the pickle: Scrape out any seeds from and cut the rind off the winter melon, just deep enough so there's no green left. Cut the flesh into ½-inch cubes until you have about 1 cup / 140g and place in a heatproof bowl.

In a small saucepan over medium-high heat, combine the apple juice and celery juice and bring to a boil. Pour the hot juice over the winter melon, making sure all the chunks are submerged. Let pickle for at least 1 hour at room temperature, or transfer to an airtight container and store in the refrigerator for up to 2 days.

In a large saucepan over medium heat, combine the pork riblets, winter melon pickle, and stock and bring back to a gentle boil. Taste and adjust with salt, if needed. When serving, be generous with the broth. Top with a sprinkle of chives and lemon zest and drizzle with a spoonful of chrysanthemum oil, if desired.

CHRYSANTHEMUM OIL

Makes ½ cup / 120ml

2 oz / 55g fresh chrysanthemum leaves (tong ho),
    or chervil leaves and stems, roughly chopped
½ cup / 120ml neutral oil

Bring a small saucepan of water to a boil over high heat. Add the chrysanthemum and blanch until tender, about 1½ minutes. (If you want an especially vibrant green oil, immediately transfer the herbs to an ice bath after blanching.) Drain, let cool, and then use your hands to squeeze out as much water as possible. Transfer to a cutting board.

Coarsely chop the chrysanthemum, then transfer to a blender, add the neutral oil, and blend on high speed until smooth.

Line a fine-mesh strainer with a double layer of cheesecloth, set over a bowl, pour the oil through, and discard the solids.

Transfer the oil to an airtight container and store in the refrigerator for up to 2 days.

HOT AND SOUR SOUP

Active Time — 1 hour
Plan Ahead — You'll need overnight for soaking, and 2 hours for simmering
Makes 8 servings

Hot and Sour Broth
2½ lb / 1.1kg white-fish bones and heads
1 oz / 30g dried flounder
2 qt / 1.8L water
2 cups / 340g ice cubes
⅓ cup / 30g diced celery
¼ cup / 25g diced fennel
¼ cup / 40g thinly sliced leeks (white parts only)
4 oz / 115g ginger, peeled, sliced, and smashed
1½ tsp ground white pepper
1½ tsp toasted sesame oil
¼ cup / 60ml light soy sauce (生抽, sāng chāu)
½ tsp dark soy sauce (老抽, lóuh chāu)
Kosher salt

24 dried lily buds or flowers
2 Tbsp neutral oil
¼ tsp celery seeds
1 cup / 100g trimmed fresh nameko mushrooms
1 cup / 70g fresh wood ear mushrooms
Kosher salt
4 oz / 115g firm doufu, cut into ¾-inch cubes
½ cup / 80g cooked, shredded crab meat
¼ cup / 60ml distilled white vinegar
3 Tbsp Chinese black vinegar, plus more as needed

Our version of this soup will taste familiar but new to anyone who has ever tasted Chinese sour-hot or Chinese American hot and sour soup. We use sharp and pungent white vinegar, as well as earthy black vinegar for its rich, deep molasses acidity. The only "hot" quality comes from white pepper for a slow warming heat. Grind the pepper super-finely so that it dissolves into the soup, then give it a few minutes to steep and bloom before you taste. Pepper and vinegar change as they infuse a hot broth. Keep tasting and adjusting until both the "sour" and the "hot" come through. You may need one last tweak with vinegar right before serving. It will all come together as a singular flavor and delicately punch you in the face. Garnish with cilantro and nasturtium leaves and flowers for a special touch.

To make the broth: Trim away and discard any guts and large blood vessels from the fish bones and remove and discard the gills from the heads; rinse the bones. Place everything in a large bowl, cover with cold water, and let soak overnight in the refrigerator.

Preheat the oven to 300°F

Place the dried flounder on an oven rack and toast until fragrant, about 5 minutes.

Drain the fish bones and then place them in a 6-quart or larger pot. Add the dried flounder, 2 qt / 1.8L water, and ice cubes and bring to a simmer over medium heat, skimming off any foam that floats to the top and never letting it come to a boil. Add the celery, fennel, leeks, and ginger; turn the heat to medium-low; and simmer, skimming occasionally as needed, until intensely flavored, about 2 hours.

Fit a fine-mesh strainer over a large bowl and then strain the broth and discard the solids. Stir the pepper, sesame oil, and both types of soy sauce into the broth. Taste, season with salt, and let cool. (At this point, you can transfer to an airtight container and store in the refrigerator for up to 2 days, or in the freezer up to 1 month.)

Bring a kettle of water to a boil.

Place the lily buds in a heatproof bowl, cover with boiling water, and let soak for 10 minutes.

Meanwhile, in a large frying pan or wok over medium heat, warm the neutral oil for a few seconds. Add the celery seeds and cook until fragrant, about 30 seconds. Add all the mushrooms, season with salt, and cook until just tender, about 5 minutes. Set aside.

Drain the lily buds. Divide the sautéed mushrooms, lily buds, doufu, and crab among serving bowls. Bring the hot and sour broth back to a simmer. Add the white and black vinegars, then taste for balance and re-up the black vinegar as needed. Ladle the hot broth into each bowl (at the table, if you feel inspired) and serve immediately.

ON HOT AND SOUR

In 1945, Buwei Yang Chao wrote *How to Cook and Eat in Chinese*, a book introducing the diversity of regional Chinese cuisines to American home cooks. In it, she—with help from her daughter and husband—coined the terms "stir-fry" and "pot sticker" and described "sour-hot soup" (酸辣湯) as "a very famous soup that sometimes will help you get rid of leftovers."

Most readers had never tasted anything such as sour-hot. Spicy Chinese food didn't enter mainstream American consciousness until after 1965, when a critical mass of people with roots in Sichuan and Hunan, among other provinces, made this country home. In San Francisco, Cecilia Chiang served a version when she opened the Mandarin on the other side of the hill from Chinatown in 1961. Chiang's restaurant was among the first to introduce the crossroads cuisine of Beijing, with its pan-China, Muslim, and Mongolian influences, as well as the regional cuisines of Shandong, Zhejiang, and other northern provinces. "Mandarin" (until then, the term for the language of imperial court officials and a type of orange) became synonymous with northern Chinese cuisine, which essentially came to mean anything other than what the first wave of immigrants had been cooking in Chinatown. New restaurants capitalized on the perception that some cooking was more "authentic" than others.

In 1974, *California Living* magazine explained that this new regional cuisine tended to have "a dry texture" that required chewing long enough to "taste all the underlying explosions within it." The primer suggested earning your server's trust by not trying to order Cantonese-style food and promising not to send back dishes that were too spicy.

Sour-hot was one of the earliest of the so-called authentic, regional Chinese dishes to catch on in this country. At first, cooks made it as close as they could to what they knew, using available ingredients—numbing, lemony, green Sichuan peppercorns were technically banned from import by 1968 for more than four decades. The Sichuan version was a mix of white and red rice vinegars, white peppercorn, and smuggled Sichuan peppercorn, perhaps topped with fermented mustard greens and soft sheets of pork blood. Beijing-style included white pepper and black rice vinegar and bits of ham and seafood, with wontons or noodles. Soon it appeared, mellowed, alongside Cantonese staples in Chinatown—the gateway spicy dish.

As customers developed preferences, chefs edited and found flavor in new sources. But eventually, sour-hot's American identity converged toward a standard—strips of pork and doufu, egg ribbons, mushrooms (usually mu'er, a black tree fungus), and dried lily buds in a broth of black peppercorn and white vinegar. It became "hot and sour," not "sour-hot," rebranded to emphasize what seemed to matter most. In the United States, with a new form and a new name, hot and sour came to represent a cuisine that didn't exist before in the old country.

OXTAIL SOUP

Active Time — 1 hour

Plan Ahead — You'll need 6 hours for salting and simmering, plus time to make a double batch of Chicken Stock. If you can, leave the oxtails in the broth and chill overnight for maximum tenderness and flavor.

Makes 6 servings

Special Equipment — Cheesecloth, kitchen twine

5 lb / 2.3kg oxtails, cut into 2-inch-thick pieces

Kosher salt

2 tsp black peppercorns

2 tsp white peppercorns

2 star anise pods

3 bay leaves

Two ¼-inch-thick slices unpeeled ginger

5 qt / 4.7L cold Chicken Stock (page 34)

8 oz / 230g daikon or other radish, peeled and then roll cut

8 oz / 230g carrots, peeled and then roll cut

4 oz / 115g fresh shiitake mushrooms, stems trimmed, halved if very large

1 Tbsp neutral oil

Fresh watercress or Chinese or regular celery leaves dressed in peanut or nut oil for garnish

Oxtail, a favorite of resourceful immigrants everywhere, is now among the priciest specialty cuts at the butcher's counter. Even back when it was cheap, my busy mom knew to treat it right. She blanched it in boiling water, then braised it for hours in our slow cooker. When I started cooking professionally, I tried new techniques on oxtail, but the results were never as succulent or as satisfying as hers. I came to my senses and, aside from salting before blanching, I basically do it her way, coaxing out flavor with patience rather than a hard sear. This recipe is a variation on what we do at the restaurant, where we take the meat off the bone, fold in bone marrow, and roll it into a mustard-leaf torchon. But deep down where it matters, both restaurant and home versions keep my mom's dish in mind.

Season the oxtails all over with 1 Tbsp salt and let sit at room temperature for 2 hours.

In a small frying pan over medium heat, combine all the peppercorns and the star anise and toast, tossing or stirring frequently, until fragrant, about 2 minutes. Immediately transfer to a plate and let cool. Make a sachet of the spices and bay leaves by wrapping in a double layer of cheesecloth and tying closed with kitchen twine. Add the ginger to the same pan over medium-high heat and char until blackened in spots, 3 to 4 minutes per side.

Fill a 10-quart or larger pot halfway with heavily salted water (it should remind you of seawater) and bring to a vigorous boil over high heat. Add the oxtails and blanch for 1 minute, then transfer them to a colander and rinse under cold water. Discard the blanching water and rinse out the pot.

Return the oxtails to the pot. Add the sachet, ginger, and chicken stock and bring to a simmer over high heat. Turn the heat to medium-low and very gently simmer, uncovered and skimming every hour or as needed, until the oxtails are tender but not falling off the bone, about 4 hours. About an hour before the oxtails are done, taste the broth and season with salt.

Preheat the oven to 425°F. Place the daikon, carrots, and mushrooms on a rimmed baking sheet, drizzle with the neutral oil, and toss to combine. Roast until they start to brown on the bottom, about 20 minutes, then remove from the oven and let cool. Transfer to an airtight container and store in the refrigerator for up to 1 day.

Transfer the oxtails to a large bowl. Line a colander with a double layer of cheesecloth and fit over a 5-quart pot. Strain the broth and discard the solids.

If serving the same day, skim the fat from the surface of the broth. If serving the next day, return the oxtails to the broth. Let cool, then cover and refrigerate. When ready to finish the soup, skim the hardened fat from the surface of the broth. Warm over medium heat until the broth liquefies, then transfer the oxtails to a large bowl.

Bring the broth back to a simmer. Add the roasted vegetables and continue to simmer, uncovered, until just knife-tender, about 15 minutes. Return the oxtails to the broth and simmer until they are warmed through, about 5 minutes more. Taste the broth and season with salt.

Serve the soup hot, garnished with the dressed watercress.

4

My Ying Ying, my grandmother on my dad's side, you couldn't hold her down. "I'm taking the 11 bus," she'd say, making her index fingers dance. That meant, after she was done teaching tai chi, she was walking through the markets in Richmond and then all the way through the markets in Chinatown. When I was lucky, she took me along (with a backup plan for the bus).

Shopping with Ying Ying in Chinatown was a competitive sport, because all the grannies wanted the best ingredients. We'd make a dozen stops to find what we needed in the markets that spilled out onto Stockton Street's sidewalks. The vegetables drew the biggest crowds, and you had to get there early. The produce was stacked neatly around 7 a.m., just in from small farms around the Sacramento Delta down through Gilroy and the Central Valley, but by early afternoon, the grocers were slashing prices on what was left.

Many of the vegetables in the markets first grew on this side of the Pacific in backlot gardens in Chinatown and hidden corners of farms around California. Early Chinese brought varieties of ginger, greens, and alliums; squashes such as sī gwā (loofah), bitter melon, and mòuh gwā (hairy gourd); pears, plums, and loquats; and at least nine new varieties of citrus, among other produce. Chinese could rent but not own land, so many worked as migrant farmers, soon picking and planting the entire West Coast, and in the off-seasons carving wine caves in Napa and Sonoma or canning salmon in the Pacific Northwest, all while scattering the seeds of what they liked to eat. If vegetables hadn't been such a big part of the Cantonese diet, our agricultural landscape would probably look very different today.

Ying Ying taught me to notice not just varieties and degrees of freshness but stages of growth, each with their own qualities and uses. The pea shoots with large leaves and long tendrils were sweetest when stir-fried; small leaves and wisps on crisp stems were better cooked in liquid. Chives weren't just green stalks but flowers, buds, or pale yellow stems grown out of the sun. There were rows of bok choy varieties that looked completely different from each other. The attention she put into choosing her ingredients was as intense as I am with picking ingredients now, and I'm an ingredient nerd.

Some days, I still find my place among the grannies, looking to pick up something to experiment with or chatting with Candy Lu at ProduceLand about what's just come in. I can confirm not much has changed since my mornings with Ying Ying.

I remember that after eating my grandparents' food, I felt good. Cooking, in the traditional Chinese sense, is as much about pleasure and nourishment as it is about restoring balance to the body and mind. Cooks were considered doctors, too, and I take that responsibility seriously. It's important to me to know that this is the best ingredient in all ways that I can get for you. For instance, there is such a difference in the energy of biodynamically grown plants just plucked from the stem, compared to lettuces cut, washed, and then shipped in bags a week later. I work with farmers who can bring us our greens the day they are harvested.

Our restaurant's seasonal vegetables all come direct from small organic farms. At the farmers' market, I stop by to see Annabelle Lenderink at Star Route Farms, one of the first organic farms in the country, for her sweet celtuce and stunning chrysanthemum greens. I call up Vince Trotter at Kibo Farms to brainstorm vegetable varieties with just the right dimensions, colors, and flavors I need. For a couple years, I was looking for the right white-stemmed varieties of bok choy. Now we're working on Chinese celery; and soon, Chinese mustard greens. Sometimes I send seeds to farmer friends, like Scott Chang-Fleeman up at Shao Shan Farm in Bolinas, to see what grows best and with what methods in their terroir. A plot with the dry desert heat or an inland one basking in coastal breezes can completely change a plant's character.

Not everything is a success, and it takes faith on both ends. Together, we plan what we hope to use a season from now. When unpredictable weather strikes, we pivot together. When someone brings in something incredible and fleeting, we find a way to use it on the menu for a few days until it is gone. This give and take is how we get the best ingredients and how small farmers get to take more risks. Also, it's my small nudge against the decline in biodiversity in agriculture. The Chinatown markets first showed me the endless ingredients out there. Ten years from now, I hope to go to the farmers' market and see even more varieties of vegetables with which to experiment, grown by farmers just as diverse, and that taste at least as good as the produce from those days with Ying Ying.

Chef's Note: Sourcing Vegetables

When buying vegetables in Chinatown (or anywhere), Ying Ying would advise to look and listen. Any hint of yellow on a leafy green is out. Check crispness down the length of the stem. Generally, the longer the stem, the better, since grocers trim throughout the day to keep things looking fresh. No nice snap? Move on.

When it comes to choosing among the leafy greens, look both at the variety and stage of growth. Is it a tiny shoot just seeing the sun, or is it climbing or trying to cover more ground by shooting out tough tendrils? Is it bolting, meaning sending up its thick stalk to go to seed? Generally, where it's putting all its energy is what will taste the best. Once a plant has flowered or climbed, the leaves and stems are less sweet and less tender. What is closest to the sun is usually most important (and most delicious).

There is beautiful produce in Chinatown markets and some of it is effectively, if not officially, organic. Because demand for the varieties of Chinese produce is so low, relatively speaking, Chinatown markets rely on small farms and wholesalers that operate independently from the network that supplies big market chains, which means some unpredictability. But if you don't need crates of organic bok choy a week like we do, you should shop for produce in Chinatown. Come early. Look through the chaos to the piles of just-picked greens still wet with morning dew. Whenever you find yourself overwhelmed, just follow the crowd of grandmas.

Miuh Bok Choy (苗白菜)

Buddha's Hand (佛手柑)

Chinese Eggplant (茄子)

Young Ginger (子薑)

Kohlrabi (苤藍)

Long Beans (豇豆)

Romanesco Broccoli (羅馬花椰菜)

Kabocha Squash (南瓜)

Celtuce (萵筍)

Chinese Pink Celery (芹菜)

Chinese Mustard Greens (芥菜)

Jujubes (紅棗)

Matsutake or Pine Mushrooms (松茸)

Nasturtium (旱金蓮)

Dry-Farmed Early Girl Tomatoes (番茄)

Winter Melon (冬瓜)

MUSTARD GREEN SALAD

Having all this raw, unique, and vibrant produce available in San Francisco is truly a privilege. This recipe calls for jujubes, or red dates (紅棗, hóng zǎo in Mandarin), a softly sweet buckthorn fruit. We get ours from Twin Girls Farm in early fall with a little green on them, so they're still juicy and crunchy, like little apples. If you use dried jujubes, bring ½ cup / 170g honey, ¼ cup / 60ml water, and 2 Tbsp apple cider vinegar to a simmer and soak the jujubes in the syrup overnight before using.

Start with dry greens and test your dressing first on a leaf to check acid and salt levels. Dressing the salad in phases protects delicate greens and ensures everything is seasoned correctly.

Active Time — 25 minutes

Plan Ahead — You'll need time to make 10 Spice and Pickled Mushrooms

Makes 4 to 6 servings

Special Equipment — Microplane

Ginger Vinaigrette

2-inch piece ginger

⅓ cup / 80ml rice vinegar

4 tsp white (shiro) miso paste

1 Tbsp honey

½ cup / 120ml neutral oil or sunflower oil

8 oz / 225g frilly red or baby mustard greens (not Chinese mustard greens), or mizuna

Kosher salt

½ small Asian pear (such as Ya Li), peeled, cored, and thinly sliced

½ medium kohlrabi, peeled and thinly sliced

¼ cup / 40g sliced Pickled Shiitake Mushrooms (page 44)

8 fresh jujubes, cut away from pit and thinly sliced

¼ cup / 25g Spiced Walnuts (recipe follows)

Petals from 2 edible calendula, marigold, or mustard flowers (optional)

To make the vinaigrette: Peel the ginger and grate it with a Microplane. Over a small bowl, squeeze the pulp with your hands and collect 1 Tbsp ginger juice. Discard the pulp. Add the vinegar, miso paste, and honey to the bowl and whisk together. Slowly add the neutral oil while quickly whisking until emulsified. Transfer to an airtight container and store in the refrigerator for up to 1 week. Re-whisk just before using.

In a large bowl, use your hands to toss the greens with ⅓ cup / 80ml of the vinaigrette. Taste and adjust with a pinch of salt, if needed. In a medium bowl, toss together the pear, kohlrabi, pickled mushrooms, and jujubes with 2 Tbsp vinaigrette, taste, and season with salt.

Layer the dressed greens with the fruit and vegetables in a pleasing pile on a serving bowl or platter. Crush the walnuts with a mortar and pestle (or coarsely chop). Sprinkle the crushed walnuts and flower petals, if desired, over the top and serve with any remaining vinaigrette on the side.

SPICED WALNUTS

Makes 4 cups / 380g

1 egg white, at room temperature

⅓ cup / 65g granulated sugar

4 tsp 10 Spice (see page 36)

1½ tsp kosher salt

4 cups / 320g walnut halves

Preheat the oven to 300°F. Line a baking sheet with parchment paper.

In a medium bowl, whisk the egg white until stiff peaks form. Gently fold in the sugar, 10 Spice, and salt. Gently fold in the walnuts until evenly coated. Spread the walnuts in a single layer on the prepared baking sheet.

Bake for 20 minutes, stir the nuts to loosen, and then bake until no longer shiny, 10 to 15 minutes more. Let cool, transfer to an airtight container, and store at room temperature up to 2 weeks.

MANDARIN AND CHINESE ALMOND SALAD

Chinese almonds aren't actually almonds but the white kernels of apricot pits. Toasted, they taste of floral frangipane with a sweet vanilla perfume. Chinese cooking (and medicine) uses two varieties; the southern (南杏, nàahm hahng) is sweet and bitter, while the northern (北杏, bāk hahng) is even more bitter, slightly plumper looking, and more prone to releasing cyanide in your digestive tract if not properly handled (so I don't use them here). My affinity for Chinese almonds must come from all the almond gelatin that I ate growing up. When I got my wisdom teeth out, my mom made me three huge bowls of almond jelly and left them in the fridge to consume at my leisure. The cooling, silky texture kept me going during my recovery. It didn't require chewing, or really even opening my mouth. Another example of the healing power of food! In this salad, the milky texture of the bitter almonds coats the mandarins and greens and lends them an unexpected richness. Adding the anise and fennel brings a savory quality that ties it all together in a refreshing winter salad.

Active Time — 15 minutes

Plan Ahead — You'll need overnight for soaking the almonds, plus time to make Chrysanthemum Oil

Makes 4 servings

Special Equipment — Cheesecloth, blender

Chinese Almond Milk Vinaigrette

1 tsp anise seeds

3 Tbsp extra-virgin olive oil

3 Tbsp champagne or apple cider vinegar

1½ Tbsp Chinese Almond Milk (recipe follows)

½ tsp kosher salt

Six 4-oz / 115g satsuma mandarin oranges

1 cup / 100g thinly shaved fennel bulb (⅛ inch thick, shaved on a mandoline)

4 fresh chrysanthemum (tong ho) green stems

2 tarragon sprigs

Chrysanthemum Oil (see page 118) for drizzling

To make the vinaigrette: In a small frying pan over medium heat, toast the anise seeds, tossing or stirring frequently, until fragrant, about 2 minutes. Immediately transfer the seeds to a mortar and pestle and let cool. Crush the seeds to the texture of cracked pepper.

Transfer the crushed seeds to a small bowl, add the olive oil, vinegar, almond milk, and salt and whisk to combine. Set aside.

Peel the oranges and cut four of them crosswise into ⅓-inch-thick rounds (3 or 4 slices per orange). Separate the remaining two oranges into segments like you would for snacking. Arrange the slices and segments on a serving platter.

Dress the fennel with 2 Tbsp of the vinaigrette and scatter over the oranges. Tear the tender greens from the chrysanthemum stems and place on the salad. Pick the leaves from the tarragon sprigs and sprinkle on top. Drizzle the salad lightly with the remaining vinaigrette and chrysanthemum oil before serving.

CHINESE ALMOND MILK

Makes ¼ cup / 60ml

3 Tbsp sliced southern Chinese almonds (南杏, nàahm hahng)

½ cup / 120ml filtered water

Place the almonds and water in a blender. Cover and let soak overnight at room temperature. The next day, line a fine-mesh strainer with cheesecloth and place in a small bowl. Blend the soaked almonds on high speed until creamy, about 1 minute. Pour through the strainer, gather up the sides of the cheesecloth, and gently squeeze the solids to extract more almond milk. Discard the solids. Transfer to an airtight container and store in the refrigerator for up to 3 days.

I used to be weird about cornstarch. It felt like an unnecessary shortcut. A filler. But then I compared it to the modern chef's arsenal of xanthan gum, methylcellulose, gellan, and other "derived" stabilizers that are not otherwise found in such concentrations in nature, and I got over it. A little starch made from ground corn kernels is worth it for everything gained.

Chinese cooking calls on starches from corn, tapioca, arrowroot, lotus, sorghum, sweet potato, water chestnut, rice, sago, and many other sources for sauces, soups, jiggly cold dishes, noodles, and pastry. Cornstarch can quickly tighten up a delicate sauce to get that satisfying, velvety mouthfeel. Cornstarch is everywhere in Chinese American cuisine, since it's the most readily available starch in this country.

Starches can be overused, though where you draw that line is personal. Critic Jonathan Gold credited tasting a "mucusy" soup at a popular Chinese restaurant early in his career for teaching him how much cultural preconceptions shape what tastes good to each of us. For context, thick, saucy soups called gāng (羹, often translated on Chinatown menus as "potage") are a carry-over from slow-braising rich meats and vegetables in bronze vessels a few thousand years ago.

If you don't use it already, add tapioca starch to your pantry. I reach for it whenever I'm working with sugars, because it makes everything glossy and stretchy, like the delicious mouthfeel of sweet and sour sauce. It stretches sīn flavors as well in a way that leaves sauces still feeling light. Tapioca starch helps a batter on fried chicken stay put and crunchy. Adding tapioca to a wheat-flour dumpling wrapper turns it magically translucent once steamed.

Every starch has a superpower. Grain starches, like corn, set firmly when brought to boiling and can handle being reheated. They are clear only when warm, so they are great for stir-fry sauces and soups. Root starches, like tapioca, set loosely at lower temperatures (138° to 150°F) and are clear at any temperature, so they are well-suited for room-temperature sauces and cool desserts. They also freeze and thaw well. Using too much of any starch or adding it to a pan that's too hot will turn everything gummy. All starches have to be heated enough to thicken and not taste raw. Try using them to:

THICKEN Cornstarch instantly gives a broth body for a soup or sauce. Mix about 1 Tbsp of cornstarch with just a little bit more water or stock to make a thin slurry. Cornstarch doesn't dissolve, so you'll need to stir again right before using, or keep the slurry in a squeeze bottle and shake it up between douses. Stream the slurry into the wok or pan at the last possible moment of cooking. Simmer for a few seconds just until you see the liquid thicken and the cornstarch is cooked through. Take off the heat if needed to keep the starch from scorching.

COAT AND SAUCE Adding a starch slurry to a stock in a wok makes an instant sauce without concentrating flavor. In European cooking, you reduce, reduce, reduce to approach this consistency, or emulsify a sauce with butter, but both techniques affect the flavor of the dish. Cornstarch is our fat-free, super-efficient, flavorless beurre monté. It keeps flavors clean and the color light without wasting a drop of stock. Also, oil suspended in an emulsification with cornstarch makes leafy greens positively gleam.

VELVET Starch has the amazing effect of tenderizing meat for stir-fries and soups. The beef in beef broccoli, for instance, is usually lightly dusted with cornstarch (or tapioca) right before stir-frying. This creates a barrier between the frying oil and the moisture in the meat. Marinating chicken or seafood in a slurry of cornstarch, egg white, and some soy sauce and/or Shaoxing wine before blanching in boiling water or oil does the same thing (see Chef's Note: Blanching with Oil, page 138).

TENDRILS, GREENS, AND STEMS

In Chinatown markets, there's an endless variety of what the USDA calls "assorted Oriental vegetables." Walk into a Chinese restaurant between lunch and dinner, and you'll find the whole staff carefully cleaning greens for their wok cooks. The following method works for leafy greens when their leaves are at their most tender, sweet, and flavorful. For some, this means when they are young; for others, when they have just flowered.

Start by rinsing the greens well in a large bowl of cold water before trimming. Swish them around, but avoid letting them soak. If the leaves are tightly bunched, as with bok choy, part them gently to get at the dirt at the base and center. Pare or prune away tough, woody outer layers, trim the bottoms, and discard bruised and discolored parts. Then dry your greens. If you have an hour or two, leave them to drain in a colander while you turn to other things. Otherwise, use a salad spinner. Moisture will impede caramelization and the smoky character of wok hei. Clean and dry, well-groomed greens will cook up crisp on the outside and tender through the middle.

I suggest some seasonings here, but don't worry as much about measurements as the order of things and keeping the cooking vessel hot. Get your mise en place of greens, oil, aromatics, and seasonings ready before you begin (see "A Pan is Not a Wok," page 25).

Active Time — 20 minutes, plus time to make stocks and seasonings
Makes 2 to 4 servings

½ tsp cornstarch
1 tsp water or stock, plus 2 Tbsp (see tables, pages 136 to 137)
1 Tbsp oyster sauce
1 tsp light soy sauce (生抽, sāng chāu)
Neutral oil or other oil (see tables, pages 136 to 137)
4 garlic cloves, peeled and crushed (see tables, pages 136 to 137)
1 tsp peeled and minced ginger (see tables, pages 136 to 137)
8 oz / 225g prepped and dried greens (see tables, pages 136 to 137)
Kosher salt
Seasonings (see tables, pages 136 to 137)

In a small bowl, stir together the cornstarch and 1 tsp water. If cooking thick-stemmed greens, in a small bowl, stir together the oyster sauce and soy sauce. Keep everything else separate.

Warm a wok or large frying pan over high heat. Add the neutral oil and let it heat up for a few seconds. Tilt the wok away from the flame so the oil pools. If using garlic, add it to the oil, letting it fry until just starting to brown, 15 to 30 seconds. Put the wok back on the flame, add the ginger (if using) and toss.

With the wok still on the flame, add the greens, starting with any thicker stems and bunches, and toss well until evenly coated in oil. Once the larger pieces begin to sweat, about 20 seconds, add the leaves and toss again.

Season with salt. Add about 2 Tbsp water to the vegetables and continue to toss until most of the water evaporates and the greens are crisp-tender, 1 to 2 minutes. Hardier greens may need more time to soften and more liquid too. Aim for about 1 Tbsp liquid left at the bottom of the wok. Remove any extra liquid as necessary.

Add the oyster sauce–soy sauce mixture, or whatever the specified seasonings, one at a time, to the vegetables, tossing to incorporate each addition well but briefly, for just a few seconds. If you want to thicken the sauce to coat, stir the cornstarch slurry again and add to the top of the vegetables, tossing well but briefly, removing the pan from the heat as soon as the sauce starts to thicken.

With the wok off the heat, add any last seasonings to finish the dish, tossing to distribute evenly.

Pile the greens high in a serving bowl or platter and drizzle with any sauce left in the pan.

STREET NAMES	LOOK FOR	PREP AND COOK	OIL	AROMATICS	SEASONINGS
Amaranth or Chinese spinach, yin choy (莧菜)	Bright magenta and green round leaves, like spinach's minerally cousin. Solid green varieties tend to be tougher.	Trim off stem ends. Make similarly sized bunches as with chrysanthemum.	Neutral	Garlic and ginger	Finish off heat with 1 Tbsp sweet wheat paste (甜麵醬, tián miàn jiàng in Mandarin)
Celtuce greens, A choy (AA 菜)	Crispy, long green leaves shaped like slender romaine without buds; in the early warm season. Also nice raw.	Trim off stem ends; cut into 2-inch pieces.	Neutral	Garlic and ginger	Finish off heat with a douse of Shaoxing wine or a squeeze of lemon
Chrysanthemum, tong ho (茼蒿)	Aromatic and herbal. Serrated leaves and long stems. A less-common variety with broad leaves is milder.	Trim off a couple inches of tough stems. Pluck away flower buds. Cut or tear into similarly sized bunches by cutting stems into 2-inch pieces and separating some leaves from sturdier stalks.	Neutral	Garlic and ginger (optional)	Fish Fumet (page 36); 1 Tbsp Shacha (page 275); cornstarch (optional)
Napa cabbage, wòhng ngàh baahk (黃芽白), daaih baahk choi (大白菜)	Tight barrels and juicy, not spongy, leaves. Best in the cool months. Avoid black spots or sheaves that have been pared down a lot. Mellow king of the bok choys.	Remove one or two layers of outer leaves, rinse dirt from base, cut out core. Cut or tear into 2-inch pieces.	Chicken, duck, or bacon fat	Garlic and ginger	Supreme Stock (page 34); finish off heat with a douse of Shaoxing wine or a squeeze of lemon
Pea tendrils, wūn dauh mìuh (豌豆苗)	Older plants with larger leaves and tender tops, which are sweet, and more flavorful than young spring shoots. Best in warm months.	Trim off stem ends. Pluck off hard tendrils, bolting shoots, and tough leaves at the bottom.	Neutral	Garlic and ginger	Supreme Stock (page 34); cornstarch (optional)
Sweet potato leaves, fāan syú yihp (番薯葉)	Heart-shaped leaves with long, juicy stems. Mild.	Tear stems and leaves from the thick main stalk.	Neutral	Garlic and ginger	None
Water spinach, ung choi (蕹菜), tūng sām choi (通心菜)	Full arrow-shaped leaves with hollow stems. Pale green variety with triangular leaves tend to be most tender.	Trim off a couple inches of woody stems. Make similarly sized bunches as with chrysanthemum.	Neutral	None	1 Tbsp white fermented doufu (白腐乳, baahk fuh yúh); 1 Fresno chile, small-diced; finish off heat with 1 Tbsp Fermented Mustard Greens (page 41)

THICK-STEMMED GREENS

STREET NAMES	LOOK FOR	PREP AND COOK	OIL	AROMATICS	SEASONINGS	
Chinese broccoli, gai lan (芥蘭)	Slender stems and tightly closed tightly buds without yellow blooms. Sweet in spring and early summer. The asparagus of Chinese greens.	Trim off stem ends on the diagonal, then peel the outer skin from the bottom couple inches. Cut or tear large bunches into similarly sized pieces and separate some leaves from sturdier stalks.	Neutral	Garlic	Oyster sauce and light soy sauce (生抽, sāng chāu)	
Chinese mustard, gai choy (芥菜)	Crisp, juicy, slender ridged stems in cooler months. Bitter and bright. (We ferment the short, wide ones, see page 41.)	Remove damaged outer leaves, wash dirt from base, cut lengthwise into halves or thirds without separating the leaves.	Neutral	Garlic with extra ginger to balance bitterness	Finish off heat with 1 Tbsp sweet wheat paste (甜麵醬, tián miàn jiàng in Mandarin)	
Miuh bok choy (苗白菜), includes varieties such as hàahm choi (鹹菜), náaih yáu baahk choi (奶油白菜)	Short white stems and ruffled, dark-green leaves, like a bok choy corsage. Best in the warm months, before they flower.	Remove damaged outer leaves, wash dirt from base, cut lengthwise into halves or thirds without separating the leaves.	Peanut or other flavorful nut oil	Garlic and ginger	Oyster sauce; cornstarch (optional); finish off heat with a few drops of toasted sesame oil	
Yu choy (油菜), choy sum (菜心)	Young summer stalks just a few inches long with no buds, otherwise they are crazy-bitter and tough.	Trim off stem ends on the diagonal, then peel the outer skin from the bottom couple inches. Cut or tear large bunches into similarly sized pieces and separate some leaves from sturdier stalks.	Neutral	Garlic and ginger	Oyster sauce; cornstarch (optional)	

Oil-blanching, gwo yáuh (過油), is the Chinese technique of passing vegetables and meats through oil before the actual cooking. It's not the same as deep-frying, where you cook to doneness. This only takes a few seconds. Oil can be heated to higher temperatures than water, but because heat passes more slowly through oil, it transfers heat to food more gently. Delicate ingredients don't overcook. Oil also won't draw out water-soluble nutrients (the flavor) as water does. If the temperature of the oil and the wok are hot enough, there's no oil slick left anywhere.

After learning to oil-blanch, you'll never look at eggplants the same way. Forget leathery, gray pieces of meat or dry, disintegrated gailan. Now you can stir-fry to succulent perfection.

Oil-blanching vegetables: This is the way to cook vegetables with shiny, waxy skins such as eggplants (see page 140), green beans, and long beans, which have built-in waterproofing that makes cooking them through difficult. A quick dip in hot oil instantly shatters the skin's cell walls while leaving the rest of its structure intact. If the oil temperature stays steady, the steam inside the vegetable keeps most of the oil out. For green beans, this takes, maybe, 4½ seconds. This is the technique behind blistered garlic–green beans that are bright green and both tender and crisp.

Oil-blanching meats: Oil-blanching meats is all about tenderizing and washing off gamey flavors. It generally calls for velveting the meat (see Chef's Note: Cornstarch, page 134) first. The time in the oil is short—for beef, pork, and chicken, maybe 2 minutes; for shrimp, maybe 1 minute. Keep everything in motion the whole time and remove with a spider to drain before finishing in the hot wok with seasonings. We don't actually do this much at the restaurant, because with the quality and cuts of meat we choose, it's unnecessary.

You can oil-blanch with one wok, but it's easier with two. This is admittedly fussy for home cooking because you need two woks (or at least one wok and a large pot), two burners on high, and enough oil to cover whatever you're cooking. Safety first, speed next time.

1. Fill wok #1, or a deep pot such as a 5-quart heavy-bottom Dutch oven, with enough oil to cover the ingredients. You want the oil to fill the pot only one-third of the way, as it will rise and roil. Find a deeper pot if needed. Warm over medium-high heat to a steady 375°F.

2. Set up wok #2 on your hottest burner for stir-frying.

3. Make sure your ingredients are dry (pat with a paper towel, if necessary). Slide them into wok #1. The oil will roil as steam comes out. Aim for two-thirds cooked through, though how long this takes depends on the size of the ingredients, water content, protein and fat, and so on. If thickness and size vary a lot, add ingredients in order of what takes longest to cook, such as thick stalks and then leaves. If the oil drops in temperature, give it time to recover before adding anything else. Look for colors to intensify as a sign.

4. Remove the ingredients with a spider and drain well for a few seconds, giving a few vigorous shakes.

5. Make sure wok #2 is hot. Add the ingredients to wok #2, again starting with what will take longest to stir-fry. Finish with any seasonings and sauces.

TAIWANESE-STYLE EGGPLANT

Active Time — 25 minutes

Plan Ahead — You'll need
1 hour for brining

Makes 4 servings

Special Equipment —
Deep-fry thermometer, spider

2 medium Chinese eggplants
1 qt plus ¼ cup / 1L water
2 Tbsp kosher salt
2 qt / 1.9L neutral oil
3 Tbsp oyster sauce
4 tsp fish sauce
2¼ tsp granulated sugar
5 garlic cloves; 2 thinly sliced,
   3 finely chopped
1 red Fresno chile, cut into
   thin rings
¼ cup / 5g packed Thai or
   opal basil leaves, torn in half
   if large

For this recipe, I prefer medium Chinese eggplants, the pale purple, slender ones that are ten to twelve inches long, over similar-looking but more bitter varieties. This calls for oil-blanching (see Chef's Note: Blanching with Oil, page 138) and, because eggplant is basically a sponge, brining them for an hour first until they are saturated but not bloated. During frying, the water turns to steam and makes the eggplant creamy and not at all oily.

Cooking is really the study of water. It takes water to grow everything, of course, and so the amount of water that remains in an ingredient after it is harvested or butchered dictates how it will heat through in the pan, whether it will soften, seize, crisp, or caramelize. You're adding water when you use stocks, vinegars, or alcohol. You're creating barriers to water with starches. How you cut ingredients and the order in which you add them to the pan is about controlling how and when they release the water inside them. Even the shapes of cooking vessels are about releasing or retaining moisture. When cooking with a wok, changes to water happen so quickly that split-second timing is essential.

Trim and discard the eggplant ends, then cut into thick wedges, like steak frites—first cut crosswise into three 3-inch chunks, then halve those lengthwise repeatedly until you have 1-inch-thick wedges.

In a large bowl, combine 1 qt / 950ml of the water and the salt and whisk until the salt is dissolved. Add the eggplant, making sure it is submerged, and let sit at room temperature for 1 hour.

Fill a 5-quart or larger Dutch oven with the neutral oil and secure a deep-fry thermometer on the side. Set over medium-high heat and warm the oil to 375°F.

Meanwhile, drain the eggplant and dry very well with paper towels. In a small bowl, combine the remaining ¼ cup / 60ml water, oyster sauce, fish sauce, and sugar and stir until the sugar is dissolved. Set this sauce aside.

Add the sliced garlic to the oil and fry until crisp and light golden brown, about 30 seconds. Use a spider to transfer them to a paper towel to drain.

Check that the oil in the Dutch oven is still at 375°F. Set up for the second fry by setting a dry wok or large skillet over high heat.

Carefully slide all the eggplant into the oil. Stir until the eggplant has darkened and caramelized at the edges, about 1 minute. Remove the eggplant with the spider and drain well over the Dutch oven, then transfer to the screaming-hot wok.

Immediately add the chopped garlic and most of the chile rings (reserve a few for garnish) to the eggplant in the wok and toss everything to combine. Add the reserved sauce and continue to toss until the sauce thickens to a glaze and the eggplants are browned at the edges, about 1 minute. Add most of the basil leaves and toss until wilted.

Transfer the contents of the wok to a serving platter. Crumble the fried garlic and scatter it over the eggplant with the rest of the basil and chile rings. Serve immediately.

SEARED NAPA CABBAGE

Active Time — 1½ hours

Plan Ahead — You'll also need time to make Chicken Stock. Start making the sauce, potato crisps and purée, and relish 1½ hours before serving.

Makes 4 servings

Special Equipment — Deep-fry thermometer, blender, kitchen twine, Microplane

Yuzu Sauce

1 cup / 240ml Chicken Stock (page 34)

5½ tsp premium soy sauce (頭抽, tàuh chāu)

1 Tbsp plus ½ tsp 100% yuzu juice

Potato Crisps

1 qt / 950ml neutral oil

1 medium russet potato

4 garlic cloves, peeled

Kosher salt

Chinese Chive Relish

1 Tbsp raw white sesame seeds

¼ cup / 20g thinly sliced Chinese chives

½ tsp peeled and minced ginger

½ tsp kosher salt

¼ tsp ground white pepper

¼ cup / 60ml neutral oil

1 Tbsp finely chopped cilantro leaves and stems

Potato Purée

1 large russet potato, peeled and cut into large dice

1 large Yukon gold potato, peeled and cut into large dice

Kosher salt

1 Tbsp duck fat

⅓ cup / 80ml unsweetened soy milk

This is a recipe that lavishes the humble napa cabbage with some overdue decadence. If you treat a cabbage as you would a dry-aged steak, it will morph into tender sheaves with varied degrees of sweet and smoky caramelization, full of complex flavor and texture. When charring the cabbage in duck fat, take it to the edge of burnt. The wok or cast-iron pan must be very hot to quickly draw out all the sugar and water in the cabbage leaves. As your kitchen fills with smoke (turn on the fan and open the windows), reassure everyone nearby that this is all part of the plan (especially any Chinese people—deeply caramelized vegetables are not so customary in Chinese cuisine). Right when you think the cabbage may be getting too dark, give it another long 5 seconds before pulling it from the pan.

To make the sauce: In a small saucepan over medium-high heat, simmer the chicken stock until reduced to ¼ cup / 60ml, about 12 minutes. Remove from the heat and stir in the soy sauce and yuzu juice. Let cool, transfer to an airtight container, and store in the refrigerator for up to 5 days.

To make the crisps: Fill a wok or large saucepan with the neutral oil and secure a deep-fry thermometer on the side. Set over medium-high heat and warm the oil to 350°F, being careful to maintain this temperature as you fry.

Meanwhile, peel and then grate the potato on the large holes of a box grater. (You can simply dice the potato if your blender can handle it, but grating releases starchy juices that better bind the crisps.) In a blender, combine the potato and garlic and blend on high speed, scraping down the sides of the blender jar often, into a smooth paste. Transfer to a piping bag, squeeze bottle, or zip-top plastic bag (snip off a corner of the bag to create a small hole when you're ready to go).

Line a plate with a double layer of paper towels.

Squeeze some of the potato purée into the hot oil in a zigzag motion about 4 inches long. Fry, stirring occasionally, until dark golden brown and crisp, about 1 minute. Using a slotted spoon or spider, transfer the finished crisp to the prepared plate. It will break up into pea-size irregular pieces. Immediately season with salt and set aside to cool. Repeat with the remaining purée. Once cool, transfer to an airtight container and store at room temperature for up to 1 week.

To make the relish: In a small frying pan over medium heat, toast the sesame seeds, tossing occasionally, until fragrant and light golden brown, 2 to 3 minutes. Transfer to a small heatproof bowl and stir in the chives, ginger, salt, and pepper. In a small saucepan over medium-high heat, warm the neutral oil just until it starts to smoke. Immediately pour the oil over the chive mixture and stir to combine. Set aside to cool. Stir in the cilantro, transfer to an airtight container, and store in the refrigerator for up to 5 days.

To make the purée: Place both potatoes in a small saucepan and cover with cold water by 1 inch. Stir in 1 tsp salt and bring to a simmer over medium-high heat. Simmer until knife-tender, about 10 minutes. Drain the potatoes and set aside.

CONTINUED

SEARED NAPA CABBAGE continued

One 1½-lb / 680g napa
  cabbage (about 5 inches
  wide and 10 inches long)
¼ cup / 50g duck fat
1 Buddha's hand or
  Meyer lemon

In the same saucepan over medium-low heat, warm the duck fat until melted. Add the potatoes back to the pan by passing through a ricer or mashing them with a potato masher until very smooth. Stir to be sure the starch and fat are thoroughly combined, then stir in the soy milk and ½ tsp salt. Taste and season with more salt if needed. Keep warm, or let cool, transfer to an airtight container, and store in the refrigerator for up to 5 days. Rewarm gently over low heat.

Preheat the oven to 425°F.

Starting about 2 inches from the stem end of the cabbage, tie pieces of kitchen twine tightly around the cabbage every 2 inches, then cut the cabbage into three 2-inch-thick cross-sections, keeping the twine intact and centered. Wrap more twine around each cabbage steak a few times (perpendicular to the first twine) to keep the leaves tight. This will ensure the steaks develop an even, crisp crust.

In a large oven-safe frying pan over high heat, warm the duck fat until just starting to smoke. Add the cabbage to the pan and don't disturb them until they are charred on the bottom, 3 to 4 minutes. Leave them in the pan (don't flip), transfer to the oven, and roast until crisp-tender, 5 to 7 minutes.

Spread the potato purée on a wide, rimmed serving platter. Settle the cabbage on the purée, then cut and remove the twine. Gently open up the cabbages so they look nice, like little flowers. Drizzle a few spoonfuls of the yuzu sauce and Chinese chive relish on top and in between the leaves. With a Microplane, generously grate the zest of the Buddha's hand over everything. Crown with a handful of potato crisps and serve immediately.

ON NAPA CABBAGE

Napa cabbage (*Brassica rapa*, subsp. *Pekinensis*) goes by many names. During the toughest years of China's economic reforms, it was called 愛國白菜 (ài guó bái cài, in Mandarin, "patriotic cabbage"), because it was free and because some winters meant eating your share and not much else. In print, the Cantonese name, wòhng ngàh baahk (黄芽白), was often Romanized as ngo bok, nga pok, nappa, and naba, but it was napa that took off. Though the name isn't tied to wine country, that is where Chinese migrant farmers likely worked the first commercial farms that grew it in the United States. It traveled in cargo holds of the ships that carried early Chinese to San Francisco. It can last through a season, stacked like firewood by the door, and even longer, indefinitely really, fermented or pickled. In hard times, napa cabbage meant survival. So why do some Chinese families keep napa cabbages carved out of jade on display? "Cài," meaning "leafy greens," is also a pun for prosperity.

MUSHROOM MU SHU

The roots of this dish are in northern China around Shandong, where "mu shu" was named for the wood ear fungus, mù'ěr (木耳), and the eggs, which when cooked properly resemble wispy, sweet osmanthus (xī, 樨). But when the dish got to Chinatown, it was probably printers making the menus who swapped in the woodblock for the more common word "whiskers," xū (須). Close enough.

On the nights my family ate out, my parents let my sister and me pick the dishes. At Chinese restaurants, I'd usually choose something new or one of the house specials, but my sister always ordered mu shu pork. (These days, whenever I'm caught up in finding peak, seasonal ingredients and eighty-sixing dishes left and right, I think of my sister and make sure we keep some long-standing favorites for our regulars.) As kids, we learned quickly that whether the pancakes could stand up to the juicy bits of pork and strips of wood ear, vegetables, and egg without disintegrating was a good predictor of the care a restaurant put into all its food. But even when the roll fell apart in our hands, we were happy to eat everything with chopsticks straight off the plate. Like its name, this dish is all about making the most of what you've got. Use any variety of fresh, wild, or cultivated mushrooms you like. Just avoid dried varieties, which cook up soggy and will test any pancake to its limits.

Active Time — 1½ hours

Plan Ahead — You'll need 1½ hours for simmering, and time to make Chinese Pancakes, Peanut Butter Hoisin Sauce, and 10 Spice

Makes 4 to 8 servings

Mu Shu Filling

1 egg
Kosher salt
1 tsp neutral oil, plus 1 Tbsp
1 cup / 50g fresh black trumpet mushrooms, torn into bite-size pieces
1 cup / 50g fresh beech mushrooms
1 cup / 50g fresh cauliflower mushrooms, torn into bite-size pieces
Freshly ground white pepper
⅓ cup / 30g thinly sliced fresh wood ear mushrooms
⅓ cup / 30g peeled, matchstick-cut jicama
⅓ cup / 30g Braised Burdock (page 146)
½ cup / 115g Mushroom Broth (page 146)
1 tsp cornstarch
Cilantro leaves for topping

1 recipe Chinese Pancakes (page 51), warmed
½ cup / 120ml Peanut Butter–Hoisin Sauce (page 37)

To make the filling: In a small bowl, whisk the egg with 1 tsp water and a pinch of salt. In a wok or large frying pan over medium heat, warm the 1 tsp neutral oil until shimmering. Add the egg mixture and quickly, with a twist of the wrist, swirl the pan to coat with the thinnest layer you can. When the egg is set but not browned on the bottom, flip and cook until the other side is just set (this happens in seconds). Transfer to a cutting board and cut into ¼-inch-wide ribbons.

Warm the same pan over high heat for another fast stir-fry. Add the remaining 1 Tbsp oil and let it heat up a few seconds. Add the trumpet, beech, and cauliflower mushrooms; season with salt and white pepper; and keep everything in motion until browned and the liquid from the mushrooms has evaporated, about 2 minutes. Add the wood ear mushrooms, jicama, and burdock and stir-fry for 30 seconds. Add the mushroom broth and bring to a boil. Whisk the cornstarch with 1 tsp water, add to the juices at the bottom of the pan, and keep stirring everything until a brown sauce coats the mushrooms.

Pour it all into a shallow bowl or platter and top with the egg ribbons and cilantro.

Serve with the warm pancakes and the hoisin sauce in a little dish with a spoon. Spread some hoisin on a pancake, followed by a generous heap of filling. Wrap by folding both sides of the pancake inward, then wrapping the bottom edge up, leaving the top open. OGs eat them one-handed.

BRAISED BURDOCK

Makes 1 cup / 90g

1½ tsp neutral oil
½ tsp peeled and minced ginger
2¼ tsp packed light brown sugar
1 cup / 80g peeled, matchstick-cut
    burdock root
⅓ cup / 80ml Shaoxing wine
¼ cup / 60ml water

1 Tbsp light soy sauce
    (生抽, sāng chāu)
2¼ tsp dark soy sauce
    (老抽, lóuh chāu)
1½ tsp Chinese black vinegar
¾ tsp 10 Spice (see page 36)
½ tsp granulated sugar

Warm a wok or large frying pan over medium-high heat. Add the neutral oil and let it heat up for a few seconds. Add the ginger and cook, stirring, until fragrant but not browned, about 15 seconds. Add the brown sugar and cook, stirring, until caramelized, about 30 seconds. Add the burdock and keep everything in motion for another 30 seconds. Carefully add the wine and stir to combine, then stir in the water, both soy sauces, vinegar, and 10 Spice. Cover and simmer until the burdock is almost tender but still snappy when you bite it, about 9 minutes.

Strain the burdock mixture through a fine-mesh strainer into a medium bowl. Clean and dry the wok. Return the strained liquid to the wok, add the granulated sugar, and bring to a simmer over medium-high heat. Cook until reduced to the consistency of thin maple syrup, about 18 minutes. (At this point, you can drizzle some of this sweet-savory syrup over Steamed Kabocha Cake, see page 257.)

Remove the wok from the heat, add the strained burdock, and toss to coat. Let cool, transfer to an airtight container, and store in the refrigerator for up to 5 days.

MUSHROOM BROTH

Makes 1¾ cups / 415ml

1 qt / 950ml water
½ cup / 15g dried
    shiitake mushrooms
½ small yellow onion,
    cut into small dice
½ small fennel bulb,
    cut into small dice

½ stalk celery, roughly chopped
⅓ cup plus 2 Tbsp / 110ml
    Shaoxing wine
3 Tbsp light soy sauce
    (生抽, sāng chāu)
1 Tbsp Chinese black vinegar
1½ tsp granulated sugar

In a medium saucepan over medium-low heat, combine the water, mushrooms, onion, fennel, and celery and simmer until the liquid is reduced to 1 cup / 240ml, about 1½ hours.

Strain the liquid through a fine-mesh strainer into a medium bowl; discard the solids. Add the wine, soy sauce, vinegar, and sugar and stir until the sugar is dissolved. Let cool, transfer to an airtight container, and store in the refrigerator for up to 5 days, or in the freezer for up to 2 months.

MOO GOO GAI PAN

Moo goo gai pan (蘑菇雞片) is one of the dishes in the Chinese American canon that I had zero contact with until Anna Lee's sweet grandma, Coco, said it was her favorite Chinese food of all time. It's a simple dish of mushrooms (the moo goo) and velveted chicken slices (the gai pan) in a shimmery brown gravy. I can see why it would have been such a treat in the 1940s and '50s, when meat otherwise came in steaks. Restaurants such as Woey Loy Goey on Jackson Street made the dish famous, adding crunch with water chestnuts, snow peas, almonds, and whatever else they imagined their bohemian patrons craved. (The Beats lovingly called this favorite subterranean joint, "The Hole.") The restaurant got a refresh in the 1990s, but fortunately New Woey Loy Goey still serves moo goo and "chop suey noodles," another dish Coco loves. Here, I use a silky chicken sausage that is reminiscent of velveted chicken and brings a pleasing, hot-doggy texture. I also add rehydrated scallop and its liquor to bring in some Chinese decadence.

Active Time — 50 minutes

Plan Ahead — You'll need time to make Dried Scallops, Chicken Stock, Chicken Boudin Blanc, and Pickled Sunchokes

Makes 2 servings

Special Equipment — Steamer

4 Dried Scallops (page 39; optional)

8 whole chestnuts in shell

Up to 2 cups / 480ml Chicken Stock (page 34)

1 Tbsp oyster sauce

1 Tbsp peeled and minced ginger

3 Tbsp neutral oil or peanut oil

One 2-inch piece Chicken Boudin Blanc in hog casing (see page 90)

2 oz / 55g fresh trumpet mushrooms; caps left whole and stems cut into ½-inch-thick rounds

1 oz / 30g fresh wood ear mushrooms

1 oz / 30g fresh nameko or beech mushrooms, separated into individual mushrooms

8 slices Pickled Sunchokes (page 213)

5 fresh jujubes, pitted and halved

½ tsp cornstarch

¼ tsp Chinese black vinegar

1 green onion, thinly sliced crosswise on the diagonal (light green part only)

If using dried scallops, cover them in warm water and soak until pliable, 30 minutes to 1 hour. Preheat the oven to 400°F.

Using a sharp paring knife, cut an X through the shell and skin on the flat side of each chestnut. Place X-side up in a single layer on a baking sheet and roast until the shells start to peel back from the X, about 12 minutes.

Meanwhile, prepare a steamer in a wok or a large, lidded pot following the instructions on page 167 and bring the water to a boil over medium-high heat.

Wrap the chestnuts in a kitchen towel. Working with one chestnut at a time, use your fingers and another towel to loosen their shells a bit by squeezing and rolling, until you can pick the shell and thin, papery skin away from the chestnut. When all the chestnuts are peeled, place them in the steamer, cover, and steam until tender, about 20 minutes.

Strain the scallops and reserve the liquid. Add enough chicken stock to the liquid to get 2 cups / 480ml and transfer to a small saucepan. Place over medium-high heat and boil until reduced to 1 cup / 240ml, about 10 minutes. Remove from the heat and stir in the oyster sauce and ginger.

Warm a wok or large frying pan over medium heat. Add 1 Tbsp of the neutral oil and let it heat up a few seconds. Add the boudin blanc and sear until browned on two sides, 2 to 3 minutes per side. Transfer to a cutting board and cut crosswise into eight rounds.

Wipe out the wok or pan and return to high heat. Add the remaining 2 Tbsp neutral oil and let heat up a few seconds. Add the trumpet and wood ear mushrooms and cook, tossing occasionally, until starting to brown, 2 to 3 minutes. Add the nameko mushrooms and broth mixture and simmer for 1 minute. Add the scallops, sunchokes, chestnuts, and jujubes and simmer, tossing occasionally, until the sauce starts to thicken, about 3 minutes.

In a small bowl, stir together the cornstarch and 1 tsp water to make a slurry.

Add the sliced boudin blanc to the pan and cook until heated through, about 30 seconds. Add the vinegar and cornstarch slurry and toss until the sauce thickens and just clings to the food. Transfer to a serving plate and garnish with the green onions. Serve immediately.

GONG BAO ROMANESCO

Gong bao (宮保, a.k.a. kung pao) is one of those dishes that you grow up loving in the States, but if you're lucky to ever eat it in China, specifically in Chengdu, it will blow your mind. The Chinese American version is tamed, made without Sichuan peppercorns and only a little chile. It tends to be saucy, not dry like on the mainland. Mine leans toward the original, though purists would question the Romanesco, which was probably first bred near Rome. It's a fast, easy dish for any night, and if this vegetarian version doesn't make it clear enough, Chinese food is as healthful as you want to make it. I love the density and brocco-cauli flavor that Romanesco, my favorite late-summer brassica, brings. Break up the florets by hand into little fractal pine trees and make sure all the components in this dish are about the same size. Eat it with however much rice you'd like.

Active Time — 30 minutes
Makes 2 to 4 servings
Special Equipment —
Deep-fry thermometer

Gong Bao Sauce
2 Tbsp plus 1 tsp oyster sauce
2 Tbsp water
2 tsp fish sauce
1 tsp granulated sugar

1 qt / 950ml neutral oil
4 dried árbol chiles, stemmed
    and coarsely chopped
3 garlic cloves, thinly sliced
2 Tbsp roasted, unsalted
    peanuts, coarsely chopped,
    plus ¼ cup / 30g roasted,
    unsalted peanuts
1 cup / 100g ¾-inch
    Romanesco broccoli florets
¾ cup / 90g large-diced
    firm doufu
1½ cups / 150g diagonally
    sliced celery
½ cup / 50g thin-sliced peeled
    purple daikon (¼-inch-thick
    slices, quartered)
½ red Fresno chile, thinly sliced
    into rings
Cilantro for garnishing

To make the sauce: In a small bowl, combine the oyster sauce, water, fish sauce, and sugar and whisk until the sugar is dissolved. Set aside.

Line a plate with a double layer of paper towels.

Fill a large saucepan with the neutral oil and secure a deep-fry thermometer on the side. Set over medium-high heat and warm the oil to 400°F, being careful to maintain this temperature as you fry. Add the árbols and fry until darkened slightly, about 10 seconds. Using a slotted spoon or spider, transfer the chiles to the prepared plate. Add the garlic to the oil and fry until crisp and light golden brown, about 30 seconds. Transfer to the plate. Reserve the oil to fry the Romanesco and doufu.

Crumble the fried garlic into a small bowl. Stir in the chiles and coarsely chopped peanuts. Set aside.

Rewarm the frying oil to 375°F. Pat the Romanesco and doufu very dry with a paper towel. Add the Romanesco to the oil and fry, stirring occasionally, until golden brown, 2 to 3 minutes. Using a slotted spoon or spider, transfer to a plate. Repeat with the doufu.

Warm a wok or large frying pan over high heat until it is just starting to smoke. Add 1 Tbsp of the frying oil, then add the celery and daikon and stir-fry until crisp tender, about 2 minutes. Add the Fresno chile, ¼ cup / 30g peanuts, and fried Romanesco and doufu and toss to combine. Drizzle in the sauce and toss until it thickens and coats everything and then garnish with the chile-garlic peanuts and cilantro. Serve immediately.

ON THE GONG BAO PERIL

In 1993, the Center for Science in the Public Interest (CSPI) published a report on the caloric content of popular Chinese dishes that concluded, "Chinese kung pao chicken is as bad nutritionally as a McDonald's Quarter Pounder." To get the numbers, CSPI blended orders of gong bao from twenty restaurants "most frequented by Americans" in San Francisco, Chicago, and Washington D.C. and then measured the total calories. Every major news outlet ran with the story: "Eating Dangerously with Chinese Takeout" (*San Francisco Chronicle*); "Some Chinese Should be Suey-Cidal" (*Chicago Tribune*); and "Kung Pao Chicken Menaces Human Race" (*The Baltimore Sun*). David Letterman joked that his fortune cookie told him he was due for a triple bypass (it would be a quintuple, actually).

In Chinese restaurants across the country, business plummeted. Philip Chiang (future co-founder of P.F. Chang's and son of Cecilia) said that the Mandarin in Beverly Hills sold only one order of gong bao the day after the headlines. Lee and Rose Au Yong, owners of two local restaurants in Allentown, Pennsylvania, offered this defense, "We face a catch-22 situation if we try to serve people a dish in true Chinese style—two-thirds vegetables and one-third meat. Our customers still want two-thirds meat and one-third vegetables. If we don't do it that way, they complain about not getting their money's worth."

For the record, CSPI found San Francisco's version to be the lowest in calories, probably since it used the fewest peanuts and was the smallest portion. Despite the study's questionable scientific method and racist overtones, the results haunt Chinese restaurants' bottom lines to this day. In 2007, CSPI released a follow-up on sodium in Chinese food based on two national chains' published data, this time acknowledging how healthful your food is depends entirely on the restaurant and how you eat.

ASPARAGUS, OLIVES, AND SMOKED DOUFU

Active Time — 1½ hours

Plan Ahead — You'll need time to make Fermented Mustard Greens. Start preparing the doufu and relish 2 hours before serving.

Makes 4 servings

Special Equipment — 1 cup apple-wood smoking chips, soaked in water at least 1 hour

Smoked Doufu

3 Tbsp dark soy sauce
 (老抽, lóuh chāu)
6 oz / 170g firm doufu,
 drained and cut into
 2-inch-long blocks

½ bunch (½-inch-thick)
 asparagus, ends trimmed
2¼ oz / 60g ramps or
 Chinese chives
Kosher salt
1 Tbsp neutral oil
2 Tbsp light soy sauce
 (生抽, sāng chāu)
4 tsp fresh lemon juice
2 Tbsp Black Olive and
 Fermented Mustard Green
 Relish (page 155),
 at room temperature
Chervil for garnishing

I get inspiration for creating dishes from recalling childhood memories, wisdom passed down from chef mentors and through books, and traveling to new places. But this one came from a Sunday spent watching Netflix. I always thought Chinese fermented black beans had a lot in common with Italian oil-cured olives in the way salt and time made them more complex. A show called *Flavorful Origins* confirmed my hunch. In Chaoshan cuisine, they process Chinese white olives (青果, cên guê in Teochew) much in the way that Italians do with their own to make the tannic bitterness edible. Chinese olives are technically in a different plant family than European olives, but they too get dried, pressed, stewed, braised into sauces, and eaten as snacks. I fell asleep to a dish of braised fermented mustard greens and white olives. The next day, I found my sous chefs had seen the episode too. When we tried it with our own mustard greens and my favorite black olives from the Central Valley, we knew it belonged on the menu.

Choose a high-protein, nutty-flavored doufu (or tofu, bean curd, or bean cheese—whatever you'd like to call it), such as Hodo Soy's organic firm, and thin asparagus stalks, which are packed with grassy, green chlorophyll flavor.

To make the doufu: Pour the soy sauce into a shallow bowl that will fit the slices of doufu in a snug single layer. Add the doufu and let marinate for 15 minutes, flipping the doufu halfway through. Meanwhile, set up your work for smoking following the instructions on page 59.

Remove the doufu from the soy sauce and arrange in a single layer on the rack in the wok.

Smoke the doufu with the pan on the flame for 10 minutes, then remove from the flame and leave for another 20 minutes. Get the wood chips smoldering again and repeat the steps, for a total of two rounds of smoking. Once cooled, the doufu can be transferred to an airtight container and stored in the refrigerator for up to 3 days.

Split the asparagus spears lengthwise, then cut into 2-inch-long pieces. Trim and discard the roots from the ramps. Cut to separate the green ramp tops from the white ends, then split the green tops lengthwise, reserving both green and white parts. (If using Chinese chives, trim and discard the roots, then cut into 2-inch pieces.) Cut the doufu into 2-inch-long matchsticks that are about ½ inch wide and ¼ inch thick.

Warm a wok or large frying pan over high heat until it is just starting to smoke. Add the asparagus and white ramp bottoms (or Chinese chives), season with salt, and cook, tossing occasionally, until starting to char, about 1 minute. Add the neutral oil and toss to coat. Add the soy sauce and lemon juice and cook until almost completely absorbed, about 1½ minutes. Add the doufu and green ramp tops and toss until heated through, about 30 seconds. Transfer to a serving dish and garnish with the relish and chervil. Serve immediately.

BLACK OLIVE AND FERMENTED MUSTARD GREEN RELISH

Makes ¾ cup / 170g

¼ cup / 60ml neutral oil
1 tsp minced garlic
⅓ cup / 55g coarsely chopped
    dry-cured pitted black olives
3 Tbsp coarsely chopped drained
    Fermented Mustard Greens
    (page 41)

1 tsp granulated sugar
1 tsp light soy sauce
    (生抽, sāng chāu)

In a small saucepan over low heat, warm the neutral oil for 2 minutes. Add the garlic and cook until fragrant but not browned, about 2 minutes. Add the olives and cook until the garlic is light golden brown, about 10 minutes. Add the mustard greens, sugar, and soy sauce and cook until the garlic is deep golden brown and the relish is very fragrant, about 15 minutes more. Remove from the heat and let cool. Transfer to an airtight container and store in the refrigerator for up to 1 week.

SILKEN DOUFU WITH RIB-EYE CAP MAPO

When I see all the love for Sichuan food now, I see what a dish such as mapo doufu can do to open up the world. There are so many regional Chinese cuisines that aren't represented in Chinatown or anywhere in this country yet. I really hope other dishes hit it big, and cooks from Yunnan, Xinjiang, Anhui, and elsewhere move in nearby, and bring more regional ingredients to the markets.

It was that way with doufu for a long time. In Chinatown, fresh doufu was made in basement shops and sold from baskets, which peddlers balanced on the ends of a long pole, to people in the neighborhood. Now doufu is in every grocery store. I love doufu in every form (fresh, fermented, dried, smoked, molded, whatever) so much that I initially fantasized about opening Mister Jiu's as a doufu shop. We make our version with especially nutty yellow soybeans from Hodo Soy and add just a touch of gypsum so it sets as a soft custard. If you want to make your own, start by reading the classic *Book of Tofu* by William Shurtleff. When buying doufu, choose flavorful, organic, or at least non-GMO, versions.

Active Time — 35 minutes

Plan Ahead — You'll need time to make Fermented Chile Paste and Basic Chile Oil

Makes 4 servings

Special Equipment — Spice grinder or mortar and pestle, steamer

Mapo Powder

1 tsp white peppercorns
1 tsp black peppercorns
1 tsp green peppercorns
1 tsp red Sichuan peppercorns

1 Tbsp fermented black beans
2 Tbsp Fermented Chile Paste (page 43)
1 Tbsp red miso paste
2 tsp minced garlic
1 tsp granulated sugar
2 tsp cornstarch
1 Tbsp water, plus ½ cup / 120ml
One 16-oz/ 450g block silken doufu
1 Tbsp tallow or rendered beef fat
6 oz / 170g small-diced dry-aged fatty steak, such as rib-eye
Kosher salt
2 Tbsp Spicy Beef Chile Oil (page 41), at room temperature
⅓ cup / 25g thinly sliced (crosswise) green onions
Steamed Rice (page 229) for serving

To make the powder: Warm a wok or a small frying pan over high heat. Add all the peppercorns and toast, tossing frequently, until fragrant and starting to make popping sounds, about 2 minutes. Immediately transfer to a dish and let cool. Smash the peppercorns in a mortar with a pestle or grind with a spice grinder into a very fine powder. Transfer to an airtight container and store at cool room temperature for up to 3 months.

Place the fermented black beans in a medium bowl and cover with hot water. Let soak for 10 minutes and then drain.

In a small bowl, stir together the fermented black beans, chile paste, miso paste, garlic, and sugar. In a separate small bowl, stir together the cornstarch and 1 Tbsp water to make a slurry.

Prepare a steamer in a wok or a large, lidded pot following the instructions on page 167 and bring the water to a boil over medium-high heat. Drain the doufu and place in a shallow heatproof bowl or pie plate. Place the dish of doufu in the steamer, cover, and steam until warmed through, about 8 minutes. Turn off the heat and leave in the steamer to keep warm.

Warm a wok or a large frying pan over high heat. Add the tallow and let it melt. Add the steak in a single layer and season generously with salt. Sear until well browned on the bottom, about 1½ minutes. Add the black bean mixture and toss to coat the beef. Add the remaining ½ cup / 120ml water and toss constantly to make sure the miso is very well distributed. Stir the cornstarch slurry again, add to the pan, and toss until the sauce thickens, about 30 seconds. Add the chile oil and toss until well combined. Immediately remove the pan from the heat.

Remove the doufu dish from the steamer and carefully pour off any accumulated liquid. Pour the mapo sauce over the doufu, sift some mapo powder over the top, and sprinkle with the green onions. Serve hot with plenty of rice.

ON HOW MÁ AND LÀ
TOOK OVER THE WORLD

When you think Sichuan food, you think mapo doufu. It's the posterchild for má là (麻辣, in Mandarin), the distinctive central-basin flavor profile made possible by Sichuan peppercorns and every type of chile (fresh, dried, or pickled), backed usually by green onions, fermented black beans, and dòubànjiàng (豆瓣醬, in Mandarin), an earthy paste of fermented broad beans and more chiles.

Mapo doufu got its name from "the pockmarked granny" (the po po with the ma on her face) who cooked soft doufu and minced beef with a fiery sauce for the workers crossing Wanfu Bridge in north Chengdu in the 1870s. Chen Liu Shi (陳劉氏) was her name.

When more chefs started cooking mapo doufu in Chinatown after Nixon visited China in 1972, they called it "hot bean curd" and "Szechuan spicy cheese," but even with the name change, it didn't stand a chance. Doufu was, at that point, "weird," and so was the physical sensation of eating the dish. If you weren't sweating from the chiles, your lips and tongue were tingling from the Sichuan peppercorn. The compound hydroxy-alpha-sanshool in Sichuan peppercorn stimulates the touch receptors on our lips in a way that makes our brain think they are vibrating at 50 hertz. The flavor profile was still so new to most of America that even Julia Child, when eating at Kan's in 1974, commented, "Isn't this far better than that hot Szechwan stuff? . . . Paul and I lived in China for a year and a half and never had it. I wonder if it really exists there."

Sichuan cuisine was until recent decades still something you had to travel to find, but that's totally changed. It's hard to pinpoint all the causes in this country, but a critical mass of Americans with Sichuan roots, Fuchsia Dunlop's writing, Iron Chef Chen Kenichi's celebrity, and Danny Bowien and Anthony Myint's Mission Chinese must all have something to do with it. From 1968 to 2005, the USDA banned Sichuan peppercorns from import supposedly to protect American citrus, so restaurants here were working with powders, infused oils, or the occasional stash that made it through the mail. As of 2015, importers are no longer required to heat-treat Sichuan peppercorns, so you can increasingly find them at full potency. In this Chinatown, Sichuan specialist Z & Y on Jackson Street led the boom. Now every Chinese restaurant serves spicy food, even if it isn't focused on Sichuan, Chongqing, or Hunan cuisine. It's this way in China, too, where Sichuan has supplanted Cantonese food as the most popular choice for a night out.

CARROT MA JIANG MIAN

Active Time — 1 hour, 10 minutes

Plan Ahead — You'll need time to make Pickled Shiitake Mushrooms, Basic Chile Oil, and Fermented Mustard Greens

Makes 4 servings

Special Equipment — Stand mixer, pasta machine, food processor, pasta cutter (optional)

Carrot Noodles

1¾ cups / 245g bread flour, plus more for dusting

1 tsp kosher salt

½ cup plus 1 Tbsp / 135ml carrot juice, plus more as needed

Sesame-Peanut Sauce

¼ cup / 30g raw white sesame seeds

⅓ cup / 85g natural, unsalted smooth peanut butter

⅓ cup / 80ml Chinese black vinegar

1 Tbsp Basic Chile Oil (page 40)

1 Tbsp light soy sauce (生抽, sāng chāu)

¼ tsp cayenne pepper

8-inch piece ginger, peeled

¾ cup / 175ml carrot juice

4 tsp Basic Chile Oil (page 40)

1 tsp Le Ferre Bergamot Extra-Virgin Olive Oil

¼ cup / 50g coarsely chopped Fermented Mustard Greens (page 41)

½ recipe Pickled Shiitake Mushrooms (page 44), drained and thinly sliced

1 cup / 100g matchstick-cut young carrots, plus leafy carrot tops, stems removed

Part of the fun of researching the regions of Chinese cuisine is imagining how classic combinations might taste with the ingredients I have available. Má jiàng miàn (麻醬麵, in Mandarin) is a sesame-peanut noodle dish often spiked with Sichuan peppercorn. The foundation of the sauce in this version similarly uses sesame and peanut paste that is reinforced with black vinegar, chile oil, and soy sauce. It's thick and coats the noodles. But it's balanced with a thin sauce of ginger juice, carrot juice, and bergamot oil that keeps the noodles cold. I find that bergamot has some of the same floral qualities as Sichuan peppercorn, and has the same effect of prolonging flavors on your palate; in this case, the sweetness of the carrots and the spiciness of the ginger. I like serving this cooling dish in the spring or late summer when the sun is out.

To make the noodles: In the bowl of a stand mixer fitted with the dough hook attachment, combine the flour and salt. With the mixer on medium-low speed, slowly pour in the carrot juice and mix until a dough forms a fairly smooth ball around the hook, about 5 minutes. If mixing by hand, in a bowl, mix the flour and salt and then add the juice a little at a time, kneading the dough until smooth. If the dough is dry and doesn't come together, add more carrot juice, 1 tsp at a time. Knead the dough into a smooth ball and let rest, covered with a damp kitchen towel, for 30 minutes. The dough should feel soft and hold an indentation when pressed.

Divide the dough into four pieces. If using a pasta roller, start at the thickest setting and progressively go one setting thinner with each pass until at slightly less than 1⁄16 inch thick (setting 5 on a KitchenAid pasta roller). If rolling by hand, roll each piece out until 1⁄16 inch thick. Lightly dust the sheets with flour and let rest for 10 minutes.

Cut the pasta sheets into ⅛-inch-wide noodles (about the width of linguine) using a pasta cutter or by hand with a knife. Toss the noodles with additional flour so they don't stick. (At this point, you can transfer to an airtight container and store in the refrigerator for up to 1 day, or divide into four portions and freeze for up to 2 months. Cook from frozen; do not thaw first.)

To make the sauce: In a medium frying pan over medium heat, arrange the sesame seeds in a single layer and toast until lightly browned, 3 to 5 minutes. Remove from the heat and let cool, then transfer to a food processor fitted with the blade attachment.

Add the peanut butter, vinegar, chile oil, soy sauce, and cayenne to the food processor and process, scraping down the sides of the bowl occasionally, until smooth—it will take a few minutes. (At this point, you can transfer to an airtight container and store in the refrigerator for up to 1 month. Bring to room temperature before using.)

CONTINUED

Grate the ginger on the fine holes of a box grater. Using your hands, squeeze the pulp over a bowl and collect ¼ cup / 60ml ginger juice. Discard the pulp. In a small bowl, combine the ginger juice, carrot juice, chile oil, and olive oil and whisk together. Cover and transfer to the refrigerator so that it is cold for serving, about 30 minutes.

Bring a large saucepan of heavily salted water (it should remind you of seawater) to a boil over high heat. Meanwhile, prepare an ice bath in a large bowl by filling it with ice cubes and a little water.

Add the noodles to the boiling water and cook, stirring occasionally, until just tender, about 1½ minutes, if using fresh noodles, or 3 minutes, if frozen. Drain and transfer to the ice bath. Let chill for a few minutes, then drain the noodles again, shaking off as much water as possible.

Divide the noodles among four bowls and drizzle with the sesame-peanut sauce. Top with the fermented greens, pickled mushrooms, carrots, and carrot tops. Drizzle the chilled vinaigrette around the inside rim of each bowl. Toss it all together before taking a bite.

MOUTHWATERING TOMATOES AND LIANG FEN

Active Time — 20 minutes

Plan Ahead — You'll need time to make Basic Chile Oil, Lanzhou Chile Oil, and Mapo Powder

Makes 4 servings

Special Equipment — 8½ × 4½-inch loaf pan

⅓ cup plus 1½ Tbsp / 100ml cold water

1 Tbsp mung bean starch

Kosher salt

8 oz / 225g dry-farmed Early Girl or other heirloom tomatoes

8 cherry or grape tomatoes

1 Tbsp Basic Chile Oil (page 40)

1 Tbsp Lanzhou Chile Oil (page 40)

1 Tbsp unrefined peanut oil

2 tsp Chinese black vinegar

2 tsp light soy sauce (生抽, sāng chāu)

8 small Thai or opal basil leaves, or shiso leaves

8 cilantro leaves

Mapo Powder (see page 156) for dusting

Mouthwatering flavor (口水味, kǒu shuǐ wèi in Mandarin) is a má là and tart chile oil from Sichuan that is often paired with rabbit or chicken. For a dish with red chile oil, this version is more refreshing than intense, because of all the cooling elements—tomatoes, fresh herbs, and liáng fěn (凉粉), a gelatinous square "noodle" we make with mung bean starch. It's a cold dish that feels hot. Wait until tomatoes are at their best in summer to make this. We use cherry tomatoes and dry-farmed Early Girl tomatoes with a briny intensity that comes from having the deep roots necessary to reach an underground spring at Dirty Girl Farm in Santa Cruz. Look for juicy, not mealy tomatoes with a good balance of sweetness and acidity.

In a small saucepan over medium heat, combine the water, mung bean starch, and a pinch of salt and whisk constantly until it bubbles and forms a gelatinous mass, about 3 minutes. Scrape into a loaf pan and smooth into an even layer. Press a sheet of plastic wrap directly onto the surface of the gel. Set aside to cool.

Bring a large saucepan of heavily salted water (it should remind you of seawater) to a boil over high heat. Meanwhile, prepare an ice bath in a large bowl by filling it with ice cubes and a little water.

Using a sharp paring or serrated knife, score an X through the skin at the bottom of all the tomatoes. Add half of the larger tomatoes to the boiling water and blanch until the skin around the X starts to shrink back, 15 to 30 seconds. Using a slotted spoon or spider, transfer to the ice bath. Repeat with the remaining larger tomatoes and then the smaller tomatoes, which will take about 15 seconds. When cool enough to handle, peel the skins from all the tomatoes. Cut the larger tomatoes into 1-inch wedges, or mix things up and leave a few whole.

In a medium bowl, whisk together both chile oils, the peanut oil, vinegar, and soy sauce. Set this sauce aside.

Flip the mung bean gel onto a cutting board and cut into 1-inch squares. Transfer to the bowl with the sauce, add all the tomatoes, and toss gently to coat. Using a slotted spoon, transfer to a serving dish. Drizzle the sauce left in the bowl over everything. Garnish with the basil (tear a few first, if desired) and cilantro leaves and dust with mapo powder. Serve immediately.

5

When I cook fish, I often think of Judy Rodgers, then owner of Zuni Café. We didn't cook a lot of seafood at Zuni, but with fish, and shellfish especially, there is no room for error. Judy taught me how complicated even simple food can be; *everything* matters.

With fin fish and shellfish, the flavors begin so pristine and subtle, there's not much on which to improve. You usually just muddy them up. Every second you mess with these kinds of ingredients, you're trading the most delicious thing, freshness, for whatever you're trying to accomplish. This is why Chinese seafood markets are so lively and crammed with tanks. In Chinese, the words for *freshness*, *deliciousness*, and *seafood* all share the same root—*sīn* (鲜), the ephemeral, essential flavor of an ingredient at its peak.

The guiding principle of classic Cantonese cuisine is to use technique to bring out the best of an ingredient's innate characteristics. It's the antithesis of a lot of modern cooking, which is about bending ingredients to our will. Cantonese cooks start with a great ingredient and look to understand how to complement it or to balance it to bring out its best qualities. That's what Judy believed too.

When I worked for Judy, she was already respected as a pioneer of California cuisine. She had grown up thinking about food as fuel but fell in love with cooking after living her junior year abroad with the Troisgros family in France. Brothers Jean and Pierre pioneered nouvelle cuisine, which redefined European fine dining and was deeply influenced by Asian cuisine's emphasis on seasonality and lightness. But Judy always said it wasn't their cooking that inspired her so much as the Sunday dinners that their sister Madeleine cooked at home. When I walked into Zuni, I had never worked for an American chef who cared as much about ingredients and precision as Judy did.

A misconception about California cuisine is that we have a million choices when it comes to ingredients, because we live in a place with such incredible resources. Actually, a lot of the work is finding the right ingredient for each particular application. Then you make constant adjustments as that ingredient changes over the season. For a million reasons, there's actually no other broccoli except this broccoli, no other squid except these squid. Of the chickens that I roasted at Zuni, we would use only those raised according to Judy's specifications and that weighed 2½ pounds, no more, no less.

Judy had an incredible palate, of course, and would taste the gnocchi that I made and notice the most micro-change in texture and say something like, *Were the eggs older today?* (Old eggs are more watery and cook up more densely.) Her precision wasn't ego. She just knew exactly what her ideal for each dish was. But she didn't want an emotionless kind of perfection. One time, after I had painstakingly layered all the toppings on a pizza into a perfectly symmetrical, robotic landscape, Judy pointed out that people like to be surprised with each bite. Unpredictability actually makes things more delicious. It keeps your palate enticed for the next bite. Chaos is a part of nature, she said.

When you walk through the Chinatown markets, you start to understand the Chinese commitment to freshness and acceptance of nature's chaos. The seafood markets source from farms, but also from local boats. Live deliveries arrive on trucks. Guys wheel in sloshing barrels of fish and lug crates of crab and buckets of frogs. When everyone arrives to buy, there is more to do. There is the catching, the stunning, and the cleaning. Scales fly. Someone wants a certain live crab but it keeps grabbing the tongs. There are easier ways to sell seafood. But all the markets here still do it this way, because everyone in Chinatown knows there is no fish but *this* fish, the one you saw with its bright eyes and smooth scales, the one the fishmonger chased with his net for you, and pulled from the tank, bristling with life.

Chef's Note: Steaming

Steaming is gentle cooking with moist heat. Steam temperatures actually reach much higher than boiling, but the cooking is gentle and steady. It's the classic Chinese method for preparing extremely fresh fish and seafood. It's the only way to cook dumplings and bao without turning the wrappers or bread into a soggy mess. If you're Chinese, you always have a steamed dish on the table. I use this technique whenever I have to use heat but want to leave flavor pristine.

To steam, you just need boiling water and a sealed vessel. In Chinese cuisine, some soups call for double steaming in tureens, sealed with two lids or bound tightly with cloth, set in a large, deep pot. Fragrant leaves can also serve as the vessel (see Noh Mai Gai [Quail with Sticky Rice], page 237). Most of the time at the restaurant, we use perforated flat pans set in round stainless-steel or bamboo steamers. Look for a domed lid that lets steam circulate without condensing onto the food, which causes uneven cooking and leaves puckers and divots on dumplings and bao. When you're done, just rinse and air-dry the steamers before storing.

When steaming something such as a crab or a fish that won't fit in a steamer, set a platter or pie pan on a heatproof rack in a Dutch oven or other large pot with a domed lid. If you don't have a rack, do as Chinese grandmas do and make a trivet with three chopstick pieces across the bottom of your vessel. Here's how to set up a wok or large pot for steaming.

1. Set the steamer in the wok or large pot to test for fit. A 12-inch bamboo steamer will fit in a 14-inch wok just right. Line the steamer with cheesecloth or loose cabbage leaves (leaving a few gaps between them for steam to come through). If you're using a platter, set it on a rack or a chopstick trivet, so that it is not touching the sides of the pot or the lid.

2. Add just enough water to reach the bottom rim of the steamer, not so much that boiling water will touch the food inside it. If using a platter, aim for at least ½ inch of space between the food and the surface of the water (you may need to weigh it down until you add what you're cooking).

3. Turn the burner to medium-high. For the recipes in this book, you want a medium-high simmer; but with some delicate ingredients, a low simmer is best. Keep another pot of water boiling on a second burner for topping off if doing multiple batches.

4. If using cabbage leaves to line the steamer, wait until they have wilted and flattened. Add whatever you're steaming in a single layer, leaving at least 1 inch between each item and the sides of the steamer for the steam to circulate. Stack multiple steamers, if you need more space.

5. Once the water comes to a high simmer, cover tightly with the steamer lid or pot lid. Resist the urge to lift the lid. Instead, monitor water levels by the quality of the steam escaping and the simmering sounds.

6. If you find too much steam is escaping from your bamboo steamer or pot, wrap a damp, clean cloth around the lid to seal.

7. When done, individually lift items out with chopsticks or a serving spoon, or remove the entire steamer basket with the help of tongs and dry towels.

SIZZLING FISH

Active Time — 20 minutes

Makes 4 servings

Special Equipment —
Steamer, 9-inch pie plate

1 Tbsp fermented black beans
(optional)
One 1½-lb / 680g whole fish
(such as black bass or Tai
snapper), gutted and scaled
1 large handful aromatics (such
as thinly sliced ginger, green
onion tops, and/or strips of
fresh citrus zest)
¼ cup / 60ml high-smoke-
point oil (such as peanut oil)
2 Tbsp premium soy sauce
(頭抽, tàuh chāu) or light soy
sauce (生抽, sāng chāu)
1-inch piece ginger, peeled and
thread cut
3 green onions, thread cut
(white parts only)
Young cilantro sprigs
for garnishing

On a weekly basis, my mom would cook corned beef with cabbage, or chicken à la king, or sausage lasagna. It was too expensive to travel internationally, but we got to eat all over the world from our kitchen table. When she cooked food from her childhood, though, she would make us this steamed fish, topped with ginger, green onions, and fermented black beans. The flavor of steamed fish in Cantonese cuisine is all about sīn tìhm (鮮甜), the essential flavor of a fresh ingredient in combination with a pure, smooth sweetness. The final lashing of hot oil in this dish infuses the green onions and ginger into the flesh of the fish and enriches the soy. Take care not to overcook the fish; I like to turn off the heat in the last minutes of cooking and let the steam finish the job. The flesh should pull off the bone in tender morsels, not flake. I always score round, fleshy fish to help it cook evenly. Then I steam the fish only until the thickest flesh right behind the gill area is not quite opaque or, as Cantonese cooks say, "translucent like white jade."

In a small bowl, cover the black beans (if using) with water, let soak for 30 minutes, and then drain.

Prepare a steamer in a wok or a large, lidded pot following the instructions on page 167 and bring the water to a boil over medium-high heat.

Meanwhile, using kitchen shears, cut off the gills and the fins (careful, sharp!) on the top, bottom, and sides of the fish. Run your fingers over the skin, especially near the gills and belly, toward the head to check for any last scales; remove the scales with the edge of a spoon or the back of a knife.

On both sides of the fish, make eight 2-inch-long parallel slits into the flesh, not quite deep enough to hit bone, starting about 1 inch from the gills. Place the fish in a pie plate. (The fish can hang over the edges so long as everything fits in the steamer. If not, cut the fish in half to fit and hope none of your guests are superstitious.) Tuck some of your chosen aromatics into each slit, then stuff the remaining aromatics in the cavity. Top the fish with the black beans.

Place the pie plate in the steamer, cover, and steam until the eyeball is opaque and the flesh of the fish is white and flaky at the thickest part near the head and first slit, 10 to 12 minutes.

While the fish is steaming, in a small heavy-bottom saucepan over low heat, slowly warm the oil.

When the fish is ready, remove it with the pie plate from the steamer. (Reassemble as a whole fish if you cut it in two.) Drizzle with the soy sauce, then top with the ginger and green onions. Turn the heat under the oil to high and warm until it just starts to smoke. Immediately pour the oil over the fish, getting as much of the ginger and green onions to sizzle as you can. Garnish with the cilantro and serve with a spoon big enough for drizzling the juices.

SALT-BAKED TROUT

Slow cooking a fish is not an easy task. Most American restaurants will train their cooks to portion a fish, then sear it, grill it, or fry it, all of which require high heat in an attempt to build exterior flavor while hopefully leaving the center just cooked enough. Chinese cooks think more about how to use a gentler and slower approach that results in the fish retaining more of its own flavorful fat. This recipe borrows from the techniques of beggars' chicken, which cooks in an insulating layer of clay, and Hakka salt-baked chicken, which is buried in rock salt that softens and disperses dry heat more evenly than turning or flipping the fish ever would. Wrapping the fish in a lotus leaf provides more insulation and imparts a pleasant tea aroma. It was by total luck that we found the lotus leaf also gently lifts off the fish skin, exposing all the luscious fat in which the trout has been slow cooking. Adding ginger–green onion sauce and trout roe, that's plain decadence that just gets better with a hot bowl of rice.

Active Time — 30 minutes, plus 4 hours for soaking the lotus leaf

Makes 3 or 4 servings

Special Equipment — Stand mixer

Salt-Crusted Trout

1 dried lotus leaf, about 12 inches wide, soaked in water for 4 hours

One 1- to 1½-lb / 450 to 680g whole cleaned trout, fins cut off

1 cup / 240ml egg whites, at room temperature

2 lb / 900g kosher salt

¼ cup chopped fennel or dill fronds (optional)

Charred Ginger–Green Onion Sauce

3 green onions

1 Tbsp peeled and finely chopped ginger

½ garlic clove, finely chopped

¼ cup / 60ml sunflower oil or grapeseed oil

1½ Tbsp toasted sesame oil

1 Tbsp light soy sauce (生抽, sāng chāu)

1 Tbsp cured trout roe or caviar, plus more for serving

To make the trout: Preheat the oven to 450°F. Line a baking sheet with aluminum foil and coat generously with cooking spray.

Remove the lotus leaf from the water and arrange vein-side up. Place the trout on the lotus leaf toward the leaf's bottom edge. Fold the sides and bottom edge over the fish, then flip the fish over until it is completely and tightly wrapped. You may not need the whole leaf; trim the excess so that the trout is wrapped in only one layer or so.

In a stand mixer fitted with the whisk attachment, whisk the egg whites on medium-high speed until soft peaks form, about 2 minutes. Turn the speed to low, add the salt and herbs (if using), and mix until the salt is evenly moist and holds together like brown sugar, about 1 minute.

Pour about one-fourth of the salt mixture on the prepared baking sheet and pat into a roomy bed for the fish. Lay the wrapped trout, seam-side down, on the salt. Use about half of the remaining salt to pack around the sides of the fish, then pack the rest on top of the fish. Pat down the salt so that it is evenly thick and has no gaps, cracks, or loose bits. (At this point, you can refrigerate for a few hours before finishing.)

Roast the fish until the flesh is just cooked through, firm but not tough, 20 to 30 minutes. You can test the fish by sticking a cake tester or metal skewer through the crust into the center of the fish for 5 seconds or so. When you pull it out, it should feel lukewarm, not cold or ripping hot. A thermometer reading from the center of the flesh should be 125°F.

To make the sauce: Meanwhile, thinly slice the green onions crosswise, separating the whites and light green parts from the dark green tops, which cook a little faster. Warm a wok or a small frying pan over high heat. Add the white and light green parts of the green onions and stir-fry until starting to char, about 2 minutes. Remove from the heat and stir in the dark green parts until wilted, about 2 minutes more. Stir in the ginger and garlic. Transfer to a small serving bowl and then stir in the sunflower oil, sesame oil, and soy sauce.

CONTINUED

Using a spoon, crack a lid in the salt crust by tapping a rectangular outline along the length of the fish. You should be able to remove the salt in just a few pieces. Cut down the middle of the lotus leaf with a pair of scissors. Gently pull back the leaf, which should also remove the skin, to reveal pink flesh. Drop three large spoonfuls of the ginger–green onion sauce on the trout. Top each dollop with a small spoonful of trout roe. Serve with more sauce and trout roe on the side.

Chef's Note: Prepping Fish

Most Chinese fish recipes call for whole fish, which stay fresher than fillets and retain all the flavor and richness that comes from the head and bones. Serving a whole fish also lets you experience the subtle differences in the fatty belly versus the muscular tail meat.

Chinatown seafood markets sell all kinds of fish live, mostly from the ocean but sometimes freshwater species too. Pick a frisky one with sleek scales and a gleam in its clear eye. Ask the fishmonger to clean and scale it. Chinese generally leave the fins and tail on, but feel free to ask for those trimmed as well. The fishmonger will pull it from the tank and kill it humanely with a strong blow to the head just above the eyes. Keep it on ice and use within a day. To clean it yourself:

1. Rinse the fish under cold water. If preferred, trim the fins with kitchen shears. I don't worry about them if they're not particularly sharp, as with trout, or if I'm serving people who expect an intact, whole fish. Lift the collar flap on both sides to cut out the gills.

2. Remove the scales with a descaler, the dull side of a thin knife, or the edge of a spoon, scraping from the tail toward the head. Feel for any last scales (even if a fishmonger did a first pass), especially around the collar flap and belly. Rinse the fish again.

3. Use a knife tip to make a shallow cut from the fish's collar flap to the vent. With flat fish such as petrale, cut from the white belly side, starting near the collar flap and following along the bottom fin a few inches until you hit bone. Gently pull out the entrails so that you do not rupture the gall bladder, a small yellow-green sack that contains bitter bile, and discard. Rinse the fish inside and out. If you want to remove the head, lift the collar flap to sever the spine.

4. For round fish, on both sides of the fish starting about an inch from the gills, cut a few parallel slits in the flesh, not quite deep enough to hit bone, to help it cook evenly. Skip this with flat fish.

"HUNAN-STYLE" CRISPY PETRALE SOLE

Active Time — 1 hour

Plan Ahead — You'll need time to make Fermented Chile Paste, Basic Chile Oil, Fermented Kohlrabi, and Fermented Mustard Greens. Start at least 2 days before serving by pickling the ramp bottoms. The day before, salt the fish and make Fish Fumet.

Makes 4 to 6 servings

Special Equipment — Deep-fry thermometer

Green Sauce

2 Tbsp neutral oil

2 serrano chiles, seeded and cut into small dice

1½ tsp peeled and minced ginger

¼ cup / 30g Dehydrated Fermented Kohlrabi (see variation, page 43)

2 Tbsp Fermented Mustard Greens (page 41), finely chopped

1 recipe Pickled Ramp Bottoms (recipe follows), drained and thinly sliced crosswise, plus 1 tsp pickling liquid

1 tsp distilled white vinegar

½ tsp premium soy sauce (頭抽, tàuh chāu)

Red Sauce

5 garlic cloves, peeled

1 to 1½ cups / 240 to 360ml neutral oil

8 dried árbol chiles, stems trimmed

2 tsp fermented black beans

1 red Fresno chile, seeded and cut into small dice

2 Tbsp Fermented Chile Paste (page 43)

1 Tbsp Basic Chile Oil (page 40)

They say absence makes the heart grow fonder, and sometimes I have to free myself from my obsession with Chinese food by leaving town with Anna Lee, and going somewhere where Chinese food is not on my agenda. On one of these trips, we went to Mexico City to enjoy some art, tacos, and mezcal. The mental vacation didn't last long. One night at Contramar, many tables had a splayed-out fish, half green and half red, and it immediately reminded me of the dish suān cài yú (酸菜鱼, in Mandarin). (Also, it turns out, Mexico City's Barrio Chino is one of the first Chinese enclaves in the Americas.) In Hunan, they pile a crimson mountain of spicy and sour fermented mustard greens, chile, and garlic over the fish. For this variation, I like a flat fish such as petrale sole or monkfish and hold back on the heat to let their delicate flavors shine. We cook one large two-pounder at the restaurant. This recipe is for a pair of fish, which is more manageable at home.

To make the green sauce: In a wok or small frying pan over medium heat, warm 1 Tbsp of the neutral oil until shimmering. Add the chiles and cook until softened but not browned, about 2 minutes. Stir in the ginger and cook until fragrant, about 30 seconds. Scrape into a small bowl. Stir in the remaining 1 Tbsp neutral oil, the kohlrabi, mustard greens, ramp bottoms, pickling liquid, vinegar, and soy sauce. Let cool, then transfer to an airtight container and store in the refrigerator for up to 1 week.

To make the red sauce: Place the garlic in a small saucepan and add enough of the neutral oil so that the garlic is fully submerged. Cook over a low heat so the oil around the garlic is barely bubbling, until the garlic is very tender but not browned, about 30 minutes. Remove the garlic from the pan and smash into a rough consistency.

Secure a deep-fry thermometer on the side of the pan, place over medium-high heat, and warm the garlic oil to 350°F. Add the árbols and fry until just starting to darken in color, about 30 seconds. Remove to a paper towel and reserve the oil.

In a medium bowl, combine the black beans with enough hot water to cover and let soak for 5 minutes, then drain and rinse.

Warm a wok or medium frying pan over medium heat. Add 1 Tbsp of the garlic-árbol oil and let it heat up for a few seconds. Add the Fresno chile and cook until softened but not browned, about 2 minutes. Stir in the black beans and cook until shriveled looking, about 5 minutes. Remove from the heat.

With your hands, crumble the fried árbols into a bowl; add the smashed garlic, chile paste, and chile oil; and stir to combine. Let cool, then transfer to an airtight container and store in the refrigerator for up to 1 week.

Check that the fishes are scaled and completely gutted. Trim the fins and tail with kitchen shears. Cut each fish in half crosswise, place in a single layer on a rimmed baking sheet, and season all over with the salt. Cover and refrigerate 1 day to firm the flesh and let everything sink in.

Two 1-lb / 450g whole cleaned
   petrale soles or other flat
   white fish
1 Tbsp kosher salt
2 qt / 1.9L neutral oil
½ cup / 120ml Fish Fumet
   (page 36)
2 Tbsp light soy sauce
   (生抽, sāng chāu)
2 tsp coarsely chopped cilantro

Fit a wire rack over a baking sheet.

Fill the wok or a large Dutch oven with the neutral oil and secure a deep-fry thermometer on the side. Set over medium-high heat and warm the oil to 375°F, being careful to maintain this temperature as you fry. Pat the fishes very dry with paper towels.

Gently slide the top halves of the fishes into the oil. Fry until cooked through, golden brown, and crispy, about 5 minutes, and then transfer to the prepared rack. Repeat with the bottom halves of the fish. Let the fried fish rest for 5 minutes.

While the second batch is frying, in a small saucepan over medium heat, combine the fish fumet and soy sauce and bring to a simmer. Remove from the heat and stir in the cilantro.

Arrange the fish on a serving platter, fitting the halves back together. Dollop a spoonful of the green sauce on one of the fish, do the same with the red sauce on the other fish, and then pour the soy-fumet around both fish. Serve immediately with the remaining red and green sauces on the side.

PICKLED RAMP BOTTOMS

Makes about ½ oz / 15g

Six 1½-inch white ramp bottoms
¼ cup / 60ml rice vinegar
2 Tbsp water

1½ tsp granulated sugar
1¼ tsp kosher salt

Place the ramp bottoms in a small heatproof container. In a small saucepan over medium-high heat, combine the vinegar, water, sugar, and salt and bring to a simmer, stirring to dissolve the sugar and salt. Pour the liquid over the ramp bottoms and make sure they're submerged. Let cool, cover, and store in the refrigerator for up to 3 days.

WHOLE DUNGENESS CRAB

Active Time — 1 hour, 40 minutes

Plan Ahead — You'll need 2 days to make the salted yolks. The day you serve, you'll need about 4½ hours to make the crab, crab rice and custard, and salad, plus time to make Chrysanthemum Oil. Soak the glutinous rice while making the crab stock and crab oil.

Make 2 servings

Special Equipment — Cheesecloth, high-speed blender, steamer, 6-ounce ramekin, seafood cracker, 8½- or 9-inch loaf pan

Sesame Vinaigrette

2½ Tbsp apple cider vinegar
⅛ tsp coriander seeds
⅛ tsp fennel seeds
1½ Tbsp well-stirred tahini
¾ tsp light soy sauce
   (生抽, sāng chāu)
¼ tsp kosher salt
⅛ tsp granulated sugar

One 2- to 3-lb / 900g to 1.4kg
   whole, live Dungeness crab
1 tsp neutral oil,
   plus 1 cup / 480ml
¼-inch-thick slice
   unpeeled ginger
1 qt / 950ml water
½ cup / 100g short-grain
   glutinous rice (such as
   Sho Chiku Bai)
2 garlic cloves, thinly sliced
12 stalks fresh chrysanthemum
   greens, any buds removed
1 Tbsp Chrysanthemum Oil
   (page 118)
¼ tsp ground turmeric
Kosher salt
2 eggs
¾ tsp granulated sugar
1 Tbsp unrefined coconut oil,
   warmed until liquefied

Crab is the definition of regional pride in every country. Everyone knows theirs are the best. In the United States alone, there's blue crab in the Chesapeake, peekytoe in Maine, stone crabs in Florida, and king crab in Alaska. Along the cold parts of the Pacific coast, we boast about our Dungeness. I'd put my money on it against any other crab any day; but as I tell my cooks, whether our guests agree all comes down to how we cook and clean the crabs, by which I mean how beautifully we get everything out of the shell. At Chinese restaurants, you get a whole crab on a platter, and it's on you to figure out how to get at it to eat it. I came to appreciate not being told how to experience my food. But when you have less experience getting in all the nooks, you miss out. With this dish, I wanted to show off all the subtleties of Dungeness from different parts of the crab, as well as the buttery crab fat and roe, and the delicate flavor in its shells. But it calls on the cook to do the cleaning. To clean a Dungeness crab, forget clunky crackers, which can smash delicate meat. Chinese cooks do it with precise taps using a cleaver, but I recommend good strong, pointy scissors.

To make the vinaigrette: In a small saucepan over medium-high heat, bring the vinegar to a simmer. Remove from the heat and stir in the coriander seeds and fennel seeds. Let infuse for 1 hour.

Pour the vinegar through a fine-mesh strainer into a small bowl; discard the seeds. Add the tahini, soy sauce, salt, and sugar and whisk until smooth. Transfer to an airtight container and store in the refrigerator for up to 1 week. Let come to room temperature and whisk to recombine before using.

Prepare a wok or a large, lidded pot for steaming following the instructions on page 167 (which include a work-around if your crab does not fit in a steamer) and bring the water to a boil over medium-high heat. Place the crab in the steamer and steam for 6½ minutes. Twist off the claws and legs and set aside. Return the rest of the crab to the steamer and steam for another 3 minutes. Remove from the steamer and set aside.

When the crab is cool enough to handle, using your hands or the tip of a knife, remove and discard the apron (triangular piece of shell at the crab's tail). Hold the crab where the apron was and pry off the top shell—imagine a hinge at the eyes—to separate it from the rest of the body. Scrape the creamy yellow crab custard from inside the top shell into a small bowl, cover, and refrigerate until ready to use. Scrape out and discard everything else still attached to the top shell. Rinse the top shell clean, then set aside.

Clean the rest of the crab body. Remove and discard the gills. Break off and discard the mouth pieces. Under cold running water, rinse away any remaining viscera. Place the crab on a cutting board and cut in half through the center valley of the body.

CONTINUED

2 tsp fresh lemon juice

Red vein sorrel for topping

8 citrus segments (such as
white marsh grapefruit,
pomelo, Cara Cara orange,
blood orange), or 2 thinly
sliced kumquats

1 Tbsp roasted, unsalted
peanuts, crushed

1 Tbsp minced chives

½ Salted Egg Yolk
(recipe follows)

Crack and pick the meat from the legs and place in a bowl; set the shells aside. Pick the backfin meat from the body and place in a separate bowl, again reserving the shells. Cover the picked meats and refrigerate until ready to use.

Preheat the oven to 350°F.

Rinse off all the shells, spread in a single layer on a baking sheet, and bake until completely dried and crisp, about 30 minutes.

Warm a large saucepan over medium-high heat. Add the 1 tsp neutral oil and heat for a few seconds. Add the ginger and char until blackened in spots, 3 to 4 minutes per side. Add the water and two-thirds of the crab shells and bring to a simmer. Turn the heat to medium and simmer until reduced to 1 cup / 240ml, about 45 minutes. Pour through a fine-mesh strainer set over a medium heatproof bowl and discard the solids. When this stock is cool, cover and refrigerate for up to 1 day.

Line a strainer with a layer of cheesecloth and set into a small bowl.

Break the remaining crab shells into manageable pieces for a high-speed blender. On low speed, blend the shells with ½ cup / 120ml neutral oil, gradually moving to high speed and scraping down the sides as needed, until extremely smooth and a uniform orange color, about 8 minutes. Strain through the prepared strainer. This oil will keep, covered, in the refrigerator for up to 1 month.

Place the glutinous rice in a clean strainer, rinse well under cool running water, and then soak in a bowl of fresh cool water for 1 hour.

While the rice is soaking, fill a small saucepan with the remaining ½ cup / 120ml neutral oil. Set over medium-high heat and warm the oil. Add the garlic and fry until crisp and light golden brown, about 30 seconds. Use a spider to transfer to a paper towel to drain.

Bring a small saucepan of heavily salted water (it should remind you of seawater) to a boil over high heat. Meanwhile, prepare an ice bath in a medium bowl by filling it with ice cubes and a little water.

Tear a few of the chrysanthemum stalks into 2-inch pieces and add to the boiling water. Blanch until tender, about 1 minute, then transfer to the ice bath. Once cool, use your hands to squeeze out as much water as possible and transfer to a cutting board. Finely chop and combine with the chrysanthemum oil.

Drain the rice well and return to the bowl. Add the turmeric and ½ tsp salt and stir to combine. Pack the seasoned rice into the crab top shell.

In a medium bowl, whisk together the eggs, sugar, 1 tsp salt, custard from the crab, and ½ cup / 120ml of the crab stock. Pour this custard through a clean fine-mesh strainer into a ramekin and press on the solids with a spoon to extract as much liquid as possible. Discard the contents of the strainer. Cover the ramekin tightly with plastic wrap.

Place the custard and rice in the steamer, then pour the remaining ½ cup / 120ml stock into the crab shell. Cover and steam over medium-high heat until the rice is tender and the custard is set, about 20 minutes. Remove both from the steamer.

Place the crab-leg meat in a small heatproof bowl and dress with 1 Tbsp crab oil. Season lightly with salt and toss to combine. Place the backfin meat in another small heatproof bowl and dress with the coconut oil. Season lightly with salt and toss to combine. Place both bowls in the steamer, cover, and steam until warmed through, about 2 minutes. Remove both bowls from the steamer. Dress the backfin meat with the lemon juice. Taste and season with more salt.

Uncover the custard and top with the blanched chrysanthemum, half of the leg meat (use the larger pieces), and a few sorrel leaves.

Pick the leaves from the remaining chrysanthemum stalks and place in a medium bowl. Add the remaining crab-leg meat, the citrus segments, and 1 Tbsp sesame vinaigrette and toss to combine. Taste and toss with more vinaigrette as needed. Transfer to a serving bowl.

Sprinkle the crab rice with the peanuts and chives, then crumble the fried garlic over everything. Top with the backfin meat and finish by finely grating the salted yolk over the top. Serve immediately.

SALTED EGG YOLKS

Makes 4 salted yolks

1 cup / 140g kosher salt

⅔ cup / 130g granulated sugar

½ cup / 25g aonori (seaweed) flakes

4 duck or chicken egg yolks

In a medium bowl, combine the salt, sugar, and aonori and stir together to make a cure. Transfer half to a loaf pan and spread into an even layer. Create four yolk-size divets in the salt mixture, then gently drop a yolk into each. Cover the yolks with the remaining cure without packing it. The yolks should be completely covered by about ½ inch of cure. Cover and refrigerate for 2 days, until firm to the touch.

Remove the yolks from the cure and rinse with cold water. Gently rub off any residual cure with a paper towel. Place the yolks in a dehydrator set to 135°F and dehydrate until firm when pressed and opaque, about 48 hours. Let cool, then transfer to an airtight container and store at room temperature for up to 2 months.

SALT AND PEPPER SQUID

Squid might be the most consistently available and superb seafood we have in the Bay Area, thanks to the Monterey Bay. The squid in those waters are just a few inches long, with purple speckled skin and elongated bodies. Because their flesh is so thin, they don't work well for the cool Chinese techniques of scoring to turn them into flowers, but they do stay tender when cooked quickly, which makes them perfect for frying with salt and pepper. This is one of the few dishes I ever saw in Chinatown that involved green jalapeños. Now even in China, salt-and-pepper dishes use "the Aztec's chile." It's these cross-cultural exchanges materializing on the plate that make the regional cuisine here in California so exciting to me.

Active Time — 45 minutes

Plan Ahead — You'll need time to make Wok Salt

Makes 4 to 6 servings

Special Equipment — Deep-fry thermometer

1 medium jalapeño chile, thinly sliced crosswise and seeds removed

¼ cup / 60ml premium soy sauce (頭抽, tàuh chāu)

One 2-lb / 900g squid, or 1 lb / 450g cleaned squid bodies and tentacles

1⅓ cups / 185g cornstarch

1½ cups / 360ml club soda

⅔ cup / 90g short-grain glutinous rice flour (such as mochiko)

½ cup / 50g rice flour (粘米粉, jīm máih fán)

4 tsp Wok Salt (see page 37)

Vinaigrette

1 tsp neutral oil

1 green onion, thinly sliced crosswise

1 tsp roasted pecan oil or other toasted nut oil

½ tsp champagne vinegar

1½ qt / 1.4L neutral oil

Wok Salt (see page 37)

¼ cup / 7g fresh parsley leaves

¼ cup / 7g fresh cilantro leaves

Kosher salt

In a small bowl, combine the jalapeño and soy sauce and let marinate.

Separate the squid body and tentacles by cutting right below the eyes. Squeeze out and discard the hard beak from the tentacles; reserve the tentacles. Holding the body, pull out and discard the head, then the guts, ink sac, and clear skeleton. Working from the cut end of the body, grasp the thin speckled skin, peel toward the tip, and discard. Rinse well. Quarter the bodies lengthwise, then cut in half crosswise to get eight pieces from each body.

Put 1 cup / 140g of the cornstarch in a large bowl. In a separate large bowl, make a wet batter by whisking together the club soda, glutinous rice flour, rice flour, wok salt, and remaining ⅓ cup / 45g cornstarch.

To make the vinaigrette: Warm a small frying pan over medium heat. Add the 1 tsp neutral oil and let it heat up for a few seconds. Add the green onion and saute until softened, about 1 minute. Transfer to a large bowl, add the pecan oil and vinegar, and whisk to combine. Set aside.

Fill a wok or a Dutch oven with the 1½ qt / 1.4L neutral oil and secure a deep-fry thermometer on the side. Set over medium-high heat and warm the oil to 375°F, being careful to maintain this temperature as you fry.

Preheat the oven to 200°F. Fit a roasting wire rack over a baking sheet.

Toss the squid in the plain cornstarch until evenly coated. Tap off the excess and then drop the squid into the wet batter, making sure every crevice is coated. Transfer to a colander and shake the excess batter back into the bowl.

A small handful at a time, slide the squid into the oil and fry, stirring occasionally to break up any pieces that stick together, until light golden brown, crisp, and cooked through, about 2 minutes. Transfer to the prepared rack, season generously with more wok salt, and keep warm in the oven as you fry the rest.

Whisk the vinaigrette again. Add the parsley, cilantro, and jalapeño and soy sauce. Season with kosher salt and toss to combine. Add the squid and toss again. Serve while the squid is hot with additional wok salt on the side.

POACHED SPOT PRAWNS

Active Time — 20 minutes

Plan Ahead — You'll need 30 minutes, plus time to make Basic Chile Oil and Fermented Chile Paste

Makes 2 to 4 servings

Special Equipment — Instant-read thermometer, blender, cheesecloth, kitchen twine

Peel of ½ lemon, plus ½ lemon, cut into wedges

¼ cup / 10g star anise pods

2 Tbsp coriander seeds

2½ tsp red Sichuan peppercorns

3 dried árbol chiles

3 bay leaves

1 lb / 450g live spot prawns

¼ cup / 60ml neutral oil

5 tsp Basic Chile Oil (page 40)

1½ tsp Fermented Chile Paste (page 43)

Flake salt

Sometimes I daydream about having fish tanks at Mister Jiu's, so we can keep our seafood swimming until just before a customer orders it. Unfortunately, I learned, installing them would require tearing out our kitchen, so for now the liveliest seafood we serve comes whenever the sweet, sweet words "spot prawns available" show up on our seafood purveyors' list. Their boats chase down a run of spot prawns and deliver them to us the next morning, still kicking. Poached shrimp, baahk cheuk hā (白灼蝦), are classic Cantonese fare and all about enjoying the pleasures of fresh, unadulterated seafood cooked to just done. Nothing else will make these shrimp any better than a little chile oil, a squeeze of lemon, and some flake salt. The only problem is, when I taste the freshness of a prawn that was just alive a couple seconds ago, I go back to daydreaming of those tanks again.

Fill a large pot with 3 qt / 2.8L water and bring to a simmer over high heat. Wrap a double layer of cheesecloth around the lemon peel, star anise, coriander, peppercorns, árbols, and bay leaves and tie closed with kitchen twine to make a sachet. Add the sachet to the water, turn the heat to medium, and let this poaching liquid simmer for 20 minutes.

Meanwhile, check the prawns under the tail for the roe, which ranges from golden to crimson. Scrape off any eggs and set aside to add to the sauce. Refrigerate the prawns until ready to cook.

In a small saucepan over low heat, combine the neutral oil, chile oil, and chile paste and warm for a few minutes. If you have roe, stir it into this sauce and cook until the roe brightens in color, about 30 seconds. Scrape the sauce into a blender and blend briefly until it emulsifies and turns a bright orange but is still a bit chunky, about 15 seconds. Pour into a small bowl.

Secure an instant-read thermometer to the side of the pot. Set the pot over high heat and bring the poaching liquid to a boil, then turn the heat to medium until the liquid is at 180°F or slightly cooler. Add the prawns and poach gently until just cooked through—the thickest part of the tails should have just turned opaque, 1 to 1½ minutes. Drain well and transfer to a large bowl.

Drizzle the prawns with ¼ cup / 60ml of the sauce, sprinkle with ½ tsp salt, and toss until the prawns are well coated. Spoon the remaining sauce onto a serving plate and top with the dressed prawns. Pour any sauce left in the bowl over the prawns, and sprinkle with more salt, if needed.

Serve immediately with the lemon wedges and a stack of napkins. Have diners pull the head off a shrimp and suck out the creamy juices, then peel off the shell, sprinkle with lemon juice, and eat by hand.

HANGTOWN EGG FOO YOUNG

Active Time — 30 minutes

Plan Ahead — You'll need to time to make Matsutake Broth, Lap Yuk, and Potato Crisps

Makes 1 or 2 servings

Special Equipment — Oyster knife

⅓ cup / 80ml Matsutake Broth (page 213)

1 tsp water

1 tsp cornstarch

6 small raw oysters (such as Miyagis)

3 eggs

1 tsp oyster sauce

½ tsp kosher salt

1 Tbsp rendered lard or pork fat

2-inch piece Lap Yuk (page 47), cut into ¼-inch-thick, 1-inch-long matchsticks

½ cup / 30g bean sprouts

1½ Tbsp minced Chinese chives

1 Tbsp Potato Crisps (see page 143)

Early in conceptualizing the menu for Mister Jiu's, I thought about Hangtown Fry and egg foo young, two dishes born from the same place and era of hard times and division. Fùh yùhng (芙蓉) is actually classic Cantonese technique (the eggs are meant to bloom like "hibiscus" in the wok), but Cantonese cuisine leans toward light sauces. Adding brown sauce, or "Chinese gravy," was an innovation of early Chinese cooks in America. You could argue, egg foo young isn't authentic Chinese cuisine, but I don't think that makes it inherently less soulful food. Egg foo young led more people to dive deeper into Chinatown. Its popularity kept Chinatowns bumping. You can still taste the originals—egg foo young at Far East Cafe by the Grant Avenue gate, and Hangtown Fry at Tadich Grill just down the hill. In my mashup, I use creamy oysters such as kumamotos or Miyagis, and salty Virginia ham, and keep the eggs soft. These two dishes have more in common than they do differences. They should have been friends a long time ago.

In a small saucepan over medium heat, bring the broth to a simmer. In a small bowl, stir together the water and cornstarch until the cornstarch is suspended, then whisk into the broth and simmer until thickened into a gravy, 15 to 30 seconds. Remove from the heat and cover to keep warm.

Shuck the oysters, placing the oysters in a small bowl and the liquor in a separate medium bowl. Add the eggs, oyster sauce, and salt to the liquor and whisk until very well combined and no streaks of egg white remain.

In 10-inch nonstick frying pan over medium heat, warm the lard until melted, then swirl the pan to coat the bottom. Add the lap yuk and cook until lightly browned, about 1 minute per side. Add the oysters and cook 1 minute, then add the bean sprouts and cook 30 seconds more. Make sure the oysters, lap yuk, and bean sprouts are evenly distributed in the pan.

Pour the egg mixture over everything and sprinkle with the chives. As the eggs on the edge set, use a heatproof rubber spatula to gently lift those parts, then tilt the pan so that the unset eggs can run underneath. Cook until the eggs are almost set but just a little wet on top, about 3 minutes total.

Remove the pan from the heat and sprinkle with the potato crisps. Using the spatula, nudge and fold the top third of the fry over the center, then continue rolling toward the bottom. Slide the eggs onto a plate. Stir the mushroom gravy, then spoon over the fry and serve immediately.

There's nothing like Cantonese barbecue, sīu meih (燒味), the tantalizing cuts of meat basking in the golden glow of Chinatown's windows. You have your choice of glistening char siu pork, siu yuk (roast pork belly with crispy skin), roasted birds of every sort, and all kinds of offals and off cuts basted with a master stock of drippings and aromatics, compounded over time.

Cantonese barbecue demands specialized equipment, a lot of space, and late hours. Roasting is done on forks or spits over open flames, on racks in domed kiln ovens fired by coals, and, most commonly in Chinatown, hanging on hooks in a cylindrical oven with a round top and flames below. The round shape of mìhng fó lòuh (明火爐) circulates the heat automatically around a whole pig or a rack of char siu, without any help from a convection fan. These roasting ovens have been used for centuries and derive from the round tandoor brought from the west by the Silk Road.

In Chinatown, early restaurants built the distinctive cone-shaped ovens out of brick, a few feet tall and wide, covered with a piece of heavy iron, in the alleys. Locals say you could smell meat roasting and see smoke billowing from ovens tucked into the narrowest gaps between buildings into the 1960s. Eventually, wood-fired brick ovens became gas-fired and punched from steel. Now those ovens are called taai hūng lòuh (太空爐), space-age rocket ovens, but the method of roasting is still the same. (Barbecue master Eric Cheung is pictured opposite with one of Hing Lung's ovens.)

Cantonese barbecue is about controlling the fire as much as the water. With American barbecue, you might make a dry rub for the outside and then smoke the meat. You usually don't add or take away water in the process. With Cantonese barbecue, most cuts of meat include the skin, so the Cantonese way involves blanching and basting the meat while drying the skin and fat for a true roast, rather than a steam. With pork belly, you prick the skin so that the fat can render through it, an auto-marinade that keeps the meat juicy and fries the skin crisp. Westerners skewer shut the cavities of birds to lock in moisture. But with Chinese duck, you do everything possible to take away moisture, by blowing air under the skin to separate it from the meat and then hanging the bird to dry in the breeze. It's all about finding that balance of time for enough of the fat and collagen to do their thing, the proteins to cook and firm up without drying out, and the skin to develop a succulent or crackling texture that is out of this world.

To get your oven to work for you, remove all but the center rack, so whatever you're roasting has space to itself. Put the meat on a roasting rack set in a very low-rimmed sheet pan so heat can circulate and not just reflect back on certain parts. Turn on the convection, if you have it; otherwise plan to rotate the pan regularly, every 15 minutes. If you want to go all-in and your oven is big enough, hang your meat. Cut whatever you're roasting down to size. Set a rack at the highest slot of the oven, and put a pan on the bottom for drippings. Slide a meat hook through a sturdy part of the meat, like the neck or a thick muscle, and then hang it from the rack. Now you've got your own hang-roasting oven.

FOUR SEAS CRISPY CHICKEN

Active Time — 50 minutes

Plan Ahead — You'll need time to make Wok Salt or Shrimp Salt and Fermented Mustard Greens. Start 3 days before with trimming and dry-brining the chickens and making the vegetable-chip base. Then 2 days out, blanch and marinate the chickens and steam and dehydrate the vegetable chips.

Makes 4 to 8 servings

Special Equipment — Food processor, steamer, dehydrator, deep-fry thermometer, Microplane

Two 2- to 2½-lb / 900g to 1.1kg small chickens or Cornish game hens

3 tsp kosher salt

1½ Tbsp sweet potato vinegar or red wine vinegar

1 tsp brown rice syrup

1 tsp fresh lemon juice

¼ cup / 60ml water

Vegetable Chips

¾ cup / 115g drained Fermented Mustard Greens (page 41), coarsely chopped, plus 2 Tbsp liquid

⅓ cup plus ¼ cup / 95g small, white tapioca pearls

2 qt / 1.9L neutral oil

½ garlic clove

1 large handful red or green watercress

½ tsp sherry vinegar

½ tsp melted chicken fat

Kosher salt

Lemon wedges for serving

Wok Salt or Shrimp Salt (see page 37)

I always thought my grandfather Yeh Yeh disapproved of me cooking. But the week after I signed the lease to take over the Four Seas space, he gave me a clipping from the *San Francisco Chronicle* that he had carefully saved in a filing cabinet for fifteen years. It was the recipe for Four Seas Whole Crispy Skin Chicken (金牌炸子雞) by Chef Jing Yu Tan, which called for salting, blanching, and then at least a day of basting with maltose (a wheat-and-soy-based syrup) and red rice vinegar to get a crackly, golden skin. Before that moment, it hadn't totally registered that all those papers in Yeh Yeh's cabinet, all those books stacked around his recliner, were recipes and cookbooks. How had I missed the entire Time Life series of *Flavors of the World* on his bookshelf? Turns out, Yeh Yeh understood me. I've made some modifications to Chef Tan's recipe. Instead of a fryer chicken, I prefer a small choice or Cornish game hen. I baste with a brown rice syrup blend, which has more savory, caramel undertones than maltose alone, and sweet potato vinegar, which has a nice sweet sourness. We dry-brine the chickens for two days, then serve with a side of crisp watercress and lemon, or with chips (shrimp as pictured opposite or fermented mustard green as in this recipe), because Yeh Yeh loved them.

Fit a wire rack over a baking sheet.

Trim the wing tips from each chicken. Using poultry shears, cut along both sides of the backbone and remove it. (Save the wing tips and backbones for chicken stock, see page 34.) Cut each chicken into two pieces down through the breastbone (we have a huge pot and a dedicated deep fryer, so we leave it whole as pictured). Season the chicken all over with 2 tsp of the salt. ❶ Place skin-side up on the prepared rack and refrigerate for at least 8 hours or up to overnight.

Bring a large pot of heavily salted water (it should remind you of seawater) to a boil over high heat.

Meanwhile, in a small bowl, whisk together the vinegar, brown rice syrup, lemon juice, ¼ cup / 60ml water, and remaining 1 tsp salt until the salt and syrup are dissolved. Set this marinade aside.

Place half the chicken in the boiling water ❷ and blanch just until the skin turns white, about 10 seconds. Remove from the water ❸ and pat very dry with paper towels. Place, skin-side up, back on the wire rack. Repeat with the remaining chicken. Brush the skin with the marinade, ❹ then transfer the chicken and the remaining marinade to the refrigerator and chill, uncovered, for 2 days. Brush the skin with more marinade twice a day.

To make the chips: In a food processor fitted with the blade attachment, combine the mustard greens and liquid and process until finely chopped, like pickle relish, scraping down the sides of the bowl as needed. Add the tapioca and process until well combined (the tapioca will stay whole), about 45 seconds.

CONTINUED

Scrape the mixture out onto the center of a 16-inch-long sheet of parchment paper. Cover with a sheet of plastic wrap. Use a rolling pin to roll the mixture into an even rectangular layer no thicker than a tapioca pearl. Slide onto a baking sheet and refrigerate overnight so the tapioca pearls can hydrate.

Prepare a steamer in a wok or a large, lidded pot following the instructions on page 167, and bring the water to a boil over medium-high heat.

Remove the plastic wrap from the baking sheet. Using kitchen shears, cut the sheet of chips and parchment in half or into thirds so that it will fit into your steamer. Trim off any excess parchment paper so that the paper extends past the chips by about ½ inch, and so it does not cover the steamer bottom entirely. Steam one sheet at a time until the tapioca pearls are clear, 20 to 25 minutes. Add water to the pot between batches, as needed.

If you have a dehydrator, use it set to 135°F. Otherwise, preheat the oven to 150°F and place the sheets of chips, still on parchment, on a wire roasting rack.

Dehydrate or bake for 1 hour, then remove the parchment paper. The chips should feel wet and rubbery at this point. Continue dehydrating or baking until the sheets are completely dried and brittle and snap easily, 4 to 6 hours total depending on your dehydrator or oven. Let cool, then snap into roughly 2-inch pieces; they can and will be irregular in shape. (At this point, you can transfer to an airtight container and store at room temperature for up to 3 months.)

Fit a wire rack over a baking sheet. Line a second baking sheet with a double layer of paper towels.

Fill the wok or a Dutch oven with the neutral oil and secure a deep-fry thermometer on the side. Set over medium-high heat and warm the oil to 350°F, being careful to maintain this temperature as you fry. In two batches, carefully place the chicken in the oil and fry, flipping occasionally, until the skin is dark golden brown and the chicken is cooked through, about 10 minutes. Transfer, skin-side up, to the prepared rack and let rest for 5 minutes. Optional bonus move before resting—heat the oil to 400°F, then ladle the oil over the bird to make the skin extra golden and crisp. **5**

Meanwhile, reheat the oil to 375°F. Add a handful of the vegetable chips and fry. At first, they will sink to the bottom; when they start to float, stir so that they don't stick together. They are ready when they puff and float to the top, about 30 seconds. Transfer to the prepared baking sheet and repeat with the remaining chips.

Using a Microplane, grate the garlic into a medium bowl. Add the watercress, vinegar, and chicken fat; season with salt; and toss to combine.

Cut each chicken half into four pieces: drumstick, thigh, and two breast pieces. **6**–**7** Arrange on a platter, season with kosher salt, **8** and top with the dressed watercress and vegetable chips. Serve with the lemon wedges and some wok salt or shrimp salt for dipping.

WHITE-CUT CHICKEN GALANTINE

The galantine is a dish of French culinary mastery, the most notorious of cooking-school final exams. It calls for removing every bone from a chicken, grinding some of the meat to a smooth paste and carefully butchering the rest, and then forming it all into a cylinder encased in its own skin. Mike Tusk at Quince first showed me the technique, and I really enjoyed learning its intricacies. The butchering and assembling we do in this version is French, but the cooking and flavors are all Chinese, which makes this one of the most demanding recipes that we pull off in our kitchen in not just the mechanics but in controlling flavors and textures. The closest flavor inspirations are Cantonese white-cut chicken, baahk chit gāi (白切雞), and the related Hainan chicken, two dishes that require their own show of mastery. To make white-cut chicken, you poach a whole chicken (preferably small, male, and castrated) in a concentrated chicken stock multiple times until the meat is just seconds away from set, then shock it in cold water to tighten up the skin, before cleaving it just so at the bones to expose the red marrow. You serve it reconstructed with a side of green onion–ginger sauce. Both the galantine and white-cut chicken are served cold or room temperature and require precision. Both are about eating the whole animal—dark meat, light meat, skin, and bones made into stock. To me, our white-cut galantine isn't so much showing off as it is about how cultures can think differently of what's "delicious" and "refined" and still meet at the same place.

Active Time — 3½ hours

Plan Ahead — You'll need about 12 hours for chilling and poaching the meat, gelling the aspic (optional), and overnight for setting it in the refrigerator, plus time to make Chicken Stock and Wok Salt

Makes 16 servings

Special Equipment — Food processor, boning knife, cheesecloth, kitchen twine

Chicken Galantine

1 Tbsp neutral oil

¾ cup / 45g thinly sliced (crosswise) green onions

⅓ cup / 45g finely chopped celery

One 4-lb / 1.8kg whole chicken

3½ Tbsp cold heavy cream

Kosher salt

2½ to 3½ qt / 2.4 to 3.3L cold Chicken Stock (page 34)

Green Onion–Ginger Sauce

½ cup / 30g thinly sliced (crosswise) green onions

⅓ cup / 50g peeled and minced ginger

1 tsp kosher salt

½ tsp granulated sugar

⅓ cup / 80ml unrefined peanut oil

To make the galantine: Warm a wok or small frying pan over medium heat. Add the neutral oil and heat it a few seconds. Add the green onions and celery and cook until just tender but not browned, 6 to 8 minutes. Transfer to a bowl and set aside in the refrigerator.

Have a large plate or baking sheet handy for the galantine parts, as well as a plate for bones and scraps.

Position the chicken breast-side down on a cutting board with the legs facing you. Keeping the skin intact in one piece, use a boning knife to cut a vertical line down the backbone through the skin from the neck to the tail until you hit bone. ❶

Working with one side at a time, pull the skin away from the backbone and cut it and any meat, including the oyster, attached to the skin away from the bones by sliding the knife along the rib cage. ❷ When you get to the ball joint where the thigh attaches to the backbone, dislocate the thighbone by pushing it up. This will expose the ball joint; cut around it so that you can keep cutting down, stopping when you get to the skin covering the breasts.

Dislocate and pop up the ball joint where the drumette of the wing attaches to the backbone, toward you to expose it, ❸ then cut around the joint. When both sides are done, the chicken should lie flat like a book with the spine at the center. ❹

Lift the chicken at the neck to locate the V-shaped wishbone at the base. Hold on to the wishbone as you pull the neck, backbone (with the tenderloin still attached), and rib cage up and away from the rest of the bird. ❺ – ❻

CONTINUED

5 egg whites,
    at room temperature
1½ lb / 680g ground chicken
1 Tbsp peeled and coarsely
    chopped ginger
1 Tbsp thinly sliced (crosswise)
    green onions
1 tsp white peppercorns
One ¼-oz / 7g envelope
    powdered gelatin
2 Tbsp minced shallot
2 Tbsp sweet potato vinegar
1 lb / 450g haricots verts,
    tops trimmed
1 tsp light soy sauce
    (生抽, sāng chāu)
Wok Salt (see page 37)
Crushed roasted, unsalted
    peanuts for sprinkling
Chervil for sprinkling

Cut off the wings at the drumettes. There will be holes in the skin where the wings were; cut from the holes to the edge of the skin so that the skin can lay flat. Place the wishbone, backbone, and wings on the bone plate.

Using your hands and the knife as needed, carefully separate as much of the skin from the legs as you can. When you get near the bony end of the drumstick, pull the leg and skin in opposite directions so that you can remove the whole leg from the skin, like taking off a tight shirt. **7** There will be holes in the skin where the drumsticks were; once again, cut from the holes to the edge of the skin so that the skin can lay flat.

Cut between the meat on the breasts just until you hit the skin. Peel each breast from the skin. **8** Trim off any scraps of meat still clinging to the skin and place on the galantine plate. Being careful not to puncture the skin, scrape off and discard any pockets of fat or blood. **9** If you have a cooking vessel that's at least 15 inches long, like a fish poacher, keep the skin in one piece to make one long galantine. Otherwise, cut the skin in half from the neck to the tail to make two galantines, then transfer to the galantine plate.

Cut the breasts lengthwise into ½-inch-wide strips, **10** then transfer to the galantine plate. Cut the tenders (the long strips of meat) out of the breastbone, trim off any white slivers of tendon, and place on the galantine plate.

Separate the thighs and drumsticks by cutting through the joint between them (if you have trouble finding the joint, dislocate the thighbone first by pushing it up toward you). Cut and scrape the meat from the thighbone, removing any thin white slivers of tendons or bone fragments. Small-dice the thigh meat, then run your knife through it a few more times so that it's a little stickier. **11** Transfer to the galantine plate.

Cut the meat off the drumsticks the same way, again removing all the tendons or bone fragments. Small-dice the drumstick meat and any reserved scraps of meat, then run your knife through it until it's stickier than the thigh meat. Transfer to the galantine plate.

At this point, the galantine plate should have breast strips, two tenders, diced thigh and drumstick meat, and one or two pieces of chicken skin. **12** Save the wings, carcass, and any other trimmings for making stock.

Cut the tenders crosswise into 1-inch pieces. Weigh the tenders and add enough chicken breast strips until you reach 5 ¼ oz / 150g. Place back on the plate in a separate pile.

Make an ice bath by filling a large bowl with ice cubes and setting a medium bowl inside.

Transfer the thigh and drumstick meat to the bowl set over the ice bath, so that the meat stays cold. Place the chopped tenders/breasts in the bowl of a food processor fitted with the blade attachment and pulse about ten times, until it balls up around the blade. Check for and remove any stray tendons. With the motor running, slowly pour in the cream and process, stopping the motor and scraping down the sides of the bowl occasionally, until very smooth and gluey in texture, about 1 minute. Transfer to the bowl with the thigh meat, making sure to scrape everything off of the food processor blade.

Add the green onion mixture to the bowl, weigh the contents of the bowl, then calculate and add 2 percent of the weight in salt. Mix until this farce is thoroughly incorporated. Weigh the chicken breast strips, then calculate and toss with 2 percent of the weight in salt. Set both aside in the refrigerator.

Dampen the counter with a few drops of water to help sheets of plastic wrap stick. For one galantine, use two slightly overlapping sheets that are 24 inches long. (For two galantines, use two separate sheets that are 20 inches long.) Position the skin(s) smooth-side up with the legs closest to you on the bottom third of the plastic wrap, arranging gently so there are no major gaps.

Portion the farce into halves (or fourths, if doing two galantines). Spread one portion of the farce across the center of the skin(s) in a band, leaving a 2-inch border on both sides of the length of the skin. **13** Stack the chicken breast strips over the farce. **14** Spread another portion of the farce over the top, using an offset spatula or table knife to mold and smooth the farce to completely cover the strips. **15** (Repeat with the second galantine, if making.)

Fold the skin on the sides over the farce, then tightly roll up from the bottom. **16** It's okay if there are a few small patches not covered with skin, but the skin should be perfectly smooth. Roll it up tightly in the plastic wrap. Twist the plastic wrap on one end as tight as you can and tie a knot as close to the galantine as you can. **17** Holding on to both ends, roll the galantine along the counter a few times to tighten the plastic wrap. Twist and knot the other end. The bundle should feel taut like a balloon. If you find you're not getting the plastic tight enough, hold the roll vertically while twisting and let gravity help. Set aside in the refrigerator for 2 hours.

Line the counter with one 24 × 20-inch (or two 20 × 16-inch) sheet(s) of cheesecloth. Cut the ends off of the plastic wrap on the galantine(s), then carefully unwrap and place near the bottom of the cheesecloth. Working slowly and carefully, roll the galantine up as tightly as possible in the cheesecloth. After each roll, it's best to smooth the cheesecloth over the galantine and pull the remaining cheesecloth taut before continuing to roll. Twist the cheesecloth on one end as tight as you can and tie a knot as close to the galantine as you can. Tie kitchen twine between the knot and the galantine to make it even tighter. **18** Holding on to the tied end and the loose end, roll the galantine along the counter a few times to tighten the cheesecloth. Twist and tie the other end with a knot and kitchen twine. Set aside in the refrigerator for 2 hours more.

Place the chilled galantine(s) in a fish poacher, large pot, or Dutch oven wide enough that the galantine(s) sit flat. Add enough cold chicken stock to cover by ½ inch, keeping track of how much stock you use, then add 1½ tsp kosher salt for every 1 qt / 950ml stock. Bring to a simmer over medium-high heat. Remove from the heat, cover, and let sit until room temperature, about 4 hours (the galantine will cook in the residual heat). Transfer to the refrigerator, still in the poaching liquid, and let sit overnight.

CONTINUED

To make the sauce: In a medium heatproof bowl, combine the green onions, ginger, salt, and sugar. In a small saucepan over medium-high heat, warm the peanut oil until it is just starting to smoke. Pour over the green onions and ginger and stir to combine. Let cool to room temperature, about 20 minutes, then cover and store in the refrigerator for up to 3 days.

Remove the galantine(s) from the stock, unwrap and discard the cheesecloth, and then rewrap tightly in plastic wrap and return to the refrigerator. Place the stock in a large pot, preferably one that is tall instead of wide.

In a large bowl, whisk the egg whites until soft peaks form. Add the ground chicken, ginger, green onions, and peppercorns and fold until combined. Place in the cold stock and spread into an even layer. Warm over medium heat until it reaches a bare simmer and the egg mixture coagulates and forms what is called a "raft" at the top.

Poke and scoop out a hole about 3 inches wide in the center of the raft. Do not stir, but continue to cook at a low-enough temperature that the stock is moving but bubbles don't break the surface and it never comes to a boil. Occasionally ladle out some stock through the hole and pour it over the raft, which acts as a filter, until the stock is very clear and now a consommé, about 45 minutes.

Line a fine-mesh strainer with a double layer of cheesecloth and fit over a large bowl.

Ladle out the consommé through the hole into the prepared strainer (nudge the raft aside if needed), stopping when it gets too difficult to scoop out just the liquid. Discard the raft and the contents of the strainer.

Transfer 1¾ cups / 415ml of the consommé into a small saucepan. Transfer ¼ cup / 60ml consommé into a small bowl and refrigerate until chilled. (Save the rest of the consommé for sipping or using for soup.)

Sprinkle the gelatin over the chilled consommé and stir so all the gelatin is hydrated. Let sit while you bring the saucepan of consommé back to a boil. Remove the consommé from the heat and whisk in the hydrated gelatin until dissolved. Transfer to a 1-pint container. Let cool, cover, and refrigerate until it sets into a savory jelly, about 2 hours.

Bring a large saucepan of heavily salted water (it should remind you of seawater) to a boil over high heat. Meanwhile, prepare an ice bath in a large bowl by filling it with ice cubes and a little water.

In a small bowl, stir together the shallot and vinegar.

Drop the haricots verts in the boiling water and blanch until crisp-tender, 2 to 3 minutes.

Drain the haricots verts, then place in the ice bath. When cooled, remove from the water and pat dry.

Drain the vinegar from the shallots, then place the shallots in a large bowl. Add the haricots verts, soy sauce, ¼ cup / 120ml green onion–ginger sauce, and ¾ tsp wok salt and toss to combine. Taste and season with more green onion–ginger sauce or wok salt as needed.

Unwrap the galantine(s) and cut into ½-inch-thick slices. Top with dollops of aspic jelly and sprinkle with peanuts and chervil. Serve with the haricots verts salad alongside.

LIBERTY ROAST DUCK

Active Time — 2 hours

Plan Ahead — You'll need 10 to 14 days for curing, plus time to make 10 Spice, Chinese Pancakes, and Peanut Butter–Hoisin Sauce. Pull the duck out of the refrigerator to start tempering at least 8 hours before you plan to serve, so you have time for smoking, roasting, and carving.

Makes 4 to 6 servings

Special Equipment — Bicycle pump, 4 cups apple-wood smoking chips, food processor, kitchen twine, wooden chopstick or skewer, roasting pan with rack

One 6-lb / 2.7kg duck, preferably with head still attached
4 qt / 3.8L water
2 cups / 480ml distilled white vinegar, plus more for brushing
1 cup / 140g kosher salt
1½ cinnamon sticks
2 tsp juniper berries
1 tsp allspice berries
3 black cardamom pods (草果, chóu gwó)
1 tsp green peppercorns
2½ star anise pods
3 Tbsp brown rice syrup
1½ tsp dark soy sauce (老抽, lóuh chāu)
1 tsp 10 Spice (see page 36)

Duck is to Chinatown as pizza is to North Beach, chowder is to the Wharf, and burritos are to the Mission District. Whenever I pass glistening roast ducks hanging in a window, I have to stop and admire them. I wanted our roast duck to touch on this Chinatown experience but go in a new direction, of course. I knew I wanted to use Jim Reichardt's Liberty ducks (see page 207), which are about twice the size of the typical duck, with delicious, unctuous meat as delectable as the skin. In finding the best way to complement the ingredient, I ended up blending many techniques but in a new way. We use the air curing and lacquering techniques for Beijing roast duck but drawn out for a longer time, and also the smoking technique of a Sichuan camphor-tea duck but with local apple wood. We season the meat with warm spices sort of like with Cantonese roast duck, but not quite. We cook it to medium, slightly pink with a touch of gray, which is atypical of any Chinese roasted meat. Of all our recipes, this is the one that I don't think I will ever stop working on. There's so much history behind it and so many personal influences. Nudging this recipe closer to perfection is my holy grail.

Every step in this process matters to this recipe. Blanching tightens the skin and ensures it will have that crisp, satisfying texture and not turn bitter when you smoke and then roast the duck. It also helps the meat stay buttery and tender. Air curing removes most of the water from the skin and flesh, so it doesn't steam but instead caramelizes while the fat renders. When it's ready in about two weeks, the skin should be taut and sort of glow. Speeding things up with a fan or hair dryer won't have the same effect as slow, natural drying, unfortunately. You have to wait for that crispy skin/melty flesh mind-blowing experience.

If there are gizzards inside the duck, remove and set aside for gizzard confit. Remove any pockets of fat. Using tweezers (or needle-nose pliers) pull out stray pin feathers from the skin of the breast and legs. ❶

Separate the skin over the breasts from the meat, first by arranging the duck so that it is breast-side up. Working from the leg end, insert a clean bicycle pump between the breast meat and the skin, ❷ cinch it with one hand, and pump in enough air so the skin puffs up and separates from the meat. ❸ (It helps to have two people doing this—one to operate the pump and the other to keep everything airtight around the pump nozzle.) This can also be done, if you have a strong diaphragm, by using your mouth as the pump. (Send us pictures!)

If the duck has feet attached, pull the legs taut and cut off the feet through the joint where the knees meet the drumstick. Cut off the wings where the flat meets the drumette. ❹ Locate each thighbone, then dislocate by putting your thumb in the cavity and using the rest of your hand to push it up and into the cavity. ❺ Cut around one end of the bone to free it. Pull the bone out toward you and scrape off the meat along it until you can cut around the other end of the bone and pull it out. ❻ (Discard or save the trimmed parts for stock.) At this point, you will have a prepped duck with a sealed cavity ready for blanching.

CONTINUED

Duck Liver Mousse

1 lb / 450g duck livers
1 Tbsp neutral oil
Kosher salt
½ cup / 30g thinly sliced
    (crosswise) green onions
¼ cup / 30g diced shallots
4 tsp light soy sauce
    (生抽, sāng chāu)
1 tsp Shaoxing wine
1 Tbsp 10 Spice (see page 36)
1¼ cups / 275g unsalted butter,
    cut into ½-inch pieces,
    at room temperature

1 Persian or other small pickling
    cucumber, thinly sliced
⅓ cup / 80ml rice vinegar
3 Tbsp water
2¼ tsp granulated sugar
2½ tsp kosher salt
Flake salt
¼ cup / 15g thread-cut green
    onions (green parts only)
Cilantro for garnishing
16 Chinese Pancakes
    (page 51), warmed
Peanut Butter–Hoisin Sauce
    (page 37) for topping

You can blanch the duck in one of two ways. Either by completely submerging it in blanching liquid if you have a pot large enough (like a 16-quart stockpot) or by ladling the blanching liquid over the duck. If you go with submerging, sew the belly cavity closed with a chopstick or skewer by folding the tail flap up and over the cavity, ❼ then sewing through the skin and the tail flap in three places, until the cavity is as closed as much as possible. Secure the end of the chopstick or skewer by poking it into the breast meat (without piercing the skin) to anchor it. ❽ If you go with ladling, you don't need to sew the cavity closed; but fair warning, ladling does require keeping your hand very close to boiling water, or setting up some sort of rack if your duck doesn't have much of a neck to grab on to.

Fit a wire rack over a baking sheet.

In a large stockpot over high heat, combine the water, vinegar, salt, cinnamon, juniper, allspice, black cardamom, green peppercorns, and star anise and bring to a boil. Hold the duck by the head or neck and completely submerge it in the blanching liquid, or hold the duck (or set up a roasting rack to hold it) over the pot and ladle the blanching liquid onto the duck's shoulders so that it pours over every inch of skin. ❾ Continue until the skin turns white, taut, and firmer from parboiling, about 10 seconds submerged or twenty ladlefuls. Place the duck on the prepared rack and remove the chopstick or skewer if that makes things easier, but keep it handy. Brush the duck all over with a thin layer of vinegar.

Position the duck so that it is breast-side up. Push the neck-skin down into the shoulders, then cut off the head, leaving behind a little bit of neck so that the skin can be tied off around it. ❿ Using a knife, cut along the neckbone to expose the V-shaped wishbone, scrape along the top of the wishbone, put your fingers in behind the bone, and then pull it straight out. ⓫ Pull the skin on the neck back up to pull the skin over the breast taut and tie the neck closed with kitchen twine. ⓬–⓭ Pat the duck dry with paper towels.

In a small bowl, stir together the brown rice syrup, soy sauce, and 10 Spice and brush it all over the duck. ⓮ Arrange the duck so that it is breast-side down. Poke each end of the chopstick or skewer into the skin of the wing drumettes to keep the skin on the breast pulled taut. ⓯

Return the duck, breast-side up, to the rack (or if your refrigerator has room, stand the duck up on its legs and place on an unopened can of beer or soda over the baking sheet). Refrigerate for 10 to 14 days to cure, regularly dumping any liquid that collects. (A sign the bird is ready is if no liquid has accumulated on the baking sheet for 2 days.) Look for a taut, slightly translucent skin that feels dry and smooth except for some roughness of the pores.

To make the mousse: Trim any veins from the livers and drain off any blood. Warm a large frying pan or wok over medium heat. Add the neutral oil and let it heat up a few seconds. Add the livers, season lightly with salt, and cook until just pink in the middle but not browned, about 3 minutes. Using a slotted spoon, transfer the livers to a medium bowl.

Add the green onions and shallots to the pan, turn the heat to low, and cook until softened but with no browning, about 3 minutes. Remove from the heat. Add the soy sauce and wine and scrape up any browned bits from the bottom of the pan. Scrape into the bowl with the livers, add the 10 Spice and 1 tsp salt, and stir until well combined. Let cool until room temperature, about 30 minutes.

Transfer the liver mixture into a food processor fitted with the blade attachment and pulse until finely chopped, about ten pulses of 1 second each. Add the butter and process until smooth, scraping down the sides of the bowl as needed, 1 to 2 minutes. Scrape the mousse into a serving bowl and smooth the top. Press a sheet of plastic wrap onto the surface of the mousse and store in the refrigerator for up to 4 days or in the freezer for up to 2 months.

Let the duck sit at room temperature for 3 to 4 hours.

Meanwhile, remove all of the racks from the oven except one in the lowest position. Preheat the oven to 200°F. Prepare the wood chips and set up a smoking chamber for the duck with a roasting pan fitted with a roasting rack (see Chef's Note: Smoking, page 59). Line the inside of the roasting pan lengthwise with a few sheets of overlapping aluminum foil. Make sure that the bottom and sides of the pan are completely covered and that the excess foil extends over the long sides by at least 15 inches and slightly up and over the short sides of the pan.

Place the roasting pan over high heat. Once the wood chips are really smoking, turn off the flame. Place the rack back in the pan, then place the duck, breast-side up, on the rack. **16** Seal in the smoke quickly by bringing the long edges of the foil up to meet in the middle. Fold the foil down twice and then tightly crimp shut, leaving room above the surface of the duck for smoke to circulate. Bring the foil on the sides up to meet and crimp shut tightly, making sure the entire rack and duck are completely sealed in, with no foil touching the duck. **17**

Place the pan in the oven and smoke the duck for 20 minutes. (This step doesn't produce a ton of smoke, but you still may want to open a window or turn on the fan above your range.) Carefully open the foil pouch to repeat heating the wood chips, resealing the foil, and smoking twice more, for three rounds total. Transfer the pan to a heatproof surface. Carefully open the top seam of the foil and let the duck cool to room temperature, about 30 minutes. **18**

Meanwhile, preheat the oven to 450°F and turn on the convection if you have that setting. Line a rimmed baking sheet with foil.

Set the roasting rack with the duck on the prepared baking sheet. Roast for 12 minutes, rotate the baking sheet 90 degrees, and then roast for 12 minutes more. The duck should be a mahogany color at this point and cooked to medium, about 120°F. To test for doneness, insert a thermometer through the cavity to where the body meets the thigh, being careful not to puncture the skin. (A smaller bird will need less total roasting time, so test sooner.) Let the duck rest out of the oven for 15 minutes.

CONTINUED

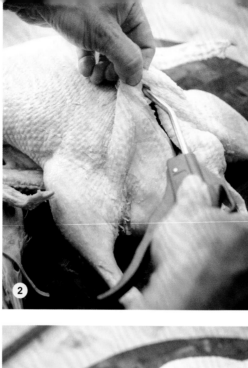

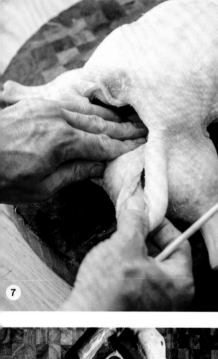

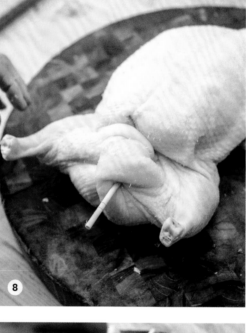

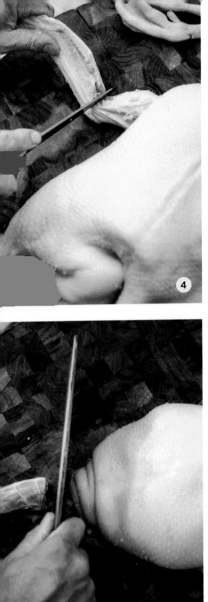

4

5

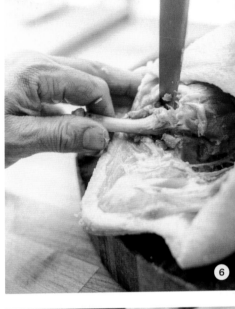

6

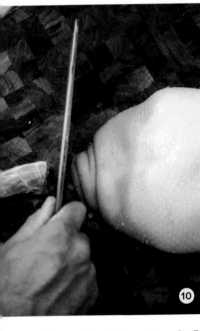

10

11

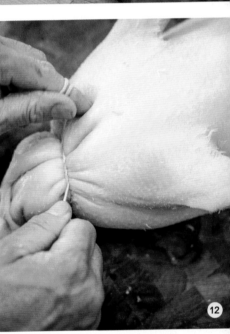

12

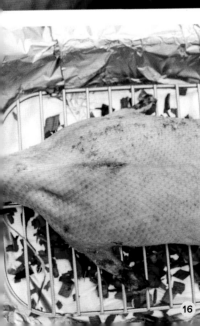

16

17

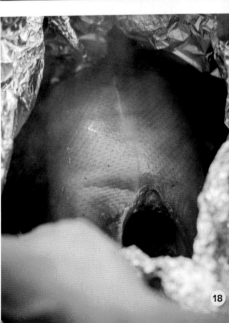

18

Place the cucumber in a medium bowl. In a small saucepan over medium heat, combine the rice vinegar, water, sugar, and kosher salt and cook, stirring, just until the sugar and salt are dissolved. Pour over the cucumber.

Remove the chopstick from the duck, drain the juices from the cavity, and then place the duck on a cutting board. Slice down either side of the breastbone, then carve around each breast, keeping as much skin from the breast and around the drumstick on the breast as possible, and remove the breasts. Season the meat side of the breasts with flake salt. Cut the tenders from the breasts and place on a serving platter. Slice the breasts crosswise into ½-inch-thick pieces and place on top of the tenders.

Carve off the legs, then cut between the thighs and drumsticks to separate them. Season the meat side of the thighs with flake salt, then thinly slice crosswise. Add to the duck platter, along with the drumsticks. Cut off the wing drumettes and add to the platter.

Drain the cucumbers and place on a plate. Add the green onions and cilantro. Serve the duck with the plate of green garnishes, Chinese pancakes, and dishes of peanut butter hoisin and duck liver mousse. Have diners spread some mousse on a pancake; top with one or two slices of duck; drizzle with peanut butter hoisin; finish with cucumber, cilantro, and green onions; and then roll up and eat.

ON LIBERTY ROAST DUCK

In 1972, US President Richard Nixon visited China and loved the roast duck in Beijing. Suddenly, there was a run on northern Chinese food and its duck in this country.

There had always been roast duck, Cantonese-style, hanging in barbecue-shop windows in Chinatown. Cantonese barbecue was grease-on-the-lips, rice-plate-for-the-people sort of food. But northern-style roast duck was billed as fine dining, subject to pre-ordering and a surcharge. Peking duck, as it was called then, appeared on Western menus after World War II brought a wave of mainland Chinese diplomats to Washington DC and New York. They arrived with private chefs who eventually opened their own restaurants. On the West Coast, Johnny Kan was one of the first to put a version of Peking duck on his menu in the 1950s. Cecilia Chiang served both tea-smoked duck and a more classic Peking duck at the Mandarin a decade later. But until Nixon, it was mainly Chinese clientele who ordered the duck.

In San Francisco, the ducks in most major restaurants and hotels came from the Reichardt family farm, which Otto Reichardt founded in 1901 with a flock descended from the first documented Pekin ducks to reach America. The original four ducks, a white-plumed variety of mallard, made it from Beijing to New York in 1873. From the start into the 1960s, the Reichardts had the keys to Chinatown's banquet restaurants and the butcher shops on Grant Avenue, delivering live birds in wooden coops every morning at 3 a.m. Chinese butchers in white coats processed and distributed the birds to restaurants around the city, from the Fairmont to Tadich Grill, a few hours later. After Nixon returned from China, the Reichardts were selling about 40,000 ducks a week to butchers and restaurants in both San Francisco and Oakland Chinatowns, and to Chinese restaurants in the South Bay.

Johnny Kan was among the Chinese restaurateurs who wanted birds raised to his specifications—fattened on corn, barley, oats, wheat, fishmeal, alfalfa, and rice to a hefty size, specifically for roast duck. His version wasn't pure northern- or southern-style. The skin of Beijing roast duck is puffed with air to separate it from the meat and lacquered with sweet maltose made from fermented barley. Then the bird is roasted, usually hanging over an open fire but sometimes slid into a charcoal kiln oven. Cantonese roast duck is marinated from the inside with warm spices and aromatics and hang-roasted in cylindrical ovens. Kan's combined the techniques and made necessary adaptations. "In Peking, the ducks hang all night while a south wind blows on them," he said. "Here we don't have a south wind, so . . . we use electric fans blowing north." In Beijing, the live ducks would be confined to baskets in their third month and force-fed grain multiple times a day to ensure tender meat streaked with fat. How they finished the birds at Kan's is lost to time; he kept the process and recipe secret.

Kan was early in the farm-to-table movement, but not the last when it came to ducks raised to order. Opening night at Chez Panisse in 1971 featured duck with olives as the main course—Reichardt ducks that Alice Waters had procured that morning from San Francisco's Chinatown. Waters and Barbara Tropp of China Moon would eventually ask for a meatier bird, which led Jim Reichardt, Otto's great-grandson, to break away from the farm and raise his own ducks in line with slow-food principles. Almost all the ducks sold in Chinatown are still raised and delivered at 3 a.m. by the original Reichardt Duck Farm, which is still one of only a handful of duck farms west of the Mississippi. Twice a week, during the early morning, Jim comes by Mister Jiu's, bringing his organic Liberty ducks.

SQUAB IN LETTUCE CUPS

Active Time — 2 hours

Plan Ahead — You'll need time to make Lap Cheong, Chicken Stock, 10 Spice, and Wok Salt. Start curing the squab 6 to 10 days out. You can pickle the sunchokes and make the glaze in advance too.

Makes 4 servings

Special Equipment — 2 unopened beer bottles (optional), deep-fry thermometer

Squab

Two 14-oz / 400g whole squabs

2 tsp kosher salt

2 Tbsp sweet potato vinegar
or sherry vinegar

2 Tbsp water

1½ tsp brown rice syrup

1 tsp fresh lemon juice

Squab Glaze

2 Tbsp oyster sauce

2½ Tbsp Shaoxing wine

4 tsp water

1 Tbsp granulated sugar

1 Tbsp packed
light brown sugar

½ tsp ground ginger

⅛ tsp 10 Spice (see page 36)

Mushroom-Jicama Filling

1 Tbsp chicken fat or schmaltz

2 tsp peeled and minced ginger

1 tsp minced garlic

¾ cup / 100g finely chopped
shallots

¾ cup / 50g small-diced fresh
shiitake mushrooms

⅔ cup / 80g small-diced
peeled jicama

Some of my closest friendships have come from cooking next to each other in high-intensity kitchens under the strict standards of our chef. Clocking out after a long day always felt like such an accomplishment that it usually meant celebrating. Most nights were drinking nights, but on occasion someone (usually me) would suggest going to Chinatown to grub down at Yuet Lee on Broadway. It serves food until 3 a.m., and sharing a feast and rounds of Tsingtao as a family all around the lazy Susan became a tradition. Once in a blue moon in fall, their cooks would hang a couple of whole squabs on hooks over their hotline, and I'd order one. I had cooked plenty of squabs in kitchens before even tasting one myself. Squabs are hard to come by, because females won't just mate with any male. They are also very delicate, so we served every precious bit, which meant nothing left to taste for ourselves. Those late nights at Yuet Lee were such a reward for a hard day's work. A dish with squab will always mean "celebration" to me.

To make the squab: Season the squabs all over with 1 tsp of the salt and let sit at room temperature for 1 hour. Meanwhile, in a small saucepan over low heat, combine the vinegar, water, brown rice syrup, lemon juice, and remaining 1 tsp salt and cook, stirring, just until the salt dissolves. Set this marinade aside.

Set up a large saucepan of boiling water and prepare an ice bath in a large bowl by filling it with ice cubes and a little water, both with room enough to submerge a squab. Dip one squab at a time, first in the boiling water for 10 seconds, and then immediately in the ice bath. Leave in the ice bath until chilled through, about 5 minutes. Remove from the ice bath and pat very dry, inside and out, with paper towels.

Brush the squabs outside and in with the marinade. Stand up the birds by propping over unopened beer bottles, or lay on a wire rack set over a baking sheet, and refrigerate, uncovered, for 6 to 10 days to cure (if using a rack, flip them daily). The squabs will shrink slightly and darken in color.

To make the glaze: In a small saucepan over low heat, combine the oyster sauce, wine, water, both sugars, ginger, and 10 Spice and cook, stirring until the sugar is dissolved. Let cool, transfer to an airtight container, and store in the refrigerator for up to 2 weeks.

To make the filling: In a wok or large frying pan over medium heat, warm the chicken fat until shimmering. Add the ginger and garlic and cook for 1 minute. Add the shallots and mushrooms and cook until just softened but not browned, about 2 minutes. Add the jicama, lap cheong, and chicken stock and cook until the liquid is evaporated, about 5 minutes. Stir in the oyster sauce, then stir in the pickled sunchokes and hazelnuts. Transfer to a serving bowl and keep warm.

¼ cup / 25g small-diced
   Lap Cheong (page 45)
¼ cup / 60ml Chicken Stock
   (page 34)
5½ tsp oyster sauce
⅓ cup / 50g drained, diced
   Pickled Sunchokes
   (recipe follows)
2 Tbsp toasted hazelnuts,
   coarsely chopped

1½ qt / 1.4L neutral oil
1 small fresh sunchoke,
   scrubbed and very thinly
   sliced to get at least 10 slices
2 tsp pickling liquid from
   Pickled Sunchokes
   (recipe follows)
1 tsp toasted sesame oil
1 tsp hazelnut oil
2 Fuyu persimmons, thinly
   sliced into rounds
1 head Castelfranco radicchio,
   or red radicchio, leaves
   separated
1 lemon, cut into 8 wedges
Wok Salt (see page 37)

Take the squab out of the refrigerator and let sit at room temperature for about 10 minutes. Line a plate with a double layer of paper towels. Fit a wire roasting rack over a baking sheet.

Fill the wok or a Dutch oven with the neutral oil and secure a deep-fry thermometer on the side. Warm the oil to 300°F over medium-high heat. Add the sliced sunchoke and fry until light golden brown and crisp, about 2 minutes. Transfer to the prepared plate to drain.

Now bring the oil up to 350°F. Add one squab at a time, making sure it is mostly submerged in the oil, and fry, turning occasionally; look for even dark-golden coloring, about 3 minutes for medium-rare. Transfer to the prepared rack. Set aside to rest for 6 minutes. (Seriously, we set a timer at the restaurant, because they carve up especially nicely at this point.)

Carve the breasts and legs off the squabs. Brush the skin with the glaze, then slice the breasts crosswise into 1-inch-wide pieces.

In a medium bowl, whisk together the pickling liquid, sesame oil, and hazelnut oil and toss with the persimmons. In a separate bowl, top the mushroom-jicama filling with the fried sunchokes. Have diners load each radicchio leaf with a slice of persimmon, a generous spoonful of filling, and a piece or two of squab. Top with a squeeze of lemon and a sprinkle of wok salt before eating.

PICKLED SUNCHOKES

4 oz / 115g sunchokes, scrubbed
   and sliced ¼ inch thick
½ cup / 120ml water
½ cup / 120ml apple cider vinegar

2 Tbsp granulated sugar
½ tsp kosher salt
½ tsp vanilla extract

Put the sunchokes in a 1-pint jar. In a small saucepan over high heat, combine the water, vinegar, sugar, salt, and vanilla and bring to a boil, stirring to ensure everything has dissolved. Immediately pour the liquid over the sunchokes. Let cool, then seal and store in the refrigerator overnight before eating, or for up to 1 month.

ON SQUAB

During the three decades that Angel Island detained Chinese arrivals, there were only a few officially documented riots. One was for soap and clean toilets; the others were in the dining hall over the food. According to historian Connie Young Yu, Chinese detainees fermented leftover rice to feed pigeons (a.k.a. squab) in the exercise yard. Once the birds were good and inebriated, they were easy enough to catch. Sympathetic Chinese cooks, hired in the dining hall following the protests, knew just how to roast them.

LION'S HEAD MEATBALLS

Active Time — 1 hour, 15 minutes

Plan Ahead — You'll need about 3 hours total, plus time to make Chicken Stock; pre-soak the clay pot for 2 hours

Makes 4 to 6 servings

Special Equipment — Meat grinder (optional), soaked 9-inch clay pot or a small Dutch oven

Lion's Head Meatballs

3 oz / 85g nettles or stemmed lacinato kale

1 tsp neutral oil

Kosher salt

4 oz / 115g skin-on pork belly

12 Savoy cabbage leaves, thick stems trimmed

12 oz / 340g pork shoulder, cut into 1½-inch pieces

3 oz / 85g pork back fat

3½ oz / 100g medium-firm doufu

4 tsp peeled and minced ginger

1½ Tbsp light soy sauce (生抽, sāng chāu)

1 Tbsp powdered milk

1¼ tsp freshly ground white pepper

1 tsp fish sauce

1½ cups / 360ml Matsutake Broth (recipe follows)

2 Tbsp neutral oil

3 oz / 85g fresh wild mushrooms (such as matsutake, black trumpets, or chanterelles), chopped if large

½ rosemary sprig, about 2 inches long

Kosher salt

Anything that needs slow braising will do well in a clay pot. The porous clay distributes an encompassing gentle heat all while sealing in the juices. The slightly alkaline clay also keeps proteins loose and tender. I appreciate a clay pot for its kindness to cooks. It holds heat so well that you can set it aside off-heat for an hour or two and come back to find everything inside still nice and toasty. And if you don't have one, a small Dutch oven with a tight lid will do. Lion's head (獅子頭, shī zi tóu in Mandarin) are a classic Chinese meatball (the bumpy texture looks like the curly manes of mythical lions). We use savory ingredients—mushrooms, seaweed, and a blend of pork—that compounds the sīn flavor exponentially. Use whatever delicious fungi you've got. Sometimes I drop a handful of fresh cordyceps (蟲草花, chóng cǎo huá) sautéed with garlic (pictured on page 216), or shave matsutake as in this recipe. For the bacon, choose an intensely smoky kind. You can use a meat grinder or hand-chop everything old-school.

To make the meatballs: While wearing thick gloves, strip the leaves from the nettles and discard the stems.

In a wok or a medium frying pan over medium-high heat, warm the neutral oil until shimmering. Add the nettles and a pinch of salt and cook until wilted but still bright green, about 1½ minutes. If using kale, this will take about 3 minutes. Finely chop and set aside.

Bring a large saucepan of water to a boil over high heat. Line a baking sheet with a double layer of paper towels.

Remove the skin from the pork belly. Add the skin to the boiling water and blanch for 30 seconds to firm up. Using tongs, remove and set aside. Add the cabbage leaves (work in batches, if needed) to the water and blanch until just wilted, about 30 seconds, then transfer to the prepared baking sheet to drain.

Place the pork skin, pork shoulder, belly, and back fat in a single layer on a plate and put in the freezer until the surface is just frozen but the center is still soft enough to be ground, about 15 minutes.

If using a meat grinder, grind the fat and skin through a fine grinding plate (⅛-inch / 3mm holes) into a large bowl. Switch to a coarse grinding plate (¼-inch / 6mm holes). Regrind about half of the fat-skin mixture back into the large bowl, then grind the shoulder and belly through the same grinding plate. Mix gently to combine. Regrind about half of the pork mixture again. Grind the doufu through the coarse grinding plate into the large bowl.

If chopping by hand, separately mince the pork belly skin, pork belly, pork shoulder, pork fat, and doufu using a chef's knife or cleaver (two if you got 'em). Transfer to a large bowl as each one has formed a sticky paste and then mix well.

Add the nettles, ginger, soy sauce, powdered milk, 1½ tsp salt, pepper, and fish sauce to the bowl and use your hands to mix until well combined and a sticky paste forms but the meat is not overworked.

CONTINUED

3 Tbsp toasted pine nuts
1 fresh matsutake mushroom,
    very thinly sliced or shaved
    with a mandoline

Divide the mixture into six portions. Roll each portion into a ball that is firmly packed and smooth. Wrap a cabbage leaf around each meatball, leaving the top exposed (save the remaining cabbage leaves for the clay pot). Refrigerate until ready to cook, up to 4 hours.

Preheat the oven to 450°F.

Place the wrapped meatballs in a single layer in a soaked 9-inch-wide clay pot or small Dutch oven. Tuck the remaining cabbage leaves between the meatballs, then add the broth. Bring to a simmer over medium-high heat.

Transfer the pot to the oven and bake uncovered until the meatballs are browned and cooked through, about 30 minutes.

Meanwhile, warm a wok or a medium frying pan over medium-high heat. Add the neutral oil and let it heat up for a few seconds. Add the mushrooms and rosemary, season with salt, and stir-fry until the mushrooms are browned, 3 to 4 minutes. Discard the rosemary.

Spoon the stir-fried mushrooms and any oil left in the pan over the meatballs and top with the pine nuts and shaved mushroom. Serve immediately.

MATSUTAKE BROTH

Makes 1½ cups / 360ml

1 slice thick-cut bacon
⅛ medium yellow onion
1 qt / 950ml Chicken Stock (page 34)
5 pieces dried matsutake mushrooms

1 small dried shiitake mushroom
One 3 × 1-inch piece kombu
1 Tbsp fish sauce

In a large saucepan over medium-high heat, sear the bacon until dark golden brown, 5 to 7 minutes. Transfer to a plate. Add the onion to the pan and sear until very browned on one side, 1 to 2 minutes. Turn the heat to medium-low; add the seared bacon, chicken stock, both dried mushrooms, and kombu; and simmer until reduced to 1½ cups / 360ml, about 1 hour.

Fit a fine-mesh strainer over a medium bowl. Strain the broth and discard the solids. Stir the fish sauce into the broth. Let cool, transfer to an airtight container, and store in the refrigerator for up to 5 days, or in the freezer for up to 2 months.

DUTCH CRUNCH BBQ PORK BUNS

Active Time — 2½ hours

Plan Ahead — You'll need 4 to 5 days for marinating the char siu, and braising and drying the pork for the floss. The day before, roast and chill the char siu, roast the beets, and make the BBQ pork sauce. The morning of serving, make the Milk Bread Dough and topping, before you finish baking the buns.

Makes forty 2½-inch buns

Special Equipment — Blender, stand mixer, spice grinder

Char Siu
One 1½-lb / 680g piece
    skinless, boneless pork belly
    or boneless pork shoulder
½ cup / 120ml strained
    beet juice
¼ cup / 60ml water
3½ Tbsp Shaoxing wine
5½ tsp oyster sauce
2 Tbsp granulated sugar
4 tsp honey
1 piece fermented red doufu
1½ Tbsp coarsely chopped
    garlic
1½ tsp dark soy sauce
    (老抽, lóuh chāu)
½ tsp 5 Spice (see page 36)
Kosher salt

BBQ Pork Sauce
1 medium red beet
1 cup / 240ml water
1 pinch kosher salt
2 Tbsp hoisin sauce
1½ Tbsp neutral oil
5½ tsp oyster sauce
1 tsp rice vinegar
1 tsp light soy sauce
    (生抽, sāng chāu)
1 tsp Chinese rose wine
½ piece fermented red doufu
¼ tsp 5 Spice (see page 36)

As kids, my siblings and I were always on the lookout for char siu bao. Either steamed white and fluffy buns that pulled apart from the center, or the golden ones baked and glazed with a domed honey top. When we found good ones, with just the right crimson-pork ratio, it was like finding a gold mine. We would tell only family where to find them. In Hong Kong, dim sum chefs tried new approaches, transplanting the tops of sweet, crunchy pineapple bao onto pork buns. Seeing those new-style buns blew my mind. I thought of Dutch Crunch, the topping native to local Bay Area delis and the bread of choice for a great cold-cut sandwich. Our pork buns draw from all these inspirations. To the tops, I added pork floss, ròu sōng (肉鬆, in Mandarin), for the intensely roasted flavor that reminds me of the crispy edges of char siu pork, which you can never get enough of. Leftover pork buns can be refrigerated up to 3 days. Reheat in a 300°F oven until warmed through, about 10 minutes.

To make the char siu: Cut the pork into roughly 3-inch-wide and 2½- to 3-inch-thick pieces (length doesn't really matter). Put into a large zip-top bag.

In a blender, combine the beet juice, water, wine, oyster sauce, sugar, honey, doufu, garlic, soy sauce, 5 Spice, and ½ tsp salt and blend until smooth. Pour into the bag, seal, and massage to coat the pork. Refrigerate for 4 to 5 days, flipping the bag every day so that the pork marinates evenly.

Preheat the oven to 250°F. Line a rimmed baking sheet with aluminum foil, then fit with a wire roasting rack.

Remove the pork from the marinade (no need to wipe off excess), season lightly with salt, and place on the prepared rack. Slow roast until the internal temperature of the pork registers 145°F, 1½ to 2 hours. Let cool, then wrap tightly in plastic wrap. Refrigerate overnight, weighed down with a heavy pot or cans to help the pork firm up.

To make the sauce: Preheat the oven to 400°F.

In a small baking dish, combine the beet, water, and salt. Cover tightly with aluminum foil and roast until knife-tender, 1½ to 2 hours. Let cool, then peel and dice.

In a blender, combine 3½ oz / 100g of the diced beet, the hoisin sauce, neutral oil, oyster sauce, rice vinegar, soy sauce, rose wine, doufu, and 5 Spice and blend to a completely smooth, burgundy-hued sauce. (Any remaining beet can be reserved for another use.) Transfer the sauce to an airtight container and store in the refrigerator for up to 5 days, or in the freezer for up to 3 months. If needed, re-whisk before using.

To make the topping: In a stand mixer fitted with the paddle attachment, combine the butter and brown sugar and beat on medium speed until light in color and fluffy, about 2 minutes. Add the bread flour, rice flour, and pork floss and mix on low speed until a sticky dough forms, about 1 minute.

CONTINUED

DUTCH CRUNCH BBQ PORK BUNS continued

Dutch Crunch Topping

6 Tbsp / 85g unsalted butter, at room temperature

⅓ cup / 65g packed light brown sugar

⅓ cup / 45g bread flour

⅓ cup / 35g rice flour (粘米粉, jīm máih fán)

⅓ cup / 30g Ròu sōng (Pork Floss) (facing page)

1 recipe Milk Bread dough (see page 48), made through Step 3

Transfer the dough to a 16-inch-long sheet of parchment paper and cover with a second sheet of parchment paper. Using a rolling pin, roll the dough out to a rough 8½ × 13-inch rectangle, about ¹⁄₁₆ inch thick. Leave the dough between the parchment and set on a baking sheet, transfer to the freezer, and freeze until firm, about 15 minutes.

Move the dough to a cutting board and uncover. Using a knife or pizza cutter, trim off any ragged edges and then cut into forty 1½-inch squares; do not separate the squares. Cover once more with parchment, place back on the baking sheet, and set aside in the freezer. (If not using within a day, wrap tightly in a few layers of plastic wrap before freezing.)

Position racks in the upper and lower thirds of the oven and preheat the oven to 425°F. Line two baking sheets with parchment paper.

Dice the char siu into ⅓-inch cubes. In a large bowl, toss the char siu with the BBQ pork sauce until evenly coated. Portion and form the milk bread dough into forty balls, each about 1½ inches across. Using your palms, flatten a dough ball and then stretch and press into a 3-inch-wide round, making the edges slightly thinner than the center. Drop a heaping 1 Tbsp of the pork filling in the middle. Gently pull the edges of the dough evenly up and around the filling and pinch together tightly at the center. (No fancy folding here, you just want it completely sealed.) Place seam-side down on the baking sheet. Repeat with the remaining dough balls and filling. Spaced evenly apart, you can fit thirteen or fourteen buns per baking sheet.

Separate the frozen Dutch crunch topping squares and, working quickly, place one on each bun.

Place both sheets in the oven and bake for 12 minutes. Rotate them front to back and between racks and bake until golden brown, 10 to 12 minutes more. Let cool for 15 minutes before serving warm.

ROU SONG (PORK FLOSS)

Makes 2 cups / 150g

1 lb / 450g boneless pork loin, trimmed of excess surface fat and cut into 2-inch pieces

2 cups / 480ml water

½ cup / 120ml dark soy sauce (老抽, lóuh chāu)

⅓ cup / 65g granulated sugar

1 tsp kosher salt

In a medium saucepan over high heat, combine the pork, water, soy sauce, sugar, and salt and bring to a simmer, stirring to dissolve the sugar and salt. Skim off any scum that rises to the surface when it starts to bubble. Lower the heat to maintain a bare simmer, cover, and cook until the pork is tender and just starting to flake apart, about 2 hours. Drain the pork through a colander and set aside until cool enough to handle but still warm.

Meanwhile, preheat the oven to 150°F. (If your oven doesn't go that low, use the lowest setting possible and plan to check progress more frequently than described, especially toward the end.) Line a baking sheet with parchment paper.

Transfer the pork to the prepared baking sheet. With your hands, very finely shred and flake the meat (aim for a fluffy texture) and spread into an even layer. Slide into the oven to dry. Every 30 minutes, slide out the baking sheet and, with your hands, shred and flake the meat into smaller and smaller pieces. The texture should move from fluffy to feathery. The floss is ready when it is just slightly damp (like chewy jerky) and a rich mahogany color, about 2 hours total. Let cool, transfer to an airtight container, and store in the refrigerator for up to 1 week, or in the freezer for up to 3 months.

SIU YUK (CRISPY PORK)

There are many ways to roast a pig. We've experimented with them. Cylindrical ovens are superb at producing even, radiant heat. The only problem with them is that they take up a lot of real estate in a kitchen and a lot of time to manage. We're lucky to have barbecue specialists in Chinatown such as our friends Simon and Eric Cheung at Hing Lung on Stockton Street. This version of siu yuk (燒肉) lends itself well to roasting in a standard oven. We blend methods from my time making Italian porchettas, my sous chef's years cooking Kauai regional cuisine, and the way southern Chinese have been doing it since before all that. We blanch and dry the skin so it will roast to a crisp and then shatter with each bite. We make a rub and brine the pig from the inside only to keep the meat tender, succulent, and flavorful. We char the skin and scrape it off, the way the Hing Lung guys showed us, to get more of the "sesame seeds," the speckles on the skin that mark a well-roasted pig. You'll need a cut of pork belly known in Chinatown as ńgh fā yukh (五花肉, wǔ huā ròu in Mandarin), which has alternating layers of meat, fat, and pork skin. I recommend boneless, so ask for the ribs to be removed if necessary.

Active Time — 1 hour, 20 minutes

Plan Ahead — You'll need 3 days for making Hot Mustard and curing the pork, overnight for blanching and resting, and 1½ hours for broiling

Makes 6 to 8 servings

Special Equipment — Spiked meat tenderizer called a cheuk jām (戳針) or sūng yuhk jām (鬆肉針), otherwise use a metal skewer (or a bundle of them)

2½ lb / 1.1kg skin-on, boneless pork belly

4 Tbsp kosher salt

1 tsp granulated sugar

1 head garlic, top trimmed off to expose the cloves

1-inch-piece ginger, peeled and sliced

1 tsp white peppercorns

1 bay leaf

Hot Mustard (page 44) for serving

Fit a wire rack over a baking sheet.

Rub the pork belly all over with 2 Tbsp of the salt and the sugar, making sure they dissolve. Place skin-side up on the prepared rack and refrigerate, uncovered, for 2 days.

When ready to cook, place the pork in a large pot or Dutch oven wide enough so that it sits flat and then add enough cold water to cover by 1 inch. Bring to a boil over high heat, then turn the heat to medium and simmer for 3 minutes. Drain and rinse off the pork with cold water. Wash out the pot.

Place the pork back in the pot and add 3 qt / 2.8L cold water, the remaining 2 Tbsp salt, the garlic, ginger, peppercorns, and bay leaf. Place over high heat and bring to a simmer, then turn the heat to medium and continue to simmer until the thickest part of the belly reaches an internal temperature of 150°F, 40 to 45 minutes total, flipping it halfway through. It should be just cooked through at this point.

Transfer the pork, skin-side up, to a rimmed baking sheet. Poke all over with a needle poker or meat tenderizer, making sure to go all the way through the skin but not into the fat. It's hard to over-poke, but you can easily under-poke. Flip the pork skin-side down. Strain and reserve 3 cups / 720ml of the cooking liquid and discard the rest. Cover the pork with a second baking sheet, weigh it down with heavy pots or pans to help flatten the pork to an even thickness, and let cool. Transfer the pork and cooking liquid to the refrigerator and let sit overnight.

When ready to broil, let the pork and cooking liquid sit at room temperature for 1 hour. Meanwhile, position an oven rack about 7 inches below the broiling element and preheat the oven to broil. Open up the kitchen windows and turn on your ventilation hood—it will get smoky!

Place the pork, skin-side up, in a roasting pan. If the pork is not evenly thick, crumple up pieces of aluminum foil and place them under the thinner sections to prop them up. Your goal is to have all the skin be the same distance from the broiling element. Pour the cooking liquid into the pan. Broil the pork until all the skin pops and is blistered with holes and crispy, 10 to 15 minutes total (keep close watch). It will make a lot of loud popping sounds and smoke—this is good! It's okay if some of the skin starts to char because you want it to be as crispy as possible.

Remove the pork from the oven and let rest until it is cool enough to handle, about 5 minutes. Drain any oil left in the pan. Use a serrated knife to scrape off any charred bits from the skin (you may want to do this over a sink). Transfer the siu yuk to a clean cutting board and slice ½ to 1 inch thick with the knife. Serve with hot mustard.

XINJIANG LAMB SKEWERS

It used to be that a spire of smoke would point you to the Muslim quarters in every Chinese town from Kashgar to Beijing and Shanghai. The chile and cumin grabbed you by the nostrils. Nowadays, clean-air ordinances are relegating street stalls to air-conditioned food courts; but if you are so lucky, you still might catch a Uyghur guy in a white cap working an old-school street-side grill. If so, get on that. To make lamb skewers at home, you'll need cuts of lamb with a lot of nice white fat. (You may need to ask your butcher to leave the fat cap intact.) Leg meat is great for this recipe, but if you can, mix it with shoulder. Then you can alternate pieces of lean leg meat with hunks of shoulder meat with streaky fat and little fat nugs from both. The fat is key to cooking these without drying everything out, and most of it melts away anyway. When it turns crisp and brown, it's perfect. Also, you want fat drips to incite those occasional flare-ups that give the skewers a nice sear. Keep the skewers close enough to the coals for high and direct heat. A narrow charcoal grill without a grate works best here. We use binchotan, a pre-burned hardwood or bamboo, for its intense and steady heat to keep serving these all night, but any clean-burning charcoal you can keep red-hot will do. A well-oiled grill pan on the stove top is your best indoor option. If you're grilling multiple batches, keep them warm on a rack over a pan in your oven set to its lowest setting, but serve as soon as possible.

Active Time — 50 minutes

Plan Ahead — You'll need time to make Lanzhou Chile Oil

Makes about 10 skewers; 2 to 4 appetizer servings

Special Equipment — Steamer, ten 12-inch skewers, soaked in water a few hours if wood; outdoor grill (preferably charcoal or binchotan)

1½ lb / 680g boneless leg of lamb or lamb shoulder
1½ tsp Xinjiang Spice (recipe follows)
1½ tsp kosher salt
Lanzhou Chile Oil (page 40) for serving

Trim any surface fat from the lamb, keeping the fat in large chunks, and set aside. Trim and discard any tough gristle, silver skin, or sinew from the meat. Cut the fat into ¾-inch pieces and cut the meat into 1-inch pieces. Set aside in the refrigerator.

Prepare a steamer in a wok or a large, lidded pot following the instructions on page 167 and bring the water to a boil over medium-high heat. Add the lamb fat in a single layer and steam for 4 minutes. Transfer to a plate and place in the refrigerator.

Prepare an outdoor grill or light the fuel in your portable firebox of choice to the highest heat possible, a glowing-red heat.

In a small bowl, mix together the Xinjiang spice and salt.

Thread the lamb and fat onto skewers, alternating a cube of fat between every couple pieces of meat, so that they are just touching but not squished, about nine pieces of meat and fat per skewer. Massage the skewers into even-shaped stacks with no gaps or stray pieces.

Space out the skewers on the grill and sprinkle generously with the spiced salt. Grill, turning the skewers as each side starts to char and sprinkling generously with the spiced salt with every turn. The time between each turn depends on your grill's heat. Wait for some char on the parts closest to the heat before each turn. With binchotan, this may take 30 seconds, while a gas grill may need 2 or 3 minutes. (If using a gas grill, keep the cover on as much as you can.)

Once the lamb is evenly browned all over and charred in spots, 4 to 12 minutes, pinch the meat; a light springiness indicates the lamb is cooked to medium. A bite test should reveal just slight pink left in the middle. Remove from the grill and let rest on a rack for a minute or two. Drizzle the skewers with the chile oil and serve.

XINJIANG SPICE

Makes ⅓ cup / 35g

2½ Tbsp coriander seeds

2 Tbsp Sichuan peppercorns

1 tsp white peppercorns

5 tsp cumin seeds

In a wok or a frying pan, large enough for everything to spread out in an even layer, over medium heat, combine the coriander seeds, both peppercorns, and cumin seeds and toast, tossing or stirring frequently, until fragrant, about 2 minutes. Immediately transfer to a mortar and pestle, or let cool in a dish and add to a spice grinder. Working in batches, smash in the mortar, or grind in a spice grinder into a fine powder. Spice dust should float in the air if you breathe over it. Transfer to an airtight container; store in a cool, dry place; and use within a month or two.

7

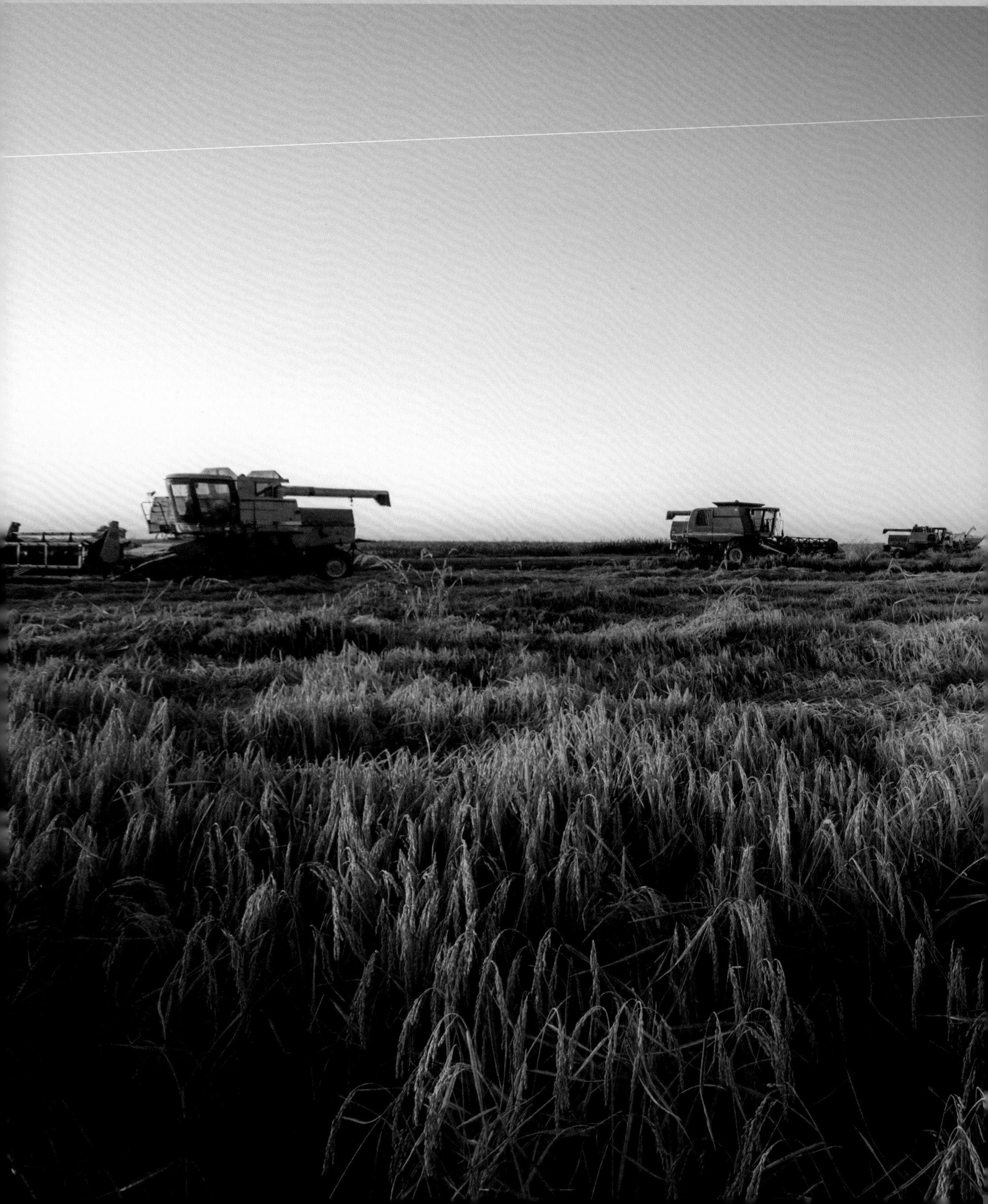

RICE

FROM THE DELTA TO THE DELTA

Rice in California is a Chinese American legacy. Soon after Chinese landed in the state in the 1850s, they started growing rice on rented plots in the Sacramento Valley, when California land was considered worthless except for the gold inside it. Around the 1880s, the government started subsidizing reclamation of land, and land barons found they could hire Chinese laborers, out of work after finishing the railroads, for cheap.

Nearly all of the first Chinese came from the Pearl River Delta, where many had experience taming waters with levees and dams and farming with sustainable, self-renewing irrigation systems. They cleared the Sacramento–San Joaquin River Delta, then a deep pit of thick peat and heavy clay filled with mosquitoes and dysentery, into a network of canals and levees surrounding fertile farmland. It was backbreaking work using hand shovels and wheelbarrows in waist-deep swamp water. They transformed eighty-eight thousand acres of "worthless" land into the "Asparagus Capital of the World" and a major supplier of every other kind of fruit, nut, leafy green, and rice. It remains one of the largest-scale, hand-engineered projects ever completed. Once reclamation was mechanized, Chinese laborers went on to planting and harvesting what grew. A majority of rice was still imported from China well into the 1900s, but California, today, grows most of the short- and medium-grain rice in this country.

Rice in California is also a Japanese American legacy. Around 1912, a Japanese farmer found that Japanese strains of rice flourished in California's climate, and rice became one of the state's most profitable crops. Keisaburo Koda bought land in his American sons' names and became the "Rice King," before he and his family were forced into an internment camp during World War II.

There were complicated feelings in Chinatown during the war. Waiters had taken to wearing buttons proclaiming American allegiance and "I am Chinese" to avoid trouble. Everyone was related to someone who had been killed by the Japanese invasion. A disproportionately high number of Chinese Americans enlisted to fight. In China, the war had been brutal. But in Chinatown, when the first Japanese arrived in San Francisco, it was the only neighborhood where they were welcomed to live and work. Some of the first Japanese restaurants in the country opened there. Together Chinese Americans and Japanese Americans had endured discrimination. In Chinatown, everyone had become neighbors.

After Japanese Americans were released from internment, they were never repaid for what had been stolen from them. The Kodas replanted their rice on the western edge of the San Joaquin Valley.

We use many varieties of rice from Guangdong and Thailand for various applications, but we use Koda's heirloom Kokuho Rose for our steamed rice. Robin Koda (pictured on page 227 at Koda Farms) tells me it's an impractical strain. It takes longer to ripen than others and can't be harvested easily of its extra-long stalks. But Robin calls it her family's "emotional legacy," and so they keep growing it.

When you properly cook an ingredient as humble as rice, it will show its character. To me, Koda's rice tastes sweet, floral, and of the California lands made fertile by Chinese and all those since.

STEAMED RICE

Perfect gleaming jewels of rice are still best made over flame, especially if you're looking for bouncy and tender grains with the bonus of a hint of crust at the bottom. But don't let me stop you from using a rice cooker. I use one at home most of the time. The stove method requires extra care so that the rice first comes to a boil and then steams. The recipes in this book work best with a medium-grain rice that cooks up just a little sticky, nutty, and sweet.

Rice is sold at different ages, and each has its applications, but for steamed rice I use new rice when it's available. The first of the season is harvested in the fall and usually marked "New Crop." Read the date and use your nose (rice contains oils that can go rancid and smell like crayons).

Active Time — 15 minutes
Makes 4 to 6 servings

2 cups / 400g short- to
medium-grain rice
2½ cups / 590ml cold water

Rinse the rice thoroughly with cool water, gently moving the grains with your fingers but not rubbing. (If you use vitamin-fortified rice, which I don't recommend, skip this step, since it will wash away everything you paid for.) Pour out the water and repeat until the water is just barely cloudy. Four or five rinses usually does it.

Transfer the rice to a heavy-bottom pot with a tight-fitting lid. Use a medium to small pot, no more than 8 inches wide. This is where one of those wooden lids fitted tightly over a clay pot would be nice but not necessary. If you use a clay pot, pre-soaking the rice for about 30 minutes gives you a wider margin of error.

Add the 2½ cups / 590ml cold water, enough to cover plus another 1 inch (the ratio will work out to be around 1 cup / 200g rice to just a bit more water, 1¼ cups / 300ml or so). The less polished, the longer the grain, and the older the rice, the more water you'll need. If you are cooking brown rice, which has not been polished completely of its husk, bran, and germ, add a little more water and allow it to boil for a few minutes more. Let the rice rest in the water for 20 minutes or so.

Bring the water to a boil over medium-high heat, about 10 minutes, stirring gently once at the start and once at the end to release any grains stuck at the bottom. Stirring more than that releases more starches, resulting in stickier rice.

Once at a boil, turn the heat to a low simmer and cover. Cook for about 15 minutes; don't touch the lid while the rice steams. If you were to open the lid (which you won't), you would see that the grains are still opaque just at the center—"fish eyes" as Chinese cooks say, meaning that the grains have not absorbed water all the way through quite yet.

Turn off the heat, and leave the rice covered for another 10 minutes or so. Gently turn the grains to mix them well and fluff them up, rest for another 5 minutes, and then serve.

FERMENTED GRAIN JOOK WITH LOBSTER

Jook (粥) is one of humanity's most ancient dishes. Rice was just a wild grass that people in southern China began cultivating some twelve thousand years ago. The earliest jook probably were made from grains such as coix seed, pearl barley, sorghum, hemp, and millet. Some tough-hulled grains were first broken down through fermentation. Slow cooking melted everything into creamy porridge. Jook has been around so long because it is nourishing, comforting, and not that hard to make. In many ways, it's the perfect food. I eat it for breakfast or lunch, whenever I'm sick or have too many leftovers, like the week after Thanksgiving. And stirring jook with a well-made wooden spoon is one of my favorite small joys in life. My wife got me into estate sales and I'm always on the look-out for wooden spoons. The nice things that are still around years later are here because of all the skill and care that went into them.

Jook is the perfect medium for improvising with toppings. I like building layers of texture and flavor with both simple and elaborate ingredients, like mushrooms, root vegetables, and seafood in this fermented-grain porridge. Aside from scorching it, you can't make a mistake.

Active Time — 2 hours

Plan Ahead — You'll need to make Fermented Kohlrabi (or buy a premade version, look for "dà tóu cài" [大頭菜]), and 4 to 5 days for fermenting the barley. Leave 4 hours the day of to make Chicken Stock and the lobster

Makes 6 servings

Special Equipment — Wooden skewer, deep-fry thermometer, blender

Jook

2 Tbsp pearl barley

Filtered water for soaking

5 cups / 1.2L Chicken Stock (page 34)

2½ cups / 590ml water

1 cup / 200g long-grain jasmine rice

1 Tbsp Korean roasted barley tea, wrapped in a cheesecloth sachet

Kosher salt

Ground white pepper

One 1½- to 2-lb / 680 to 900g live whole Maine lobster

1 Tbsp neutral oil, plus 1 cup / 240ml

¾ cup / 100g coarsely chopped shallots, plus 1 medium shallot, peeled and thinly sliced

¾ cup / 100g chopped garlic

1 Tbsp tomato paste

3 Tbsp cognac

1 qt / 950ml water

¼ tsp white peppercorns

To make the jook: Place the pearl barley in a small jar and add enough filtered water to cover by ½ inch. Cover the jar and let ferment at cool room temperature until the water is cloudy, it smells sour, and the pH is 4.6 or lower, 4 to 5 days.

Drain the barley through a fine-mesh strainer and rinse with cool water. Add the barley to a small saucepan of heavily salted water (it should taste like seawater) and bring to a boil over medium-high heat. Turn the heat to medium and simmer until tender, about 15 minutes. Drain, transfer to an airtight container, and store in the refrigerator for up to 1 week.

In a large saucepan over medium-high heat, combine the chicken stock, 2½ cups / 590ml water, jasmine rice, and barley-tea sachet. Turn the heat to medium-low, cover, and simmer until the rice is tender but not completely broken down, about 1 hour. Discard the sachet.

Taste and season the jook with salt and white pepper, then stir in the fermented barley. Let cool, then transfer to an airtight container and store in the refrigerator for up to 4 days.

Bring a large saucepan of water to a boil over high heat. Meanwhile, kill the lobster by using a heavy knife to split it through the head. ❶ Don't freak if detached parts still move even without a central nervous system in control. It's a reflex reaction. Rest assured, the lobster is still dead.

Twist off the tail and claws. Break down the claws further by twisting off the pinching claws from the knuckle segments. Refrigerate the head and any dark green roe attached to it. Starting where the tail attaches to the body, stick a wooden skewer through the tail meat to the last joint, as close as possible to the shell to minimize damage, so that it will not curl when cooked. ❷ Break off any excess skewer to help it fit in the pot.

CONTINUED

1 bay leaf

1 Tbsp red vermillion rice, rinsed, or bulgur wheat

Kosher salt

1½ cups / 60g thinly sliced Little Gem lettuce

½ ruby red grapefruit, cut into bite-size segments

2 Tbsp coarsely chopped, roasted unsalted peanuts

2 Tbsp Dehydrated Fermented Kohlrabi (see variation, page 43)

1 Tbsp roasted sunflower seeds

½ bunch chives, cut into 1-inch pieces

Drop the claws into the boiling water and cook for 2 minutes. Then add the tail and arms and cook for 5 minutes.

Meanwhile, prepare an ice bath in a large bowl by filling it with ice cubes and a little water.

Drain the lobster pieces, then transfer the pieces to the ice bath. When cooled, crack and pick the meat from the shells (reserve the shells). ❸ – ❾ Chop the meat into bite-size pieces, transfer to an airtight container, and store in the refrigerator for up to 2 days.

Remove the reserved lobster head from the refrigerator, scrape out any dark green roe, and return the roe to the refrigerator. Twist the legs from the lobster head and pull the top shell away from the rest of the body. Chop the inside body parts into smaller pieces.

Warm a large, wide pot over medium heat. Add the 1 Tbsp neutral oil and let it heat up for a few seconds. Add the chopped shallots and garlic and cook until softened, about 3 minutes. Add the head and its parts, the legs, and the reserved tail and claw shells to the pot and cook until the shells are bright red, about 5 minutes. Stir in the tomato paste and cook for 30 seconds. Add the cognac and stir with a wooden spoon to scrape up any browned bits at the bottom of the pot. Add the 1 qt / 950ml water, peppercorns, and bay leaf and bring to a boil. Turn the heat to medium and simmer until the liquid is reduced to ½ cup / 120ml, 1 to 1¼ hours.

Fit a fine-mesh strainer over a large bowl.

Strain the lobster sauce and discard the solids. Pour the sauce into a small saucepan, add the reserved lobster roe if you had any, and warm over low heat just until the roe turns bright orange or red (do not boil or the roe will turn grainy). Transfer to a blender and blend until smooth. Cover and store this sauce in the refrigerator for up to 1 week.

Line a plate with a double layer of paper towels.

Fill a small saucepan with the remaining 1 cup / 240ml neutral oil and secure a deep-fry thermometer on the side. Set over medium-high heat and warm the oil to 400°F, being careful to maintain this temperature as you fry. Add the red vermillion rice and fry until puffed and crisp, 15 to 30 seconds. Using a slotted spoon, transfer to the prepared plate and season lightly with salt.

Transfer 1 Tbsp of the frying oil to a small frying pan and warm over medium-low heat. Add the sliced shallot and cook until dark brown and caramelized, about 15 minutes.

Reheat the jook if needed and divide among individual bowls. Top with the shallots, lobster, lettuce, grapefruit, peanuts, fermented kohlrabi, a dollop of lobster sauce, puffed rice, sunflower seeds, and chives. Serve hot.

STEAK FRIED RICE

The whole point of fried rice is to showcase the ethereal charred, smoky flavor, aroma, and texture known as wok hei (see page 25). A wok makes this a lot easier to achieve, but I've made it happen with a thin cast-iron pan too. Here are the secrets.

- Use hydrated but not moist rice. This is why leftover rice fries up airy, while fresh rice turns to mush. If necessary, cook up some rice and leave uncovered in the refrigerator 1 day before frying. It should be cold when you start.

- Get your pan scorching hot. Whatever you're imagining is probably not hot enough. I set off the fire alarm whenever I cook fried rice at home (and once at a private dinner in a very tall office tower, where Anna Lee and all the office assistants threw open windows and fanned for their lives to prevent everyone in the building from having to evacuate). So turn up the flame and open your windows. Wait for that initial wok hei to hit your nose before adding the oil, then swirl the oil all around and up the sides of the pan. As you cook, unless you have a wok-burner on your gas range or a Chinese hearth stove well-stocked with firewood, you will have to turn up the heat each time you add something new and lower it again before the smoke gets out of control.

- You have to keep things moving. A wide metal spatula is good for this, and so is a 14-inch or larger wok or pan. If you don't have a big enough wok for everything to dance around in, cook in batches and combine at the end. If I'm using a cast-iron pan, I have a hand on it at all times so I can keep tossing everything up and around, since a spatula can't get in the corners fast enough. Line up your ingredients before you turn on the flame.

Cooking fried rice is all about immediacy, but you can begin with a mise of all kinds of leftovers. My mom, for instance, always packed doggy bags of the scraps of roast beef and rib-eye from Saturday nights at Sizzler to make the best fried-rice lunch the next day. This version uses tender marbled cuts of wagyu, chopped broccolini, egg, and a dusting of salty sīn beef heart that takes a few days to cure and may require a special order from the butcher.

Active Time — 30 minutes

Plan Ahead — You'll need time to make Cured Beef Heart or Salted Yolks (unless you buy bottarga)

Makes 2 to 4 servings

Special Equipment — Microplane

---

3 oz / 85g broccolini or broccoli, cut into small florets and stems cut into ½-inch pieces

1 egg

Kosher salt

1 tsp neutral oil, plus 1 Tbsp

4 oz / 115g rib-eye, hanger, or skirt steak, diced into 1-inch cubes

2 cups / 230g cold, cooked long-grain jasmine rice (see page 229)

Bring a small saucepan of heavily salted water (it should remind you of seawater) to a boil over high heat. Add the broccolini and blanch until crisp-tender, about 2 minutes. Drain and set aside.

In a small bowl, beat the egg with a pinch of salt. Warm a wok or a large cast-iron skillet over medium heat. Add the 1 tsp neutral oil, then the egg, and cook, stirring occasionally, until softly scrambled but with no browning, about 30 seconds. Transfer to a bowl and set aside.

Turn on your ventilation hood or throw open your windows now! Warm the pan over high heat until just starting to smoke. Add the remaining 1 Tbsp neutral oil, then add the steak in an even layer, and season with salt. ❶ Cook without moving until well-seared on the bottom, about

CONTINUED

STEAK FRIED RICE continued

1 Tbsp oyster sauce

2 tsp light soy sauce
　（生抽, sāng chāu)

1 tsp toasted sesame oil

1 green onion, thinly sliced
　crosswise

1 small piece Cured Beef Heart
　(page 45), Salted Egg Yolks
　(page 181), or bottarga

1½ minutes. **②**–**③** Add the rice, broccolini, and scrambled egg and toss to combine and break up any lumps in the rice. Keep everything moving until heated through, 1½ to 2 minutes. **④** Now let the rice sit without stirring until the bottom browns and lightly chars in spots, about 1 minute. Smell that wok hei? If not, stir up the rice again and let it brown once more.

Add the oyster sauce, soy sauce, and sesame oil to the rice and toss continuously until well combined, about 1 minute. **⑤**–**⑦** Transfer to a serving bowl, **⑧** top with the green onion, and use a Microplane to shave a generous dusting of cured beef heart, salted egg yolk, or bottarga over everything. **⑨** Serve it piled in a rounded mound, so it stays hot longer for the table. Eat immediately.

NOH MAI GAI (QUAIL WITH STICKY RICE)

The centerpiece of a dinner at my grandparents' was often noh mái gāi (糯米雞), sīn-rich sticky rice laced with a whole deboned chicken, lap cheong, mushrooms, and dried seafood, all wrapped in a lotus-leaf parcel. I think of it as the Chinese equivalent to turkey and stuffing, only this isn't just eaten at special times of a year. But because no one has the time to roast a Thanksgiving-size bird on the regular, finding a smaller one was key to having a couple bites of this tradition without committing to a feast.

This is where Brent Wolfe of Wolfe Ranch comes in. Brent is a legendary rancher, known especially for his quail, which he raises, processes, and delivers himself. Our version of noh mái gāi with his quail is a dish that has been on our menu from Day One. We change the fruit in this recipe to follow the seasons (poached quince is pictured on page 239) and have occasionally made a different dish entirely when ingredients aren't coming together, but his quail are always on the menu. They are that special.

If you can't find high-quality, large quail, use Cornish game hens, which will be the right size. Any bird you use must be deboned from rib cage through thigh. Quail is often sold "semi-boneless," which means you will need to remove just the thigh and trim the wing tips for this recipe.

Active Time — 1 hour, 20 minutes

Plan Ahead — You can start up to 2 days before for brining the birds, and at least 4 hours for soaking the lotus leaves, rice, and dried shrimp. Plus you'll need time to make Chicken Stock, 10 Spice, and Lap Cheong.

Makes 4 servings

Special Equipment — Steamer

Brined Birds

2 cups / 480ml cold water

1 cup / 240ml Shaoxing wine

2¼ tsp granulated sugar

1 Tbsp kosher salt

½ tsp freshly ground white pepper

4 semi-boneless large quails (about 8 oz / 225g each), or 2 Cornish game hens (1 lb / 450g each)

Sticky Rice

One 12-inch-wide dried lotus leaf

½ cup / 100g short-grain glutinous rice (such as Sho Chiku Bai)

2 Tbsp long-grain jasmine rice

1 Tbsp small dried shrimp

1 Tbsp neutral oil

2 tsp peeled and minced ginger

½ cup / 40g small-diced fresh shiitake mushrooms, stems trimmed

2 Tbsp thinly sliced Lap Cheong (page 45)

To brine the birds: In a large bowl, combine the water, wine, sugar, salt, and pepper and stir this brine until the salt and sugar are dissolved.

If necessary, debone the birds so that the meat and skin are intact and the birds can be stuffed, leaving the wings and drumsticks intact. Trim the quails' wings at the elbow (the largest joint), leaving just the drumette attached to the bird. Remove the thighbone in each leg by cutting down the length of the bone to expose it, then angling the knife to scrape the meat off the bones and joints at each end; leave the drumstick intact. Save the trimmings and bones for the chicken stock needed for the jus.

Submerge the birds in the brine and refrigerate, covered, for at least 1 hour or up to 2 days.

To make the rice: In a large bowl, soak the lotus leaf in water for 4 hours. In a strainer, rinse both rices together under cool running water, then soak in fresh water for 1 hour. In a small bowl, soak the dried shrimp in cold water for 30 minutes, then drain and finely chop.

Warm a medium saucepan over medium heat. Add the neutral oil and let it heat up for a few seconds. Add the ginger and cook until fragrant, about 30 seconds. Add the mushrooms and cook until tender, about 2 minutes more. Stir in the lap cheong, jujubes, and chopped shrimp, then transfer to a medium bowl.

Drain the rice well and add to the saucepan. Add the chicken stock and soy sauce and turn the heat to medium. Simmer until the rice absorbs all the liquid, about 3 minutes. Transfer to the bowl with the mushrooms and stir to combine.

Prepare a steamer in wok or a large, lidded pot following the instructions on page 167 and bring the water to a boil over medium-high heat.

CONTINUED

1 Tbsp pitted, finely
    chopped dried jujubes
    or Medjool dates
⅔ cup / 160ml Chicken Stock
    (page 34)
2 Tbsp light soy sauce
    (生抽, sāng chāu)
2 Tbsp thinly sliced (crosswise)
    green onions

Quail Glaze

3 Tbsp oyster sauce
3½ Tbsp Shaoxing wine
1 Tbsp water
1 Tbsp granulated sugar
1 Tbsp packed light brown sugar
½ tsp ground ginger
⅛ tsp 10 Spice (see page 36)

Quail Jus

2 oz / 55g Chinese rock sugar,
    broken into small chunks
¼ cup / 60ml water
2 Tbsp peeled and minced
    ginger
2 Tbsp minced garlic
1½ Tbsp 10 Spice
    (see page 36)
¼ tsp freshly grated nutmeg
1½ cups / 360ml Chicken
    Stock (page 34)
1½ tsp dark soy sauce
    (老抽, lóuh chāu)

Kosher salt
10 Spice (see page 36)
    for seasoning
Sixteen 1-inch pieces
    Lap Cheong (page 45),
    steamed
4 fresh figs, quartered, or
    6 halved pitted sweet
    cherries, or 6 halved
    seedless red grapes
¼ cup / 35g crushed,
    toasted cashews
Flake salt
Red veined sorrel
    for garnishing

Shake the excess water from the lotus leaf and lay it on the counter. Spread the rice mixture onto the center of the leaf to about 1 inch thick. Make a square-ish packet by folding the bottom edge and sides of the leaf over the rice so that the rice is snugly wrapped in a couple of leaf layers. Place the wrapped rice, folded-side down, in the steamer. Cover and steam until the rice is tender and cooked through, about 20 minutes.

Place the rice bundle on a plate. Carefully unwrap the rice (it will be steamy), transfer it to a bowl, and stir in the green onions. Let cool to room temperature. (At this point, you can transfer to an airtight container and store in the refrigerator overnight.)

To make the glaze: In a small saucepan over low heat, combine the oyster sauce, wine, water, both sugars, ginger, and 10 Spice and stir just until everything is melted. Transfer to an airtight container and store in the refrigerator for up to 2 weeks.

To make the jus: In a small saucepan over medium heat, combine the sugar and water and stir until the sugar is dissolved. Add the ginger, garlic, 10 Spice, and nutmeg and cook until fragrant and slightly darkened, about 2 minutes. Add the chicken stock and simmer, uncovered, until reduced to about 3 Tbsp, about 50 minutes. Stir in the soy sauce. Pour through a fine-mesh strainer into a small bowl and discard the solids. Transfer to an airtight container and store in the refrigerator for up to 1 month.

Divide the sticky rice into four portions and form each portion into a ball (don't squeeze too hard—you want the grains loose and just stuck together). Remove the birds from the brine and pat dry with paper towels. Stuff a rice ball inside the cavity of each quail, or two in the cavity of each game hen, so that the birds look plump and full.

Near the middle of a bird's thigh, cut a short slit (about ½ inch) along the tendon that runs through it. Push the opposite leg through it. (At this point, the stuffed birds can be refrigerated for up to 3 days. Let them come back to room temperature before roasting, about 30 minutes.)

Preheat the oven to 450°F. Fit a wire roasting rack over a rimmed baking sheet.

Brush the birds all over with the glaze and lightly season all over with kosher salt and 10 Spice. Place the birds, breast-side up, on the prepared rack. Roast, brushing the birds with more glaze every 10 minutes, until the birds register 145°F in the thigh and the sticky rice is hot, 20 to 25 minutes for quail and 30 to 35 minutes for game hens.

Heat the broiler, brush the birds with glaze once more, and broil until the skin is evenly dark golden brown, rotating the baking sheet as needed, 2 to 3 minutes more. Remove the birds from the broiler and let rest for 10 minutes.

Place the steamed lap cheong and the fruit on a baking sheet and broil until just heated through, about 3 minutes.

Arrange a layer of the cashews on each serving plate. You can serve one quail on each plate per guest, but a bounty of birds on a big platter looks great too. Set the birds on top of the cashews and sprinkle with some flake salt. Arrange the lap cheong and fruit around them and drizzle the jus over everything. Garnish with sorrel before serving.

DESSERT

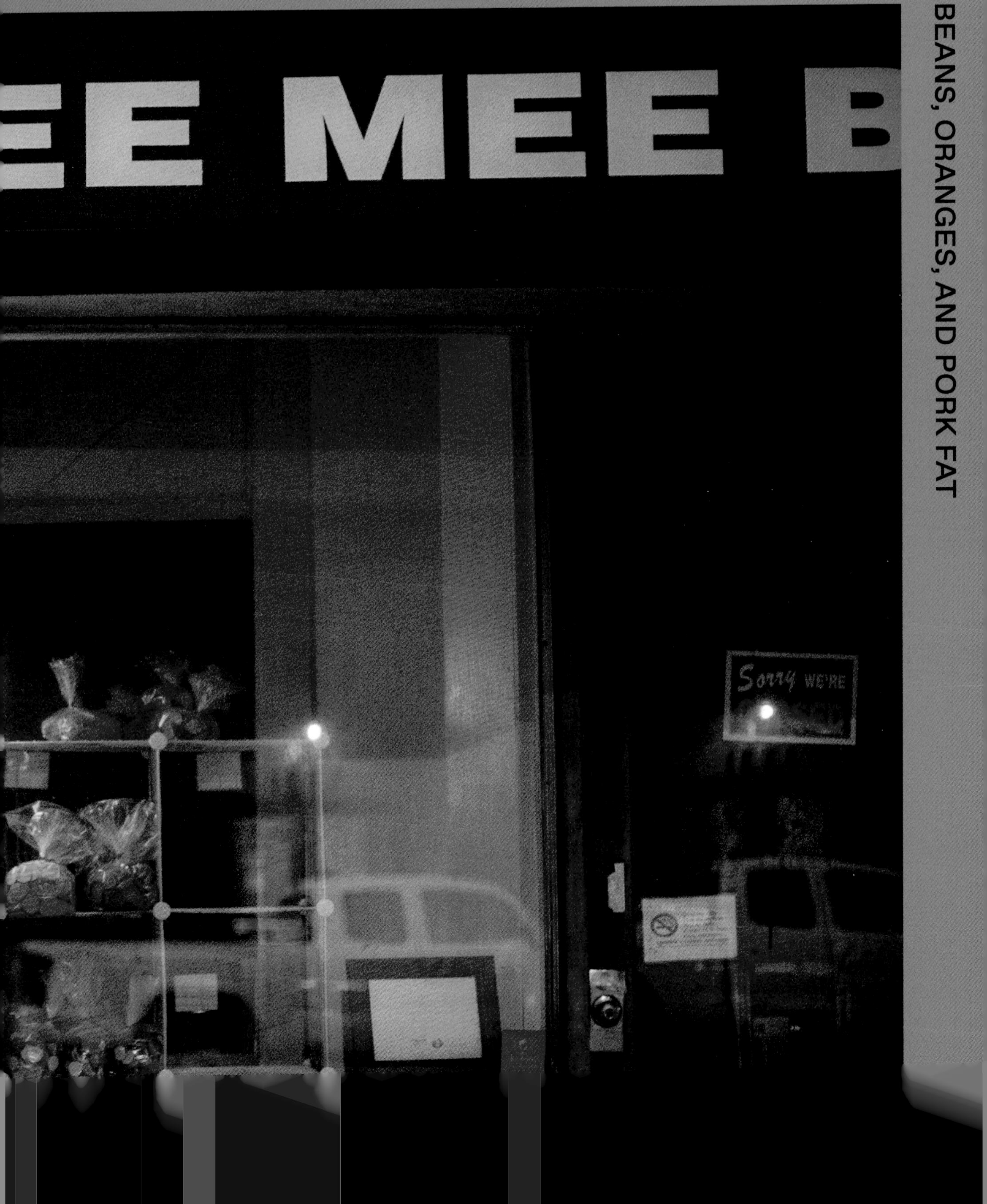

8

When Melissa Chou, the pastry chef at Mister Jiu's, and I started developing ideas for desserts, we knew we wanted to connect in new ways with the flavors and textures we think of as Chinese treats. The amazing thing is that even though she and I have ancestry in common—we both have grandparents from Toisan, grew up in San Francisco at the same time, and even share the same last name (Chou is just another way of spelling Jew and Jiu)—what Chinese food counts as comforting to us is really different at times. Because her family saved eating out for dim sum and the occasional seafood dinner, before we opened she'd never even heard of a lot of the dishes that I take for granted as Chinese American.

We wanted to play on that idea of the expansiveness of the Chinese American experience in these desserts. These pastries and sweets are inspired by strolls through Chinatown, by my memories of home, and by Melissa's memories of hers. In the following text, I'll let Melissa tell you herself and guide you through her recipes in this chapter.

• • •

When my siblings and I were kids, we ate only fruit for dessert—oranges, apples, and maybe strawberries with cream if we were lucky. Every once in a while, my mother, who was born in Chinatown, would surprise us with her banana cream pie. But other than that, there were no cookies or cake in our house, which is funny given what I do now.

I remember my dad, who grew up pretty traditionally Chinese in New Zealand until he immigrated here right before I was born, serving carrots for dinner and, alongside them, presenting the water he had boiled them in as an amazing treat. He made it sound as though it was really delicious; and you know, it was. We would eat the carrots and sip the pot liquor like tea. It tasted so sweet to us.

We talk about sugar cravings as a common human trait, but actually everyone prefers different levels and kinds of sweetness, different intensities of ingredients such as chocolate, and varying degrees of chewiness and bounce. What counts as a treat is all very cultural.

In a Chinese meal, the desserts are really just the closers. The Mandarin word for them is *tián diǎn* (甜點), which means either "a little sweet something," or "just a little bit of sweetness," depending on how you want to see it. Tián diǎn may be a flaky pastry laced with pork fat, a soup of white tree fungus and goji berries, a bowl of peach-tree sap, an almond agar-agar jelly, or a sweet mung bean soup. And they don't have to come at the end; sweetness punctuates the meal. It's there in different degrees in the fresh fish, rice, sweet and sour, flaky pastries, and condiments. There are still plenty of restaurants in Chinatown that don't serve anything like what we'd think of as a sweet dessert. You close out the meal with a plate of orange slices and a fresh pot of tea.

That open-ended structure really resonates with me. I prefer feeling satisfied at the end, not as if I've been waiting for an indulgence. I like a hit of sweetness to contrast the last bites of savory food, but dinner and dessert shouldn't compete for attention. Dessert, or whatever you want to call it, is part of a continuum, part of a beginning and an end that all ties together as a meal.

I build sweetness from a lot of sources—fruit, rice flour, and spices. It comes from fermentation, drying, and cooking things slowly to bring out natural sugars in greater concentration and more detectable forms. Even the sugars we use, like honey, sugarcane, palm, maltose from wheat, and golden rock sugar, have a much lower level of sweetness and add complexity, with their floral, spicy, and earthy background notes, than the sugars of the Western baking arsenal. I often rely on fruit for a lighter, refreshing approach to sweetness.

I also build in a lot of different textures and temperatures to my desserts. In Chinese cooking, fats are treated as delicacies. You want the texture and taste of fat without the oiliness. You can use leaf lard to create flaky, laminated doughs or blend it into bean fillings. That feeling of richness is much more satisfying to me than the decadence of Death by Chocolate or any sugarbomb. I still use milk, cream, and butter. We're always trying to bridge the gap between tradition and what we and our guests are familiar with.

All of this came to me after we opened Mister Jiu's. While my first language was Cantonese, I lost it growing up, and with that I thought I lost a lot of my heritage forever. But working with this team means being surrounded by more people of Chinese and Asian heritage than I've ever been around regularly before. I discovered I'm more Chinese than I ever imagined—in the way I eat, and the way I define a dessert.

ON DAN TAT

Dan tat (蛋撻), *dan* meaning "egg" and *tat* coming from "tart," is a textbook example of the deliciousness that comes from cultural exchange. It most likely started with Portuguese monks looking to use up egg yolks (they used the whites to starch their clothes). They came up with brûlée egg in a laminated pastry and called it pastéis de nata. (Some say they got the idea for tarts after a visit to France, which probably got the idea for laminated pastry from Austria, but that's another story.) Pastéis de nata came to China in the early twentieth century, during Portugal's colonization of Macau, where the filling became even silkier, heavy on the cream, with just speckles of brûlée. Hong Kong and the mainland brought the Chinese lamination technique yùhn sōu (圓酥), a spiraling of a water dough and a dough made with lard, that produces an especially tender, flaky crust. Dan tat have been on the world's dim sum carts since.

PARISIAN DAN TAT

Active Time — 1 hour

Plan Ahead — You'll need at least 6 hours for chilling

Makes 10 servings

Special Equipment — Food processor, 9-inch flan ring or round cake pan, pie weights, small offset spatula

Dan Tat Crust
¼ cup / 60ml whole milk

1 egg yolk

1½ cups / 210g all-purpose flour, plus more for rolling

1 Tbsp granulated sugar

½ tsp kosher salt

6½ oz / 185g cold unsalted butter, cut into ½-inch cubes

Egg Custard Filling
3 cups plus 2 Tbsp / 750ml whole milk

1 vanilla bean, split, seeds scraped, and pod reserved

1 cup plus 2 Tbsp / 265ml heavy cream

1 cup / 200g granulated sugar

1 egg, plus 4 egg yolks

⅓ cup / 45g cornstarch

1 pinch kosher salt

I've tasted many dan tat in the neighborhood. There are innovators such as Yummy Bakery on Jackson Street with egg white tarts, and traditionalists such as Golden Gate Bakery on Grant Avenue that insist on serving theirs right out of the oven. The best part of Golden Gate's tarts is the crust, which is baked perfectly all the way through and somewhere between flaky puff pastry and crispy shortbread—not quite Macau-style or Hong Kong–style but something very San Francisco Chinatown. Our version takes cues from Parisian flan with egg and cream set with cornstarch, and cold butter in the crust to tip it to the crisp, flaky side. Blind baking cuts the total oven time in half, so that the custard sets to the softest texture, and you get that proper little jiggle (dip the knife in very hot water between each slice if you want clean lines). Dan tat are best eaten warm, but I like this version chilled.

To make the crust: In a small bowl, whisk together the milk and egg yolk. Set aside.

In a food processor fitted with the blade attachment, combine the flour, sugar, and salt and pulse briefly to combine. Scatter the butter over the flour and pulse repeatedly for a second or so until cut to pea-size pieces. While pulsing, stream the milk mixture into the flour mixture. Continue with more 1-second pulses until wet clumps start to form. The dough should not be dry or form a ball. Remove the dough from the food processor, shape into a disk, and wrap tightly in plastic wrap. Refrigerate for 30 minutes.

Line a baking sheet with parchment paper and place a 9-inch flan ring or 9-inch-round (2-inch-high) cake pan on the sheet.

Unwrap and lightly flour both sides of the dough. Roll out into a 12-inch round about ¼ inch thick. Line the prepared pan with the dough, wrapping it over the rim so it will not slump during baking; trim the overhang. Using a fork, pierce the dough all over to prevent bubbling. Set aside in the refrigerator for 1 hour.

Preheat the oven to 350°F.

Press a 16-inch-long sheet of parchment paper onto the crust, then fill the crust with pie weights. Bake for 20 minutes, then remove the parchment paper and weights. Bake until the crust is very pale golden brown, about 5 minutes more. If parts of the crust have puffed up, use your fingers to flatten gently. Remove from the oven and let cool to room temperature.

To make the filling: While the crust is baking, in a large saucepan over medium heat, combine the milk and vanilla seeds and pod and bring to a simmer. Remove from the heat and let steep for 20 minutes. Discard the vanilla pod.

In a large bowl, whisk together the cream, sugar, egg, egg yolks, and cornstarch until smooth.

Prepare an ice bath in a large bowl by filling it with ice cubes and a little water.

CONTINUED

Bring the vanilla milk back to a simmer over medium heat. Whisk ⅓ cup / 80ml of the milk into the egg mixture to combine and temper the eggs, then whisk in the remaining milk. Pour the milk-egg mixture back into the saucepan and cook, stirring constantly, until the custard thickens and just starts to bubble (don't worry if it's a little lumpy), 3 to 6 minutes. Stir in the salt.

Strain the custard through a fine-mesh strainer into a medium bowl, pushing it through with a rubber spatula. Press a sheet of plastic wrap directly onto the surface of the custard so that it doesn't develop a skin. Place the bowl in the ice bath and let cool until slightly warmer than room temperature, about 30 minutes. The plastic wrap should pull off the surface cleanly. If not, let it cool further.

Meanwhile, preheat the oven to 425°F.

Stir the custard until smooth, then pour into the crust. Smooth the top with a small offset spatula or the back of a spoon. Leave on the baking sheet and bake until the surface is mostly dark brown and the custard bubbles around the edges, 40 to 45 minutes. Rotate the baking sheet as needed for even browning.

Transfer to a wire rack and let cool for 2 hours. Refrigerate, uncovered, for at least 4 hours or up to overnight before slicing and serving.

BAKED NIAN GAO

Nián gāo (黏糕, in Mandarin) are the fruitcake of Chinese desserts. The difference is that they're steamed, not baked, and made of glutinous rice flour instead of wheat flour. But like fruitcake, they show up (sometimes inconveniently) on major holidays. *Nián gāo* means "sticky cake" and is also a pun for "a year better than the last," so around the new year, you make it to bribe the Kitchen God and glue his mouth shut, as he's to report on everything he's overheard in your kitchen the past year. That classic texture can be polarizing for people who are unfamiliar with it, so for this version, I looked toward butter mochi, a favorite from the 1970s era of Oriental-style convenience baking. Baking turns nián gāo into a cake of wonderful contrasts—still chewy but topped with a golden crust. Winter is peak nián gāo season, so I use brandied cherries, like Luxardo, but feel free to use other dried fruit; rehydrate for fifteen minutes in some hot water, rum, or brandy, then chop into ½-inch pieces so they stay evenly distributed throughout the cake.

Active Time — 20 minutes

Plan Ahead — You'll need about 1 hour for baking

Makes 12 to 16 servings

Special Equipment — 9 × 13-inch baking pan (preferably metal)

½ cup / 110g unsalted butter

2½ cups / 590ml whole milk, at room temperature

½ vanilla bean, split lengthwise, seeds scraped, and pod discarded

3 eggs, at room temperature

1 lb / 450g short-grain glutinous rice flour (such as mochiko)

1 cup / 200g granulated sugar

1 Tbsp baking powder

1 pinch kosher salt

½ cup / 90g drained, pitted Luxardo cherries, or rehydrated dried fruit, drained and coarsely chopped

Powdered sugar for dusting, or clarified butter for toasting (optional)

Preheat the oven to 350°F. Line the bottom of a 9 × 13-inch baking pan with parchment paper.

In a large saucepan over low heat, melt the butter. Remove from the heat. Whisk in the milk and vanilla seeds until combined, then whisk in the eggs until smooth.

In a large bowl, whisk together the rice flour, sugar, baking powder, and salt. Pour in the milk mixture and whisk until smooth. Stir in the cherries, then pour into the prepared baking pan.

Bake the nián gāo until light golden brown and a toothpick inserted into the center comes out clean, 55 to 60 minutes. Let cool until warm, about 1 hour. Remove the nián gāo from the pan, peel off the parchment, dust with powdered sugar, and cut into squares to serve. Or skip the sugar dusting and toast the slices in a pan on the stove top with clarified butter until crisp before serving.

BANANA–BLACK SESAME PIE

Active Time — 1 hour

Plan Ahead — This is a recipe that's easiest to do over 2 days, the first for making the pastry cream and caramel, and the next for filling the pie and chilling it. Make the crust on either day.

Makes one 9-inch pie; 8 to 10 servings

Special Equipment — Instant-read thermometer, food processor, 9-inch pie plate (not deep-dish), offset spatula, stand mixer, St. Honoré piping tip (optional)

I always asked my mom to make banana cream pie when I came home from college. She'd start baking late at night, so I'd wake up to it the first morning home. She served hers cold in a crisp pie shell, but I make this with a cookie crust and bring in sesame and miso, which work so well with sweet banana. To me, the combination of gently sweet, sīn, and bitter notes makes this pie the gateway Chinese American dessert. To get this version close to what we serve at the restaurant, don't use premade graham cracker crusts or premade graham cracker crumbs, which are too fine in texture and taste dusty. Also, we grind our sesame paste with a stone mill, but if you are buying it, look for no-sugar, extra-oily black sesame paste in the sauce aisle of Asian grocery stores.

Black Sesame Pastry Cream

1 Tbsp water

1 tsp unflavored
    powdered gelatin

2 cups / 480ml whole milk

½ cup plus 2 Tbsp / 115g
    granulated sugar

2 eggs

2 Tbsp cornstarch

¼ cup plus 1 Tbsp / 75g
    unsweetened black
    sesame paste

½ tsp kosher salt

Miso Caramel

⅓ cup / 65g granulated sugar

¼ cup / 60ml water

¼ cup / 60ml heavy cream,
    at room temperature

2 Tbsp red miso paste

Graham Cracker Crust

5½ oz / 155g graham crackers
    (about 10 sheets), broken
    into 2-inch pieces

3 Tbsp packed
    light brown sugar

2 tsp all-purpose flour

¼ tsp kosher salt

5 Tbsp / 70g unsalted
    butter, melted

To make the pastry cream: Place the water in a small bowl and sprinkle with the gelatin, stirring if needed so that all the gelatin is moistened, and let it bloom. In a medium saucepan over medium heat, bring the milk to a simmer. In a medium bowl, whisk together the granulated sugar, eggs, and cornstarch until smooth.

Prepare an ice bath in a large bowl by filling it with ice cubes and a little water.

Whisk ⅓ cup / 80ml of the milk into the egg mixture to combine and temper the eggs. Whisk the remaining milk into the eggs. Pour the milk-egg mixture back into the saucepan, turn the heat to medium-high, and cook, whisking constantly, until it thickens, bubbles around the edges, and registers 180°F on an instant-read thermometer, about 1½ minutes. Remove from the heat and whisk in the bloomed gelatin, sesame paste, and salt until smooth.

Strain the pastry cream through a fine-mesh strainer into a medium bowl, pushing it through with a rubber spatula. Press a sheet of plastic wrap directly on the surface of the pastry cream so that it doesn't form a skin. Place the bowl in the ice bath and let cool until slightly warmer than room temperature, about 30 minutes. Refrigerate until completely chilled, at least 4 hours or up to overnight.

To make the caramel: In a small saucepan over medium-high heat, combine the granulated sugar and water and stir until the sugar is completely wet. Boil, swirling the saucepan occasionally to prevent hot spots but not stirring, until the sugar is caramelized and light golden brown in color, like honey (with a temperature of about 360°F), about 5 minutes.

Remove the caramel from the heat and immediately (but carefully) pour in the heavy cream (the caramel will bubble up to almost twice its volume and release a lot of steam). Whisk until the bubbling subsides and the caramel is smooth. Whisk in the miso paste until smooth. Let cool to room temperature before using, about 30 minutes. (At this point, you can transfer to an airtight container and store in the refrigerator for up to 3 days.)

CONTINUED

BANANA–BLACK SESAME PIE continued

Mascarpone Whipped Cream

1 cup / 240ml cold
   heavy cream
8 oz / 225g cold
   mascarpone cheese
1½ Tbsp granulated sugar

2 medium bananas, sliced
   into ½-inch-thick rounds
Black sesame seeds
   for sprinkling

To make the crust: Preheat the oven to 350°F.

In a food processor fitted with the blade attachment, process the graham crackers, or crush in a resealable plastic bag with a rolling pin, into crumbs. Transfer the crumbs to a medium bowl. Stir in the brown sugar, flour, and salt. Drizzle with the melted butter and stir until evenly moistened and packable, like wet sand.

Transfer the mixture to a 9-inch pie plate and press the crumbs evenly into the bottom and up the sides. Bake until golden brown and fragrant, about 8 minutes. Let cool completely before using. (At this point, you can cover with plastic wrap and store at room temperature for up to 1 day.)

To make the whipped cream: In a stand mixer fitted with the whisk attachment, combine the heavy cream, mascarpone, and granulated sugar and whip on medium speed until very soft peaks form, about 3 minutes. Do not over-whip, as it will very quickly firm up as it chills. (If you find it has become too firm to handle, gently whip in 1 Tbsp cream by hand to loosen it. You can also make by hand in a large bowl with a whisk and elbow grease.)

Evenly spread the miso caramel on the bottom of the graham cracker crust. Spoon about half of the pastry cream into the crust and use an offset spatula or the back of a spoon to spread it into an even layer. Top with a tightly packed layer of banana rounds. Spoon out and spread the remaining pastry cream over the bananas.

Spread a very thin layer of the whipped cream over the pastry cream. Dollop the remaining pastry cream onto the pie, or if you want it closer to what we do at the restaurant, pipe on a herringbone pattern with a St. Honoré piping tip. Sprinkle with some sesame seeds. Refrigerate for at least 4 hours or up to overnight before slicing to serve.

COFFEE CRUNCH CAKE

Active Time — 2 hours

Plan Ahead — You'll need about 4 hours for cooling and chilling, plus time to make Mascarpone Whipped Cream. Make the coffee mousse and nougatine the day before, then bake the cake and assemble a few hours before serving.

Makes fifteen 1-inch slices

Special Equipment — Stand mixer, instant-read thermometer

When Brandon's parents were in high school, they went on dates to Eastern Bakery on Grant Avenue to eat this cake. So really, if you think about it, we owe it all to Coffee Crunch. This sponge cake means a lot to people connected to Chinatown. It was *the* cake for Mother's Day and church functions. For a while, Eastern Bakery simply advertised theirs with a sign that read, "Coffee Crunch Cakes, Remember?" It reminds me of a Häagen-Dazs Coffee Almond Crunch bar and tiramisu. The original calls for making the toffee honeycomb with foaming baking soda, which is definitely midcentury Americana, but I went with a hazelnut crunch covered in caramel. Frosting the super-light sponge with mascarpone cream right before serving gives it body without any heft.

Coffee Mousse

1 to 1½ cups / 240 to 360ml heavy cream

¼ cup / 25g coarsely ground coffee beans

4 oz / 115g white chocolate discs, feves, or wafers

2 Tbsp water

¾ tsp unflavored powdered gelatin

1 egg, at room temperature

3 Tbsp granulated sugar

Nougatine Crunch

2 oz / 55g raw slivered almonds, or coarsely chopped skinless hazelnuts or macadamia nuts

⅓ cup plus 1 Tbsp / 75g granulated sugar

4 tsp glucose

1 pinch kosher salt

Sponge Cake

¾ cup plus 2½ Tbsp / 170g granulated sugar, plus 2 Tbsp

¼ cup / 60ml water

4 eggs, at room temperature, separated

1 pinch kosher salt

¼ cup / 60ml neutral oil

1 tsp vanilla extract

¾ cup plus 2 Tbsp / 115g cake flour, sifted

To make the mousse: In a small saucepan over medium heat, bring 1 cup / 240ml of the cream to a simmer. Remove from the heat, stir in the coffee beans, and let steep for 1 hour.

Meanwhile, in a large heatproof bowl set on top of the saucepan, use the residual heat to melt the white chocolate, stirring occasionally with a spatula until smooth. Set the bowl of chocolate aside.

Prepare an ice bath in a medium bowl by filling it with ice cubes and a little water.

Strain the coffee cream through a fine-mesh strainer into a liquid measuring cup until you have ¾ cup / 175ml (if you end up with less, top off with the remaining ½ cup / 120ml cream). Discard the coffee beans. Place the coffee cream in the ice bath and chill for 30 minutes, stirring occasionally.

Place 1 Tbsp of the water in a small bowl and sprinkle with the gelatin, stirring if needed so that all the gelatin is moistened, and let it bloom. Check that the chocolate is still melted (if not, reheat over simmering water as before until warm to the touch).

In a stand mixer fitted with the whisk attachment, whisk the egg on medium speed until foamy, about 30 seconds.

In a small saucepan over medium heat, combine the sugar and remaining 1 Tbsp water and bring to a boil, 2 to 3 minutes. Swirl the pan occasionally to melt the sugar into a syrup that reaches 235°F (soft-ball stage), but do not stir or the sugar will crystalize.

With the mixer on low speed, add the bloomed gelatin and then slowly pour in the hot sugar syrup in a thin stream. Continue to mix until the gelatin and syrup are combined. Pour the mixture through a fine-mesh strainer into the melted chocolate and whisk until smooth; it will be thick.

Wash and dry the mixer bowl and whisk attachment. Add the cold coffee cream to the mixer and whisk on medium speed to soft peaks, about 2 minutes. Fold the cream, a third at a time, into the chocolate mixture with a rubber spatula, fully incorporating before adding more. Cover and refrigerate for at least 2 hours or up to overnight.

CONTINUED

COFFEE CRUNCH CAKE continued

1 tsp granulated sugar

⅓ cup / 80ml brewed coffee, chilled

1 recipe Mascarpone Whipped Cream (see page 252)

To make the crunch: Line a baking sheet with a silicone baking mat or parchment paper.

In a small frying pan over medium heat, toast the nuts, tossing occasionally, until light golden brown, 4 to 5 minutes. Set aside in the pan, so they stay warm.

In a small saucepan over medium-high heat, combine the sugar and glucose and cook, stirring frequently with a wooden spoon, until it reaches about 325°F and has turned the color of honey, 3 to 4 minutes. Remove from the heat, then immediately stir in the warm nuts and salt. Pour onto the baking sheet and quickly spread into an even layer, about ⅓ inch thick, before it hardens. Place the baking sheet on a wire rack and let the nougatine harden and cool, about 30 minutes.

Using your hands, break up the nougatine, then chop into pieces roughly the size of popcorn kernels. If there are a lot the powdery bits, remove them by sifting in a colander. Transfer to an airtight container and store at room temperature for up to 5 days.

To make the cake: Preheat the oven to 350°F. Line a rimmed baking sheet with parchment paper.

In a small saucepan over medium heat, combine the ¾ cup plus 2½ Tbsp / 170g sugar and water and bring to a boil, whisking occasionally so the sugar dissolves, 3 to 4 minutes.

In a stand mixer fitted with the whisk attachment, whisk the eggs yolks on medium speed. Slowly pour in the sugar syrup in a thin stream. Continue to mix until the yolks are glossy, fluffy, and tripled in volume. Transfer the whipped egg yolks to a medium bowl and set aside.

Wash and dry the stand mixer bowl and whisk attachment. Add the egg whites, remaining 2 Tbsp sugar, and salt to the mixer and whisk on medium speed until firm peaks form, 3 to 4 minutes.

Meanwhile, in a large bowl, whisk together the neutral oil and vanilla.

Line the components up in this order: egg yolks and vanilla oil, cake flour, and egg whites. Whisk ½ cup / 120ml of the whipped egg yolks into the vanilla oil until smooth. Fold in the remainder of the whipped yolks in two more additions until incorporated. Fold in the cake flour until no streaks or lumps of flour remain. Gently fold in the whipped egg whites until fully incorporated.

Spread the batter onto the prepared baking sheet in an even layer. Bake until the cake is evenly light golden brown and has risen to the lip of the baking sheet, or a tester inserted into the center of the cake comes out clean, about 25 minutes.

Remove from the oven and immediately run a thin knife around the edge of the baking sheet to loosen the cake, so that it doesn't deflate. Nudge a corner of the cake up, then gently slide the cake out with the parchment onto a wire rack. Let cool completely, then finish assembling within a few hours so that it doesn't dry out; otherwise, wrap tightly in plastic wrap and store at room temperature overnight.

CONTINUED

In a small bowl, combine the sugar and coffee and stir until the sugar is dissolved. Set this syrup aside.

Flip the cake over, carefully peel off the parchment, and then gently press it back onto the cake. Flip the cake right-side up again. Press a new sheet of parchment on the top of the cake and smooth it with your palms, so that it sticks well to the entire surface. Peel off the parchment to remove the top layer of cake with it, creating a porous surface for the cake to soak up the coffee syrup. Use your fingers to gently remove any cake top remaining.

Position the cake with the long side facing you. Brush the cake with a thin layer of coffee syrup. Leaving a 1-inch border at the bottom, use a rubber spatula to spread the mousse evenly over the cake. Sprinkle the nougatine over the cake and use the spatula to gently press it into the mousse. Tightly roll up the cake starting from the bottom, using the parchment to help lift, roll, and tuck the cake before peeling the parchment away. Position the roll seam-side down. Transfer to the refrigerator and chill, uncovered, for at least 2 hours or up to 6 hours.

When ready to serve, frost the top and sides of the cake with the whipped cream. Use a serrated knife to portion into fifteen slices, wiping the knife between each cut for clean edges.

STEAMED KABOCHA CAKE WITH SOY MILK ICE CREAM

Active Time — 50 minutes

Plan Ahead — You'll need overnight for soaking the beans and chilling the ice-cream base, as well as making Braised Burdock Syrup

Makes 6 to 8 servings

Special Equipment — Blender, ice-cream machine, 9-inch round cake pan, stand mixer, steamer

Red Bean Paste

1 cup / 140g dried small
    Asian red beans
3½ Tbsp glucose
3 Tbsp packed
    light brown sugar
Kosher salt
1 Tbsp rendered lard or
    unsalted butter

Soy Milk Ice Cream

3¼ cups / 780ml fresh
    unsweetened soy milk
¼ cup / 50g granulated sugar
2 Tbsp glucose
1 tsp kosher salt

One 1¾-lb / 800g
    kabocha squash
7 Tbsp / 105ml whole milk,
    at room temperature
1 tsp vanilla extract
1¼ cups / 175g
    all-purpose flour
1 tsp baking soda
1 tsp baking powder
½ tsp ground cinnamon
¼ tsp ground nutmeg
3 eggs, at room temperature
⅔ cup / 130g packed
    light brown sugar

If you grew up Chinese American, your family probably treated the oven like the dishwasher—as a place for storing pots and pans. Tradition is hard to shake. The rare oven was saved for the extravagance of roasting meats. So instead of baking cakes, we do steamed cakes. They can range from yellow and eggy to snow-white and sour from fermented rice flour. Most are airy and moist, more sticky pudding than sponge. During one of our brainstorming sessions, Brandon mentioned his love for máh lāai gōu (馬拉糕), the brown sugarcane steamed cakes served at dim sum. Anything goes when it comes to steamed cakes, so I paired two of my favorite earthy Chinese dessert ingredients—red bean and pumpkin—to make something like an ultra-tender spice bread with a contrasting creamy layer of Chinese red bean in the middle. Red beans are labeled "紅豆" or "adzuki." Small bush (not vine) varieties usually cook up creamier than others, but it can be hard to tell before trying them. Smaller beans are usually the better bet.

To make the bean paste: Place the beans in a medium bowl, add enough water to cover by 1 inch, and let soak overnight at room temperature.

The next day, drain the beans and transfer to a large saucepan, cover with a few inches of fresh water, and bring to a boil over high heat. Turn the heat to medium and simmer until tender and starting to split open, 1 to 1¼ hours. Strain through a strainer into a medium bowl. Reserve the cooking liquid.

In a blender, combine the warm beans with ¼ cup / 60ml of the cooking liquid, the glucose, brown sugar, and a big pinch of salt and blend, scraping down the sides occasionally and adding more cooking liquid 1 Tbsp at a time, as needed, until the paste is smooth. In a sauté pan over low heat, melt the lard. Add the red bean paste and stir, cooking out some of the water, until it is thick, like canned pumpkin. Let cool, then transfer to an airtight container and store in the refrigerator for up to 5 days, or in the freezer for up to 2 months.

To make the ice cream: Freeze the ice-cream maker's canister according to the manufacturer's instructions.

In a small saucepan over medium heat, simmer 2 cups / 480ml of the soy milk, stirring occasionally, until reduced to 1 cup / 240ml, about 30 minutes. Remove from the heat and stir in the granulated sugar, glucose, and salt until dissolved. Stir in the remaining 1¼ cups / 300ml soy milk. Pour through a fine-mesh strainer into a 1-quart container. Cover this ice-cream base and refrigerate overnight.

Transfer the ice-cream base to the prepared canister and spin according to the manufacturer's instructions until it is a soft-serve consistency. Scrape the ice cream into a 1-quart container and freeze until firm enough to scoop, at least 1 hour or up to 1 week, before serving.

Preheat the oven to 400°F. Line a baking sheet with parchment paper. Line the bottom of a 9-inch round cake pan with parchment paper.

CONTINUED

¼ cup / 60ml neutral oil
Powdered sugar for dusting
Braised Burdock Syrup
   (see page 146) for drizzling
   (optional)

Halve the squash (no need to remove the seeds), then place cut-side down on the prepared baking sheet. Roast until knife-tender, about 45 minutes. Remove from the oven and let cool.

When the squash is cool enough to handle, scoop out and discard the seeds. Scoop the flesh into the blender and discard the skin. Blend the squash until smooth and the texture of canned pumpkin purée, adding water 1 Tbsp at a time if needed to get the right consistency. Measure ¾ cup / 170g puréed squash into a medium bowl, add the milk and vanilla, and whisk until smooth.

In a large bowl, sift together the flour, baking soda, baking powder, cinnamon, and nutmeg.

In a stand mixer fitted with the paddle attachment, beat the eggs, brown sugar, and neutral oil on medium speed until lightened in color, about 3 minutes. Add the squash mixture and beat until smooth. Using a rubber spatula, fold the wet mixture into the dry ingredients by hand in three additions until no dry streaks of flour remain.

Pour half of the batter into the prepared pan. Pipe or drop small spoonfuls of the red bean paste evenly over the batter. Pour the remaining batter over the red bean paste. Cover the pan tightly with aluminum foil.

Prepare a steamer in a wok or a large, lidded pot following the instructions on page 167 and bring the water to a boil over medium-high heat. Place the cake pan in the steamer and steam until the cake is set and the top springs back when poked gently with a finger, about 1 hour, adding water to the pot halfway through as needed. Uncover and let the cake cool for 10 minutes in the pan.

Remove the cake from the pan and dust with powdered sugar. Serve warm with soy milk ice cream and burdock syrup, if desired, drizzled over everything.

ON CHINATOWN ICE CREAM

Fong-Fong Bakery-Fountain opened on Grant Avenue in 1935, bringing banana splits and parfaits to Chinatown. Owner Philip Fong found a young entrepreneur named Johnny Kan to man the counter; and Kan went all in, enrolling at the University of California, Davis, Farm Dairy School to learn ice cream. "[T]ourists in Chinatown would keep coming into Fong-Fong's, and after staring at the twenty ice-cream listings they'd say, 'Cheeze, don't yuh have any Chinese ice cream?'" Kan explained in a written interview in 1971. So he came up with flavors new to those outside of Chinatown, like lychee, ginger, and Chinese fruit, which went into Chop Suey sundaes topped with a sesame cookie. Until Fong-Fong closed in 1974, it drew in young locals, the second-generation Americans, like Kan, who wanted burgers, a jukebox, and an experience as eclectic as they were.

FROZEN WHIPPED HONEY

Active Time — 4 hours

Plan Ahead — You'll need 3 days to make the ice cream and then the sorbet if you don't have two ice-cream canisters. Be sure to check your ice-cream machine's instructions, which might require freezing the canister overnight. You can save a day if you make this as semifreddo instead of ice cream. The day before serving, make the semifreddo, chocolate shards, jasmine jelly, sorbet base, roasted pineapple, and tuile base. Finish the sorbet and tuiles and serve the next day.

Makes 8 servings

Special Equipment — 8½ × 4½-inch loaf pan (optional), ice-cream machine, juicer, food processor, blender, silicone baking mats, offset spatula, acetate sheets, instant-read thermometer

Honey Semifreddo or Ice Cream

1½ tsp water

¾ tsp unflavored powdered gelatin

2 cups plus 2 Tbsp / 510ml heavy cream

¼ cup plus 2 Tbsp / 120g buckwheat or other high-quality honey

½ cup / 120ml egg whites, at room temperature

1 pinch kosher salt

Roasted Pineapple and Pineapple Sorbet

1 medium pineapple (not overly ripe)

6 Tbsp / 90ml glucose

3 Tbsp granulated sugar, plus more as needed

The star of this sundae is honey, our most ancient and cross-cultural sweet ingredient. Everyone has an understanding of honey, regardless of where they grow up. Frozen dairy desserts are surprisingly ancient too. The first on record were made in China some 4,000 years ago, though ice cream (and home refrigerators) are a relative novelty in contemporary China. I paired honey ice cream, which is not so typical at the end of a Chinese meal, with fruit, tea, and jellies, ingredients that are. The caramelized pineapple, crisp walnut, and delicate white chocolate shards are all important components, but the honey is the star. I'm lucky to have found a beautiful, local buckwheat-blossom honey that has a deep, earthy flavor. Honey can be delicate and floral or robust, musky, and even spicy. Look for a honey that has complexity, not just sweetness, made by your local bees.

To make the semifreddo or ice cream: Place the water in a small bowl and sprinkle with the gelatin, stirring if needed so that all the gelatin is moistened, and let it bloom. In a large saucepan over medium heat, bring the cream to a simmer. In a large bowl, whisk together the honey and egg whites.

Prepare an ice bath in a large bowl by filling it with ice cubes and a little water.

Add a ladleful of the cream into the egg mixture and whisk to combine and temper the eggs. Whisk in the remaining cream. Pour the cream-egg mixture back into the saucepan, turn the heat to medium-high, and cook, stirring until this base comes to a simmer and thickens (about 180°F), 5 to 6 minutes. Remove from the heat and whisk in the bloomed gelatin until fully dissolved.

Strain the base through a fine-mesh strainer into a medium bowl, pushing it through with a rubber spatula. Stir in the salt. Set the bowl in the ice bath, stirring occasionally until warm to the touch, about 15 minutes.

For semifreddo, line a 8½ x 4½-inch loaf pan with parchment paper. Pour the base into the prepared pan and freeze until solid, at least 6 hours or up to 3 days. When ready to serve, let the semifreddo sit out a few minutes; rubbing your hands on the outside of the pan will help warm it just enough to help it slide out. Invert the semifreddo onto a cutting board and cut into ¾-inch-thick slices.

For ice cream, cover the base and refrigerate overnight. Transfer to an ice-cream machine and spin according to the manufacturer's instructions until a soft-serve consistency. Freeze until firm enough to scoop, at least 1 hour or up to 1 week, before serving.

To make the roasted pineapple and sorbet: Trim the top and bottom of the pineapple, then cut the skin off the pineapple and quarter lengthwise. In a juicer, juice about three-fourths of the pineapple until you have 1½ cups / 360ml juice. Strain the juice through a fine-mesh strainer to remove any fibrous bits and set aside.

Preheat the oven to 475°F. Line a baking sheet with parchment paper.

CONTINUED

Walnut Tuile

½ cup / 60g raw walnuts

2 Tbsp all-purpose flour

8 Tbsp / 115g unsalted butter,
    cut into 8 pieces

½ cup plus 2 tsp / 110g
    granulated sugar

2 Tbsp whole milk

⅛ tsp vanilla extract

1 pinch kosher salt

Jasmine Jelly

1 cup / 240ml whole milk

3 Tbsp loose-leaf jasmine tea

1 Tbsp water

1 tsp unflavored
    powdered gelatin

1 Tbsp granulated sugar

White Chocolate Shards

8 oz / 225g white chocolate
    discs, feves, or wafers

Micro-mizuna for garnishing
    (optional)

Trim and discard the core from the remaining one-fourth pineapple, place on the prepared baking sheet, and roast until charred in spots, about 30 minutes. Let cool, then dice into ¼-inch cubes. Transfer to an airtight container and store in the refrigerator for up to 2 days.

In a medium saucepan over medium heat, combine 1 cup / 240ml of the pineapple juice, the glucose, and sugar and cook, stirring just until the sugar is dissolved. Remove from the heat, then stir in the remaining ½ cup / 120ml pineapple juice, taste, and add more sugar as needed (you still want some tartness). Pour this base into a 1-quart container, cover, and refrigerate until chilled, at least 4 hours or up to overnight.

Transfer the base to an ice-cream maker and spin according to the manufacturer's instructions until a soft-serve consistency is reached. Freeze until firm enough to scoop, at least 1 hour or up to 1 week, before serving.

To make the tuile: In a food processor fitted with the blade attachment, combine the walnuts and flour and pulse until coarsely ground, then process to a finely ground walnut flour. In a medium saucepan over medium heat, combine the butter, sugar, and milk and cook, stirring until the sugar is dissolved and the butter is melted. Stir in the walnut flour until well combined. Remove from the heat and stir the vanilla and salt into this batter.

Pour the batter into a blender and blend until very smooth, with a consistency like honey. Pour into a container, let cool, cover, and then refrigerate overnight.

When ready to bake, take the batter out of the refrigerator and let sit until room temperature, about 2 hours. Preheat the oven to 350°F.

Divide the batter among two silicone baking mats or sheets of parchment paper. Using an offset spatula, spread the batter as thinly and evenly as possible without gaps, avoiding the edges of the mat by about 1 inch.

One at a time, slide a mat of batter onto a baking sheet and bake until it has spread out and is evenly golden brown, 10 to 12 minutes. Let cool on the baking sheet until the bubbling stops, about 1 minute. Carefully slide the sheets of tuile from the baking sheets onto a flat, heatproof surface and let cool completely, about 15 minutes. Using your hands, break the tuile into shards that are about 3 × 2 inches. Transfer to an airtight container and store at room temperature for up to 2 days.

To make the jelly: In a small saucepan over medium heat, bring the milk to a simmer. Remove from the heat, stir in the tea, and set aside to steep for 15 minutes.

Meanwhile, place the water in a small bowl and sprinkle with the gelatin, stirring if needed so that all the gelatin is moistened, and let it bloom.

Pour the infused milk through a fine-mesh strainer into a small bowl and discard the tea leaves. Pour the infused milk back into the saucepan and bring to a simmer over medium heat. Remove from the heat and whisk in the sugar and bloomed gelatin until dissolved. Pour into a container, cover, and refrigerate until set, about 2 hours or up to 2 days.

To make the chocolate shards: Set out two 16-inch-long acetate sheets or wax paper.

Finely chop 6¼ oz / 180g of the chocolate and place in a medium or large metal bowl.

Prepare a double boiler by pouring an inch or two of water into a large saucepan. Bring the water to a simmer over low heat, then set the bowl of chocolate onto the saucepan and stir until about two-thirds of the chocolate is melted. Remove the bowl from the heat and stir until all of the chocolate is melted; it should be no hotter than 120°F (if it is, start over).

Let the melted chocolate cool until it registers 100°F on an instant-read thermometer, about body temperature. Add the remaining 1¾ oz / 45g chocolate and stir until it registers 87°F. (If there is any unmelted chocolate at this point, remove it.) Pour the tempered chocolate onto the acetate and use the offset spatula to spread it as thinly and evenly as possible before it hardens, which will happen quickly. Let set at room temperature until hardened. Break into shards about the same size as the tuile shards, transfer to an airtight container, and store at room temperature for up to 1 week.

Freeze individual bowls so that they are cold. Scoop 1 Tbsp jasmine jelly into each bowl. Top with a thick slice of honey semifreddo or a large scoop of honey ice cream and then a small scoop of pineapple sorbet. Scatter pieces of roasted pineapple in the bowls. Stand a few alternating pieces of walnut tuile and white chocolate shards in the pineapple sorbet like sails. Garnish with the micro-mizuna, if desired, before serving.

9

Parties are big in Chinatown, grand on the scale of hundreds of guests. A Chinese banquet entails a huge room packed with round tables for ten, as well as a stage and dais for the emcee, band, and guests of honor, usually a bride and groom, but possibly a hundred-day-old baby, an eighty-year-old auntie, or a politician. There's always an open bar with XO cognac on hand, and ginger ale for the kids, and usually a parquet dance floor, a banner announcing the celebration in English and Chinese, gigantic floral arrangements, and, when the occasion calls for it, a security guy collecting red envelopes of cash, leih sih (利是), at the door. There is at least as much talking as there is eating.

It takes an incredible range of skills, ingredients, and equipment to turn out eight or twelve multi-dish courses for the standard Chinatown dinner banquet. And that's just one kind of elaborate Chinese spread. There are New Year banquets, dumpling banquets, birthday banquets, the Confucian banquet, the sixty-sixth birthday of the emperor banquet, the single-ingredient-done-every-which-way banquet, and so on, ranging from homey to formal.

The space that Mister Jiu's occupies was a banquet hall for well over a century, hosting award nights for neighborhood bigwigs, the Chinese Sportsmen's Club annual Striped-Bass Derby Dinner, and my uncle's wedding. The menus included dim sum to the most elaborate ingredients, like hand-fed, young quail and wild mushrooms harvested just after the first spring snowmelt. Many of the last big banquet halls in Chinatown shuttered in recent years, although Far East Café and New Asia still throw down as community hubs.

Even when the ingredients are not so extravagant, a banquet always involves certain formalities and rituals to signal it as a moment for building relationships, that all-important guanxi. You eat and drink together to bind each other's hearts, as the Chinese say. The host will confer with the chef on the menu well in advance to ensure it speaks as well as it eats. The names of ingredients are often a pun for something else, so every dish says something. A dish with lòh baahk (daikon) sends a message wishing luck. A sprig of coriander represents the fate that brought everyone together. During New Year, you serve noodles for longevity; pork, chicken, and fish for wealth, health, and abundance; and citrus for continued luck and success.

Mister Jiu's banquets and celebrations are all produced by Anna Lee, co-owner and the Missus to my Mister. Sometimes I get so focused on the menu, I forget that people go out to eat for other reasons than just the food. The beauty and vibe of Mister Jiu's are reflections of Anna Lee's eye and wit. She comes up with details that bring people together and spread good vibes, from the lighting to the art, the aquariums, the soundscape, the plates, and the plants. On Valentine's Day, she brought in a photo booth. On New Year's Eve, we built the tallest champagne tower we could manage. She is always thinking of new details to keep surprising people and to make this building feel alive.

Going full-on banquet is probably not something you'll ever want to pull off at home, but the principles behind them work for planning any menu for a memorable night.

1. Invite enough guests so you have an even number, including yourself, around the table. For a party of eight to twelve, roll out a lazy Susan, if you've got one.

2. The seat of honor faces the door. The host takes the seat nearest the exit.

3. Plan on eight or twelve dishes, or at least an even number of them (not including the rice) for good luck. The usual order for a Chinatown banquet goes something like the order of the recipes in this book.

4. Try to take your guests' palates on a flavor, texture, and aroma journey. Consider both harmony and the progression of each course. For instance, it's hard to taste a subtle, mild dish after a spicy one. Make the food on the table colorful.

5. Alternate simple and complex dishes to give palates and yourself a break. It's boring if everything is steamed, overwhelming if everything is fried. You'll have to time to enjoy your party by preparing the cold, stewed, and braised dishes in advance.

6. Think about seasonality, not just in terms of what ingredients are at their best but in terms of what you crave right now on account of the weather and general state of things.

8. Serve a whole fish. A great fish always makes the night. The word for fish, *yú* (魚), is a pun for abundance. The fish's head should point toward your most honored guest.

This is how we throw down on a typical night. You can always opt for Hot Pot instead of a Soup and Mains and Veg. Start with Bites and Libations, then move on to Hot Pot, before capping it with Dessert.

BITES AND LIBATIONS
Spicy Crispy Peanuts
(page 63), Brined Celtuce
(page 60), Prawn Toast
(page 65), Smoked Oyster
You Tiao (page 56)
and Luck (page 269)

SALAD
Mandarin and Chinese
Almond Salad (page 133)

SOUP
Sizzling Rice Soup
(page 113), or Hot and Sour
Soup (page 119)

HOT POT
(pages 272–275)

or

MAINS (SEAFOOD OR MEAT) AND VEG
Sizzling Fish (page 170)
or Whole Dungeness
Crab (page 178),
with Tendrils, Greens,
and Stems (page 135)

+

Four Seas Crispy Chicken
(page 192), or Liberty
Roast Duck (page 203),
with Mushroom Mu
Shu (page 145) and
Mouthwatering Tomatoes
and Liang Fen (page 163)

RICE
Steamed Rice (page 229)

DESSERT
Jin Deui (page 103),
or Steamed Kabocha
Cake with Soy Milk
Ice Cream (page 257)

Free-flowing drinks, hot
and cold, throughout

ETERNITY

Plan Ahead — Start a day ahead to infuse the Lillet, and reserve a couple hours for the crab oil

Active Time — 10 minutes

Makes 1 cocktail

Special Equipment — Mixing glass, julep or Hawthorne strainer

1½ oz / 45ml Beefeater gin

1 oz / 30ml St. George's All Purpose vodka

¼ oz / 7ml Dill-Infused Lillet (recipe follows)

Ice cubes

4 to 6 drops Crab Oil (see page 178), at room temperature

3 pitted Castelvetrano olives, on a pick

1 jarred pickled green bean

This bold, briny martini is glorious, but takes some planning. It's crowned with orange drops of savory crab oil, so you'll need crab shells. (This is a good excuse to serve Whole Dungeness Crab.) We smoke the olives over apple wood, and pickle long beans in seasoned rice wine vinegar, but this works well with garnishes straight out of the jar too. This cocktail requires 30 seconds of shaking, so it's best for a night with friends who know it's worth the wait.

Chill a coupe glass and a mixing glass.

In the chilled mixing glass, combine the gin, vodka, and Lillet; add ice; and stir for about 30 seconds. Using a julep or Hawthorne strainer, strain into the coupe glass. Using an eyedropper (or a straw, like a pipette), slowly float drops of the crab oil on the drink's surface. Garnish with the olives and pickled bean before serving.

DILL-INFUSED LILLET

Makes 1 cup / 240ml

1 cup / 240ml Lillet Blanc   ½ bunch fresh dill

In a medium jar, combine the Lillet and dill. Cover the jar and let infuse for 24 hours. Strain out the dill. Store in a cool, dry place for up to 6 months, although it will gradually lose some potency.

LUCK

Plan Ahead — You'll need up to 1 hour to infuse the gin, plus time to freeze or buy ice

Active Time — 10 minutes

Makes 6 to 8 servings

1 cup / 240ml Lychee
    Tea–Infused Tequila
    (recipe follows)
1 cup / 240ml Tapatio
    Blanco tequila
1 cup / 240ml water
1 cup / 240ml fresh lime juice
½ cup / 120ml Giffard
    Banane du Bresil
½ cup / 120ml Simple Syrup
    (recipe follows)
Ice block
Lime wheels for floating

This warming combo of lychee, banana, and tequila is all tropical vibes. We use a lychee-scented, loose-leaf black tea. Different teas, especially black, react differently to alcohol, so taste at around the 30-minute mark and strain out the tea before it turns bitter.

In a punch bowl, combine both tequilas, the water, lime juice, Banane du Bresil, and simple syrup and stir to mix. Add the ice, then float the lime wheels on top. Ladle into cups to serve.

LYCHEE TEA–INFUSED TEQUILA

Makes 1 cup / 240ml

1 cup / 240ml Tapatio Blanco
    tequila

4 tsp loose-leaf lychee black tea

Pour the tequila into a small jar. Stir in the tea and let infuse for 30 minutes to 1 hour. Strain out the tea leaves. Store in a cool, dry place for 6 months. Chill before using.

SIMPLE SYRUP

Makes 1½ cups / 360ml

1 cup granulated
    sugar

1 cup water

In a medium saucepan over medium-high heat, combine the sugar and water and bring to a boil, stirring occasionally. Remove from the heat and let cool. Store in an airtight container in the refrigerator indefinitely.

Hot Pot

Hot pot, dá bīn lòuh (打邊爐; 火锅, huǒguō in Mandarin) is true party food. Sitting in a circle around the pot symbolizes reunion. You can't help bumping elbows and chopsticks, so you end up cooking for one another. We love hot pot for Chinese New Year, but you can serve it year-round, indoors and out.

Your hot pot can be any wide pot, such as a clay pot, set over a portable burner. I like a yuān yāng guō (鸳鸯锅, in Mandarin), a stainless-steel pot divided in the middle, so I can offer two broths at once. Set out a small bowl for sauce and a medium bowl for each guest, and a few slotted ladles or sieves for the table.

Start working on the desired add-ons such as Fish balls (page 274), Squid Ink Wontons (page 85), and Siu Yuk (page 222) at least a day before (they all keep well frozen). You'll need a couple hours before guests arrive to prep raw ingredients and make the broths and sauces. I also like whole shrimp or spot prawns (devein and trim the antennae), doufu (cut into 1-inch cubes), cellophane noodles (soak in warm water until softened, about 20 minutes), and a raw egg per person. I stack platters high with vegetables such as bamboo shoots, varieties of mushrooms (trim tough stems), mountain yam or daikon (peel and roll cut), lotus root (peel and thinly slice into disks), leafy greens such as chrysanthemum (rinse, remove any buds and woody stem ends, and cut or tear into into 2-inch pieces), napa cabbage (cut into 2-inch pieces), and water chestnuts (peel and slice into disks). Offer some meats such as thinly sliced lamb or beef (Chinese butchers can do this for you). Spread everything within easy reach across the table. Anything that can be cooked through and intact in a few minutes can go into the pot. Set out a buffet of Sesame-Garlic Sauce (page 274), Shacha (page 275), and Hot Mustard (page 44). I also like an assortment of chile oil, soy sauce, sesame oil, sesame paste, chopped fresh chiles, chopped green onions, minced garlic, and cilantro, so everyone can mix what they want.

The broth sets the scene. Get it boiling first, then throw in the first handful of aromatics, mushrooms, and whatever vegetables take the longest to cook to get everyone started. Keep the broth simmering as everyone eats, and be sure to keep a reserve heating on the stove for topping up. When cooking, hold on to ingredients that cook quickly. Thinly sliced meats need just a few swishes in the broth. Dip each bite in sauce as you go or combine everything in your bowl.

A couple rules with raw meat: Try not to eat anything else out of the pot until the meat has had at least a few seconds in simmering broth, and submerge your chopsticks in the broth for a few seconds after handling raw proteins. Once almost everything has been cooked and the broth is concentrated with flavor, add the noodles to the pot. To eat them, crack an egg into your bowl, add some noodles and broth on top, and mix it all together with your chopsticks.

HOT POT BROTHS

Active Time — 5 to 15 minutes

Plan Ahead — You'll need
time to make Supreme Stock
and the chile oil

Makes 4 servings

Special Equipment — Hot-pot
stove, deep-fry thermometer
(for Spicy Broth)

MILD HERBAL BROTH

3 qt / 2.8L Supreme Stock (page 34)
4 long slices unpeeled ginger, ¼ inch thick
8 fresh or dried jujubes
2 Tbsp dried goji berries
¼ oz / 7g dried ginseng

In a hot pot, combine the stock, ginger, jujubes, goji berries, and ginseng
and bring to a boil, then turn the heat to low and simmer for about 30 minutes.

SPICY BROTH

1 cup / 240ml neutral oil
10 dried Yunnan chiles
3 qt / 2.8L Supreme Stock (page 34)
10 black cardamom pods (草果, chóu gwó)
2 tsp green cardamom pods
4 star anise pods
1½ tsp fennel seeds
1½ tsp red Sichuan peppercorns
5 bay leaves
Basic Chile Oil (page 40), Lanzhou Chile Oil (page 40),
    or Spicy Beef Chile Oil (page 41)—these are in increasing
    level of spiciness; choose one

Fill a small saucepan with the neutral oil and secure a deep-fry thermometer
on the side. Set over medium-high heat and warm the oil to 350°F. Add the
chiles and fry until just starting to darken in color, about 30 seconds. Transfer
to a paper towel to drain. Let cool, pinch off and discard the stems, and then
crumble the chiles into 1-inch pieces.

In a hot pot, combine the chiles, stock, both kinds of cardamom pods,
star anise, fennel seeds, peppercorns, bay leaves, and chile oil (start with
a few tablespoons at first) and bring to a boil, then turn the heat to low and
simmer for about 30 minutes. (Taste and add more chile oil if desired before
adding anything to cook in the broth.)

FISH BALLS

Active Time — 30 minutes
Makes about 30 fish balls
Special Equipment — Meat grinder, deep-fry thermometer

12 oz / 340g boneless, skinless rock cod or other lean white fish fillets, cut into 2-inch pieces

6 oz / 170g cleaned and peeled shrimp

4 oz / 115g sea scallops

3 Tbsp wheat starch (look for "澄麵粉" [chìhng mihn fán], or sometimes "wheaten cornflour" or "non-glutinous flour")

1½ Tbsp cornstarch

⅓ cup / 15g finely chopped chives

1 Tbsp kosher salt

1 qt / 950ml neutral oil

If using a meat grinder, grind the fish, shrimp, and scallops through a coarse grinding plate (¼-inch / 6mm holes) into a medium bowl. Vigorously mix with a wooden spoon until it comes together as a glossy, smooth, and sticky paste.

If chopping by hand, mince the fish until it forms a paste that feels slightly grainy but contains no visible chunks. Repeat with the shrimp, then the scallops, and pile everything together and continue chopping until it comes together as a glossy, smooth, and sticky paste. Transfer into a medium bowl.

Add the wheat starch, cornstarch, chives, and salt to the fish and vigorously mix with a wooden spoon until well-incorporated into the sticky paste.

Bring a large saucepan of heavily salted water (it should remind you of seawater) to a boil over high heat.

Meanwhile, line a rimmed baking sheet with parchment paper, line a plate with a double layer of paper towels, and fit a wire rack over a second baking sheet. Drop the seafood paste, in 1½-Tbsp scoops, onto the parchment-lined baking sheet. Use damp hands to gently shape each scoop into a ball.

In two batches, drop the fish balls into the boiling water, then lower the heat and simmer until just cooked through, about 5 minutes. Using a spider, transfer the fish balls to the prepared plate and pat them very dry. (At this point, the fish balls can be transferred to an airtight container and stored in the refrigerator for up to 4 days, or in the freezer for up to 2 months. Thaw frozen fish balls and pat dry again before frying.)

Fill a wok or large saucepan with the neutral oil and secure a deep-fry thermometer on the side. Set over medium-high heat and warm the oil to 375°F, taking care to maintain this temperature as you go.

Fry the fish balls in batches of ten until golden brown, about 2 minutes. Using the spider, transfer the fish balls to the prepared rack. They are now ready to be used in hot pot.

SESAME-GARLIC SAUCE

Active Time — 15 minutes
Makes 1⅓ cups / 315ml

¼ cup plus 2 Tbsp / 90ml light soy sauce (生抽, sāng chāu)

4½ tsp granulated sugar

2 tsp minced garlic

½ cup / 120ml peanut oil or neutral oil

3 Tbsp plus 1 tsp raw white sesame seeds

½ cup / 40g finely chopped cilantro

1 Tbsp plus ½ tsp toasted sesame oil

In a medium heatproof bowl, combine the soy sauce, sugar, and garlic. In a small saucepan over medium-high heat, warm the peanut oil until just starting to smoke, 2 to 3 minutes. Carefully pour the oil into the soy mixture and stir to dissolve the sugar. Set aside to cool to room temperature.

Meanwhile, in a large frying pan over medium heat, toast the sesame seeds until light golden brown, 3 to 5 minutes; set aside to cool.

Stir the toasted sesame seeds, cilantro, and sesame oil into the sauce. Transfer to an airtight container and store in the refrigerator for up to 1 week.

SHACHA

Active Time — 30 minutes

Plan Ahead — You'll need 30 minutes for hydrating the Dried Scallops and Dried Shrimp, plus time to make 10 Spice

Makes about 1⅔ cups / 395ml

Special Equipment —
Food processor

2 oz / 55g Dried Scallops
    (page 39)
½ oz / 15g Dried Shrimp
    (page 39)
1 cup / 240ml neutral oil
1½ Tbsp minced garlic
1½ Tbsp peeled and minced
    ginger
1½ Tbsp minced shallots
¼ cup / 50g minced salt-
    or oil-packed anchovies
1 Tbsp toasted sesame oil
4½ tsp 10 Spice (see page 36)
1 tsp cayenne pepper

Place the scallops and shrimp in a medium bowl, cover with warm water, and let soak for 30 minutes. Drain, then tear each scallop into a few pieces. Add the scallops and shrimp to a food processor fitted with the blade attachment and pulse about thirty times, until shredded and fluffy. (To shred by hand, tear the scallops with your fingers, then work in a mortar and pestle with the shrimp until very finely chopped.)

In a medium saucepan or wok over medium heat, warm the neutral oil until shimmering. Add the garlic, ginger, and shallots and fry until starting to brown, about 2 minutes. Stir in the scallops, shrimp, and anchovies and cook, stirring frequently, until golden brown, about 5 minutes. Remove from the heat; stir in the sesame oil, 10 Spice, and cayenne; and let cool.

Transfer the sauce to an airtight container and store in the refrigerator for up to 6 months. Stir before using.

ACKNOWLEDGMENTS

I owe my sanity, joy, and optimism to my wife, Anna Lee; without her, Mister Jiu's would not look as it does, would not feel so thoughtful, and would be way harder to run day in and day out. I wake up every day feeling like the luckiest man ever.

Thank you to my family: my parents, Winfred and Mona, who instilled a sense of dedication, integrity, and commitment in me; my older sister, Heather, for your encouragement; and my younger brother, Travis, for your constant positivity.

Thanks to my team, past and present, at Mister Jiu's. We got better together and the food followed. Special thanks to Sean Walsh, Franky Ho, Melissa Chou, Will Do, Kim Hirota, and Kelly Teramoto for laying the groundwork for our kitchen culture, systems, sense of humor, passion, and work ethic. Special thanks to Maz Naba, Marissa D'Orazio, and Jared Feldman, who work behind the scenes to make the restaurant function.

Thank you to Betty Louie, our landlady at Mister Jiu's, who believed in my vision for the space and has been instrumental in our success. Thank you to my investors, who knew investing in our restaurant also meant investing in Chinatown.

Thank you to my cousin Ryan Lee, you put in so much work to help me design all aspects of the brand. Thank you to my Auntie Char, you didn't let me give up when I thought I had to. Thank you to Uncle Mike, who built all my crazy ideas, like a built-in lazy Susan table and a moon-gate skylight. Thank you to architects Bonnie Bridges and Stephanie Wong, who helped us design and build a space that brought back the glory that the neighborhood deserved.

Thank you to Tienlon Ho, for writing this book with me, for qualifying our ideas, and for pouring your heart into enriching these pages with Chinatown's fascinating history. Thank you to Christine Gallary, for your exacting eye and for patiently decoding all our notebooks into recipes. Thank you to Pete Lee, for being invested in our food and our staff much more deeply than just snapping photos. Thank you to Danielle Svetcov, for your enthusiasm and readiness to help; you were therapeutic. We are all grateful to Dervla Kelly, Doug Ogan, Lizzie Allen, Emma Campion, Serena Sigona, Leda Scheintaub, and Ann Martin Rolke at Ten Speed Press, for carrying us to the finish line.

We owe thanks to all our Chinatown neighbors, some of whom we had the honor of including in this book. Thank you especially for your expertise and stories to Wing, Simon, Eric, and Patricia Cheung of Hing Lung Co.; Tane Chan at The Wok Shop; Dorothy "Polka Dot" Quock; Candy Lu at Produce Land; Hon's Wun Tun House; LeeAnn Lee at Mow Lee Shing Kee & Company; Yau Kung Moon Kung Fu; Hue An Herbs and Ginseng; Mr. Zeng at Tung Fong Herbs; Jones and Judy Wong at Wong's TV & Radio Service; William

Wu at Traditional Chinese Medical and Traumatology; Henry Lam and San Francisco 9-Man; Susan Lin at Tin How Temple; Nancy and Kevin Chan at the Chinatown Fortune Cookie Factory; Zhuo Fan Ye at Stylers Art Gallery; Dot's Printing; Orlando Kuan at Eastern Bakery; Far East Café; the Ho family at Sam Wo; and Simmone Kuo at Lien-Ying Tai-Chi Chuan Martial Arts Academy.

Thank you to April Chan, for your help diving into history; I'm so glad we crossed paths again. We owe Mai Tais at Li Po Lounge to Tim Mah, Sarah Hauman, Marko Sotto, Jonathan Kauffman, Arielle Johnson, Jowett Yu, Aralyn Beaumont, Sarah Henkin, Andrea Nguyen, Albert Cheng, Chris Ying, Rachel Khong, and AJ Wang. Thank you to Ken Ho and Wenhuei Ho, for sharing your knowledge, and to Jon Adams and Quin Adams Ho, for lending me your most important person. Thank you to Martin Yan, for your commitment to Chinatown and for butchering that chicken so damn fast.

Thank you to Sik Lee Dennig and Mingfei Lau, for dialect expertise. The history in this book draws from the work of many, including Sucheng Chan, Gordon Chang, Jack Chen, Yong Chen, Thomas W. Chinn, Philip P. Choy, Andrew Coe, Marlon K. Hom, Madeline Y. Hou, Nina F. Ichikawa, Liu Junru, Him Mark Lai, Heather Lee, Rose Hum Lee, Beth Lew-Williams, Emma Woo Louie, Jennie Low, Anne Mendelson, Brett de Bary Nee, Victor G. Nee, David Shields, Diane Yee, Connie Young Yu, and Judy Yung, as well as the staffs at the Chinese American Historical Society, California Historical Society, San Francisco Public Library, and University of California, Berkeley and Irvine Libraries.

This book could not exist without the work and inspiration of the many Chinese American cooks, teachers, and visionaries before us. Thank you for paving the way.

ONE LAST THING

For many professional cooks, the work/life balance swings wildly day by day. We love cooking and the restaurant business so much that it's easy to justify all the sacrifices, so long as everything holds together.

The first case of Covid-19 in the United States was confirmed in January 2020, and everything changed for every business in Chinatown. On February 25, San Francisco declared a state of emergency, and the streets in this neighborhood emptied out. On March 16, the city was ordered to shelter in place, and all of San Francisco ground to a halt. I wrote this on March 24, when everyone in restaurants around the world were placed in a position we never imagined.

Being in Chinatown, we got hit early. But we are not going down without a fight. We are using every resource possible to support the farmers, grocery stores, customers, our staff, and our food systems. They in turn support us. We are staying nimble and trying whatever we can to stay inspired and inspire others. We are taking it day by day.

Emotionally, it has been a rollercoaster. It has been hard to figure out what to do and how to be responsible as things kept changing. It didn't help that the president keeps calling the virus a "Chinese virus." But it also makes me want to fight harder. Everyone on the team at Mister Jiu's wants to do as much as we can.

We pulled together in crises before, not on this scale, of course, but just as life changing to us as a restaurant family. On New Year's Eve 2018, my then-twenty-nine-year-old sous chef, Eric, suffered cardiac arrest while working at Mister Jiu's. He lay in our kitchen unconscious and bleeding as we stood silent and helpless around him. A 911 operator walked us through CPR until the medics arrived with a defibrillator. Over the course of a week, as Eric fought through a coma, I questioned everything about how I ran the kitchen and about our industry in general. By some miracle, Eric woke up, and walked back into the kitchen with a permanent defibrillator, as lively as ever. It's still hard to believe.

It's hard to imagine the future for Chinatown, where so much is about community, where meals are a bunch of people gathered around a lazy Susan, sharing plates of food. I worry that such experiences might be gone and never come back, and that makes me so sad. When the restaurant industry bounces back from this, we have to work together to change. Our work is physically relentless and stressful. We grind eighty hours a week. No one can live on adrenaline forever. Since that night we almost lost Eric, I have tried to be more creative in ways to support my employees, not just in terms of practical things such as salaries and retirement plans but schedules and systems, communication, mental health resources, community building, and other forms of sanity to get us all through not just the week but the next crisis, happier and healthier.

We host CPR training sessions and installed a defibrillator at Mister Jiu's. If you run a business or a household, I really urge you to learn CPR through the Red Cross or American Heart Association as a start. Order takeout from your neighbors in Chinatown. Stock up at your small, local markets and farmers' markets. We can't know what the future holds, but we can take better care of each other.

INDEX

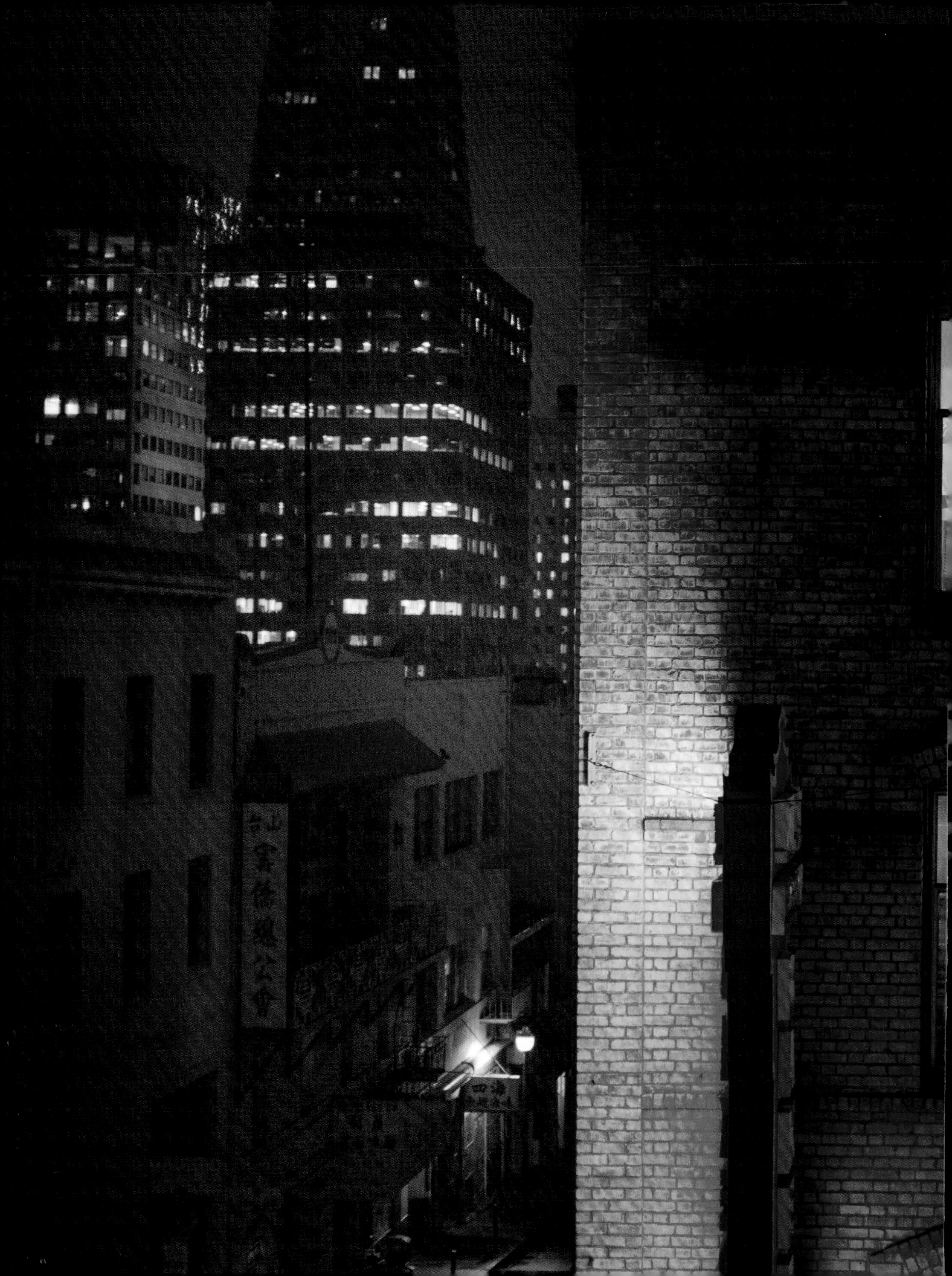
台山
四海

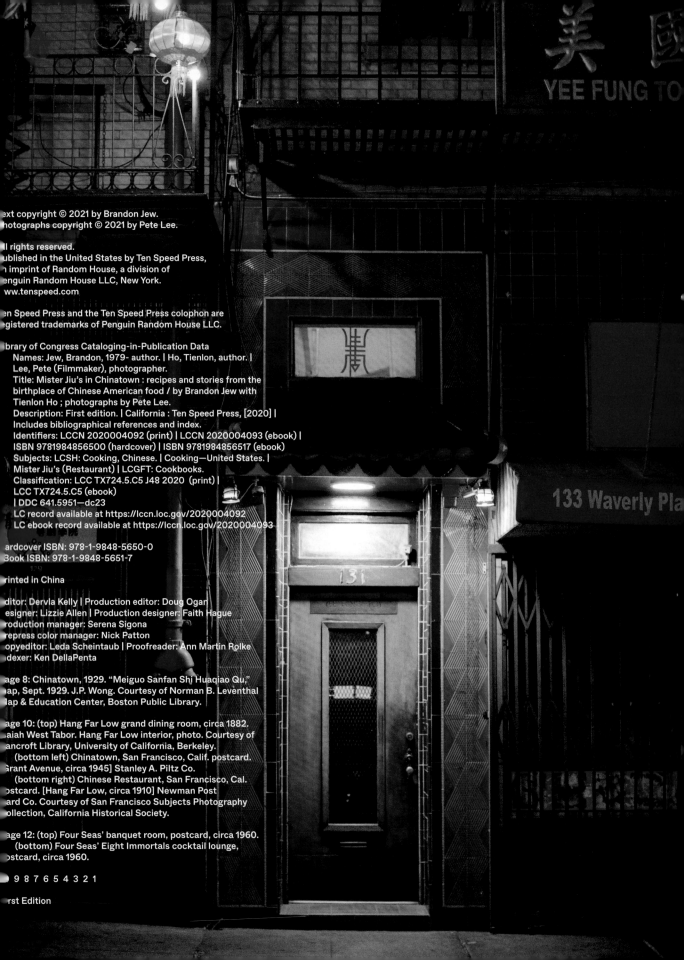

Library of Congress Cataloging-in-Publication Data
    Names: Jew, Brandon, 1979- author. | Ho, Tienlon, author. |
    Lee, Pete (Filmmaker), photographer.
    Title: Mister Jiu's in Chinatown : recipes and stories from the
    birthplace of Chinese American food / by Brandon Jew with
    Tienlon Ho ; photographs by Pete Lee.
    Description: First edition. | California : Ten Speed Press, [2020] |
    Includes bibliographical references and index.
    Identifiers: LCCN 2020004092 (print) | LCCN 2020004093 (ebook) |
    ISBN 9781984856500 (hardcover) | ISBN 9781984856517 (ebook)
    Subjects: LCSH: Cooking, Chinese. | Cooking—United States. |
    Mister Jiu's (Restaurant) | LCGFT: Cookbooks.
    Classification: LCC TX724.5.C5 J48 2020 (print) |
    LCC TX724.5.C5 (ebook)
    | DDC 641.5951—dc23
    LC record available at https://lccn.loc.gov/2020004092
    LC ebook record available at https://lccn.loc.gov/2020004093

Hardcover ISBN: 978-1-9848-5650-0
Ebook ISBN: 978-1-9848-5651-7

Printed in China

Editor: Dervla Kelly | Production editor: Doug Ogan
Designer: Lizzie Allen | Production designer: Faith Hague
Production manager: Serena Sigona
Prepress color manager: Nick Patton
Copyeditor: Leda Scheintaub | Proofreader: Ann Martin Rolke
Indexer: Ken DellaPenta

Page 8: Chinatown, 1929. "Meiguo Sanfan Shi Huaqiao Qu,"
map, Sept. 1929. J.P. Wong. Courtesy of Norman B. Leventhal
Map & Education Center, Boston Public Library.

Page 10: (top) Hang Far Low grand dining room, circa 1882.
Isaiah West Tabor. Hang Far Low interior, photo. Courtesy of
Bancroft Library, University of California, Berkeley.
    (bottom left) Chinatown, San Francisco, Calif. postcard.
[Grant Avenue, circa 1945] Stanley A. Piltz Co.
    (bottom right) Chinese Restaurant, San Francisco, Cal.
postcard. [Hang Far Low, circa 1910] Newman Post
Card Co. Courtesy of San Francisco Subjects Photography
Collection, California Historical Society.

Page 12: (top) Four Seas' banquet room, postcard, circa 1960.
    (bottom) Four Seas' Eight Immortals cocktail lounge,
postcard, circa 1960.

10 9 8 7 6 5 4 3 2 1

First Edition

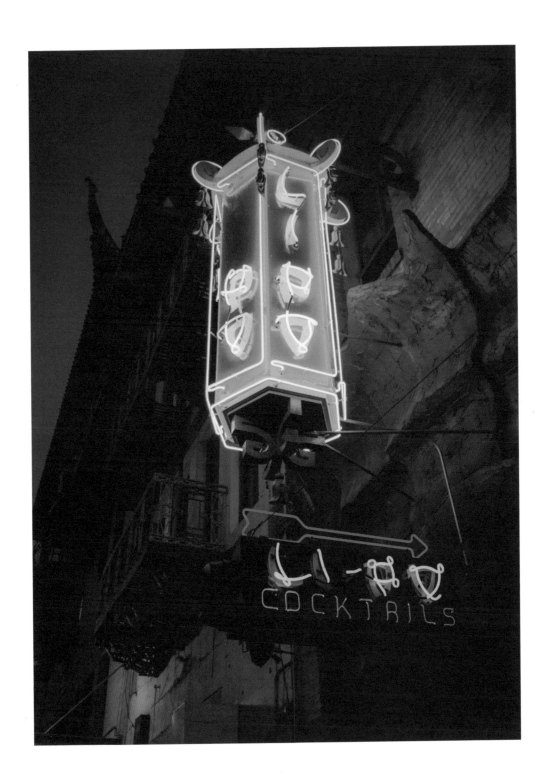